Living Language W9-CDS-519

RUSSIAN

RUSSIAN

PHRASEBOOK • DICTIONARY

Valerie Borchardt
and Anthony Richter

Crown Publishers, Inc., New York

Published by Crown Publishers, Inc., 201 East 50th Street, New York, New York 10022. Member of the Crown Publishing Group.

CROWN, LIVING LANGUAGE, LIVING LANGUAGE TRAVELTALK, and colophon are trademarks of Crown Publishers, Inc.

Manufactured in the United States of America.

Library of Congress Cataloging-in-Publication Data

Borchardt, Valerie.
    Living language traveltalk. Russian: phrasebook, dictionary/by Valerie Borchardt and Anthony Richter.—1st ed.
        p. cm.
    On t.p. the registered trademark symbol "TM" is superscript following "traveltalk" in the title.
    1. Russian language—Conversation and phrase books—English. 2. Russian language—Textbooks for foreign speakers—English. I. Richter, Anthony. II. Title.
PG2121.B67   1991
491.783'421—dc20   90-47583
                                                                         CIP

ISBN: 0-517-57651-1

10 9 8 7 6 5 4 3 2 1

First Edition

CONTENTS

11 SEEING THE SIGHTS 134

12 SHOPPING 155

13 LEISURE AND ENTERTAINMENT 170

14 GENERAL TERMS AND EXPRESSIONS 184

GRAMMAR IN BRIEF 201

ENGLISH-RUSSIAN DICTIONARY 215
RUSSIAN-ENGLISH DICTIONARY 239

ABOUT THE AUTHORS

Valerie Borchardt has a Master of Arts in Russian Language and Literature from Columbia University. Her translation of Vasily Aksyonov's "The Hollow Herring" appeared in *Formations* in 1986. She has lived and studied at Leningrad State University and has traveled throughout the Soviet Union.

Anthony Richter received a Bachelor of Arts in Russian Language and Literature from Wesleyan University and taught Russian at Wesleyan and Indiana Universities. He studied at the Pushkin Institute in Moscow, spent three years accompanying professional tours across the Soviet Union, and currently is program director of the Soros Foundation—Soviet Union.

ACKNOWLEDGMENTS

We wish to acknowledge the individuals who were helpful to us in the preparation of this work. We thank Lynn Visson for permitting us to draw materials from *The Moscow Gourmet* and Dr. Dan E. Davidson whose *Russian: Stage I* proved invaluable in compiling the grammar section of this book.

We are also grateful to Sergei Frolov, Lina Borodinskaya, Dima Litvinov, and David Gurevich for their help in reviewing this work for accuracy of language and content. We also owe our thanks to Alex Silverman; Beatriz and Alvino Fantini of the School for International Training-Experiment in International Living, Brattleboro, Vermont; Mary Seton-Watson; Tim Dunmore; and Kathryn Mintz, Crown Publishers, who helped to develop the Traveltalk ™ course. Thanks also to Fodor's Travel Publications, Inc., for portions of the book taken from *Fodor's '91 Soviet Union,* available in bookstores nationwide.

Editorial Director: Kathryn Mintz

Editorial Associate: Jacqueline Natter

Editorial Assistant: Victoria Su

The editors wish to thank the following people for their contribution to this project: Jacques Chazaud, Peter Davis, Lauren Dong, Linda Kocur, William Peabody, and Jim Walsh.

PREFACE

Are you planning a trip to the USSR? If so, this book will help you make the most of your trip. The *Traveltalk* ™ phrasebook/dictionary features more than 2,200 Russian expressions to use in the various situations you may encounter as a tourist. Each word has a phonetic transcription to help you with pronunciation.

No prior knowledge of Russian is necessary. All you have to do to make yourself understood is to read the phonetics as you would any English sentence. We also recommend using the *Traveltalk* ™ *Russian* cassette so you can hear Russian spoken by native speakers and practice pronunciation. However, this book is useful on its own, as it offers the following features:

Guide to Pronunciation and the Russian Alphabet This section presents the Russian letters and uses English equivalents to approximate their sounds. Reading through it first will help you pronounce the phrases in the subsequent chapters of the book.

Chapter 1: Essential Phrases Many common expressions are likely to be used quite frequently in a variety of contexts. For your convenience, these phrases have been grouped together in one brief chapter.

Chapters 2–13 reflect the full range of the tourist's experience. From arrival at the airport to saying farewell to new friends, *Traveltalk* ™ provides a comprehensive resource to use in every important travel situation.

Sample Dialogues at the beginning of most chapters give you a sense of how the language sounds in conversation.

Chapter 14: General Terms and Expressions provides helpful general information such as months of the year, days of the week, and legal holidays.

Travel Tips and Cultural Highlights Interspersed throughout the chapters are brief narratives highlighting cultural attractions and offering insider's tips for getting the most out of your visit. Metric conversion tables, important signs, and clothing/shoe size conversion charts are also provided.

Grammar in Brief Russian is an extremely complex language grammatically, but some of the basic structures are included in this concise summary to help expand your range of communication.

Two-Way 1,600-Word Dictionary presents all the key words that appear in this book, grouped in both English-Russian and Russian-English sections for easy reference. Both sections include the phonetic transcriptions of each Russian word.

BEFORE YOU LEAVE

You must apply for a tourist visa in order to travel in the Soviet Union. Usually your travel agent will take care of this for you. Your passport will have to be sent to the Soviet Embassy in Washington, D.C., along with three passport photographs, your visa application—including a complete itinerary and the dates you plan to be in the Soviet Union—and an application fee. If you are making your own travel plans, you may apply directly to the Soviet Embassy for an entry visa but we highly recommend going through a travel agent. The application process can be quite complicated and it is best to leave this to an expert. The address of the embassy in Washington is:

Embassy of the Union of Soviet Socialist Republics
Consular Division
1825 Phelps Place, N.W.
Washington, D.C.   20008
(202) 939-8916

This division is only open from 9:00 A.M. to 12:30 P.M.

All travel to the Soviet Union is ultimately organized through the State travel agency, Intourist Moscow Limited. They themselves have tours and a certain amount of useful information. For information on travel to the Soviet Union, get in touch with the Intourist office in New York:

Intourist
630 Fifth Avenue
New York, NY   10019
(212) 757-3884

In Canada:
1801 McGill College Ave., Montreal, Quebec H3A 2N4. Tel. 514-849-6394.

In the Soviet Union:
The head office of Intourist in Moscow is at Prospekt Marxa. For general enquiries and help in contacting other tourists call 292-2260. The American Department's phone number is 292-8670;

the British Department's 292-2697. The Excursion Department (M.E.O.) has offices in the following Moscow Hotels:

Bucharest, 232-5533, ext. 149; *Metropole* (Excursion Hall), 225-6970/1/2; *National*, 229-6224; *Rossiya*, 298-5437; *Ukraine*, 243-2690.

WHAT TO TAKE

Local shortages are common and certain items may be hard for the passing tourist to find. You might find it useful to stock up with a modest amount of the following: adhesive (Scotch) tape, ballpoint pens and refills, insect repellent, films, spare radio batteries, laxatives, anti-diarrhoea pills, indigestion tablets, travel sickness pills, aspirins, and any medicine you take regularly. Also take a spare pair of glasses or contact lenses, sunglasses, detergent, clothes pegs, toothpaste, soap, cosmetics, shampoos, a sewing kit, safety pins, buttons, chewing gum (a welcome gift), candy (ditto), a jar of instant coffee (expensive and of inferior quality in Russia), coffee creamer, Kleenex, handtowel, sanitary napkins, lavatory paper, corkscrew/bottle opener, spare baggage tags. A flat, wide suction-type bath plug might also come in very handy in some hotels and a roll of electrical tape for fixing faucets, etc. A pillow-case is useful for long rail trips. Other items that can make welcome gifts in lieu of tipping are: felt pens, cigarettes, pantyhose, cosmetics—especially eye make-up. Guides are officially not allowed to receive tips, but books—British and American classics in paperback—are appreciated.

For most tourist destinations, airline baggage now goes by size rather than weight, and the free baggage allowance is now: First class, 2 pieces up to 62 inches overall measure each piece; Economy class, 2 pieces, neither one over 62 inches, both together no more than 117 inches; carry-on baggage up to 45 inches. If you go to the U.S.S.R. by Pan Am, your baggage will be carried on this basis, with added proviso that no piece weigh over 70 pounds. Aeroflot's regulations are similar, except that the weight limitation is 45 lbs.

Packing

Travel light. This is the advice of most seasoned travelers who have learned not to take along the things that *might* be needed, only those that *will* be.

Even if you are going on a package tour with baggage handling inclusive, you will save time, money and frustration by sticking to what you can carry yourself without strain. For most people this means one suitcase with a total weight of 30 pounds or less, or two weighing 20 pounds apiece or less. A shoulder bag should weigh not more than 10 pounds. Take a light-weight collapsible one for emergencies.

Keep in mind that some package tour operators will only accept conventional hard luggage or framed soft bags. Duffle bags and the like are considered harder to fit on a tour bus.

It's a good idea to keep important papers, a camera, guidebooks, a change of underwear, your passport and shot card, other personal items, and perhaps a folding raincoat and hat in your shoulderbag. Women may wish to keep a small handbag in it as well. Carry the shoulderbag with you at all times.

Remember your luggage may be thoroughly searched at Soviet customs points. It is worth *not* wrapping up items in fancy paper or protective plastic. They are likely to be picked on.

What to Wear

Starting from the bottom up, a good pair of shoes with thick soles and firm arch supports is your best protection against traveler's limp. Many sidewalks in Soviet cities are pot-holed and poorly maintained. Make sure the shoes are well broken-in and also well-heeled. You may have trouble getting repairs done on the spot in the U.S.S.R. Clothes should be light in the summer—cotton rather than synthetic; shirts and underwear drip-dry; laundry service is slow and cleaning facilities are limited though most hotels have ironing-rooms. There are virtually no self-service launderettes except in a few new housing-estates, out of the tourist's reach. A raincoat, a cardigan or pullover (even in summer) are musts. In winter you will need a heavy overcoat plus woolen underwear, fur- or fleece-lined boots and gloves. (Fur

5

hats—*shapki*—can be bought in the country but are now fairly expensive.)

Put together your travel wardrobe by selecting one or two basic colors and coordinating other colors with them to get the most mileage out of the least amount of clothes. Trouser suits are generally acceptable for women nowadays. Beware of *over-dressing*, even for the Bolshoi Ballet. Your Intourist hotel is probably the only place where you might prefer to look really sophisticated.

For cooler weather, try the layer system. Instead of dragging along a heavy coat, wear a lighter one with a sweater, insulated underwear, and extra layers of clothing. It is a more flexible system and will keep you warmer. Also, make sure that your coat has a hook on its collar so that attendants in public buildings can hang it in the coat check. In *really* cold weather wear woolen tights, *never nylon*—it can freeze on your knees! Winter boots should be waterproof.

Light indoor clothes are a must for winter. Russian central heating is efficient and you will *swelter* at night in anything woolen.

HEALTH REGULATIONS

Tourists from other countries do not need to present any health certificates and there will be no medical examination. However, Soviet public health officers may ask for additional proof of health from tourists arriving from countries known to have an epidemic at the time of arrival. This may soon extend to an AIDS test for visitors from certain countries, mostly in Africa. The U.S. Public Health Service does not recommend cholera shots, but does urge all travelers to have had a tetanus vaccination within the last ten years. Medical service in the U.S.S.R. is free and available in any city or town. If a tourist is indisposed, he is asked immediately to call in a doctor through his interpreter or through the hotel administration. First aid treatment and doctors' visits are gratis. If hospitalization is necessary a charge of 20 rubles daily is levied; this may be waived against unused prepaid travel services.

TO KEEP IN MIND

Most visitors to the U.S.S.R. anticipate a trip for earnest reasons of political, social and cultural curiosity; few go to find the kind of relaxed fun that you would expect from a holiday in the West. Almost everyone is aware that a visit to Russia has little to do with creature comforts—sun, sand and *après ski,* or any of the other frivolous pursuits associated with having a good time. The reason for going is, pure and simple, curiosity—curiosity about a completely different way of life.

The complex world of the U.S.S.R. is fascinating beyond belief: your encounters with individual Russians, Latvians, Mongolians or Georgians (to name but a few) can be a heartwarming experience; the Soviet social order, so different from ours, will provoke the imagination if you are politically aware; the fine arts, in the form of museums, theater, dance or music, will impress you by the sheer volume of participants. On a more mundane level, you may enjoy the skill of Soviet athletics, which has more than ten million registered active participant enthusiasts, and the excitement of the very best in competition. And, despite the occasional poor service in restaurants, you will probably enjoy the various regional food and drink specialties of the country.

Special Advice for a Special Visit

Visiting the Soviet Union is like nothing you've ever done before. Our experience, and that of many other travelers, indicates that the following hints may help to prepare you for your adventure into another way of life:

1—Go to the U.S.S.R. on a group tour if you can possibly do so, especially if it's your first visit, or if you don't speak Russian. Group tourists get priority over individual tourists, even if the latter do pay more than the former.

2—Be careful not to break any laws, and if you're not sure, follow this rule: If you aren't certain something is allowed, it is safer to assume it is definitely forbidden. Sticking to your pre-arranged itinerary, not photographing any rail stations, installations, buildings, etc. which might be regarded as "sensitive," not

7

selling your blue jeans, or not offering a dollar bill or pound note for a tip, all these are covered by some law or other and, for ignoring things like these, visitors have run into trouble and some have even been expelled from the country.

3—If you are traveling individually and expect to spend more than a day or two in the U.S.S.R., register with your embassy in Moscow, preferably in person, but at least by mail or telephone, giving your full name, passport number, date and place of birth, occupation, hotel and room number, purpose and dates of visit, home address, and (if applicable) names and addresses of any relatives to be visited in the U.S.S.R.

4—Carry your hotel identity card (which you will get when you register, in exchange for your passport) with you at all times. It is officially accepted as proof of your status in foreign currency shops, restaurants, etc., and may be useful also if, for example, you get lost and want to ask someone the way to your hotel or to take a taxi. If you are allowed to keep your passport as well, keep it in a safe place on your person at all times. There is reported to be a black market in U.S. and U.K. passports.

5—Plan well ahead, meaning that *everything* you want to do in the Soviet Union, and especially all the cities you want to visit or special interests you want to pursue, is arranged before you leave your home for the airport.

6—Finally, and a very basic point, remember that you are going to a country with a very different attitude toward life from your own. Try to approach your trip with patience and an open mind and you will enjoy the adventure!

INTRODUCTION TO THE SOVIET UNION

The U.S.S.R. (Union of Soviet Socialist Republics) is by far the largest country in the world. Its area of 8.65 million square miles is greater than that of the U.S.A. and Canada combined. From its Western edge on the Baltic Sea to the Pacific Ocean on its eastern seaboard is a journey of some 5,700 miles, crossing 11 time zones. In the extreme north of the Soviet Union, within the Arctic Circle, the sub-soil is permanently frozen, while nearly 3,000 miles to the south there are deserts in the Central Asian republics.

The country spans two continents, the dividing line between the European and Asiatic parts of the Soviet Union being the Ural mountains, which rise to just over 6,000 feet. Much higher mountain ranges dominate the south of the country, notably the Caucasus in Europe (whose Mt. Elbrus is 18,481 feet high), the Pamir Mountains in Central Asia (rising to over 24,000 feet), and the Tien Shan near the Chinese border (also over 24,000 feet).

Huge rivers cut across the Soviet Union, mostly from north to south, the best known being the Dnepr, the Don, and the Volga (in Europe), the Ob in Western Siberia, and the Amur, which flows into the Pacific. The largest inland waters in the U.S.S.R. are the Aral Sea and Lake Baikal.

Preliminary results from the January 1989 census put the Soviet population at 286.7 million. The European part of the U.S.S.R. is much more densely populated than the Asiatic areas (which are three times as large). Since the industrialization drive began 60 years ago, there has been a rapid and sustained migration into the cities, where living standards are noticeably higher than in the countryside. The capital, Moscow (population 9 million) is the largest city, followed by the former capital, Leningrad (5 million) and the capital of the Ukraine, Kiev (2.6 million). There are 21 other cities with populations of over one million in the U.S.S.R. For many years official policy has sought to restrict migration into the old established European cities, but evasion of these residence permit regulations is widespread.

Only one-third of the population now lives in rural areas. There are tens of thousands of villages and small settlements all over the Soviet Union, some of which are hundreds of miles from a town and lack surfaced roads or electricity.

There are hundreds of different ethnic groups in the U.S.S.R. The most numerous peoples are the Russians, although they actually constitute only about half the Soviet population. There are other Slav nations in the west of the U.S.S.R.—mostly occupied by Ukrainians and Byelorussians. To the north of these lie the Baltic States, which along with the western Ukraine and Moldavia, were forcibly incorporated into the Soviet Union in the 1940s. The areas in the south around the Caucasus mountains and in Central Asia were colonized by the Tsars in the 19th century. They contain a variety of peoples, many of them of Turkic ancestry. The smaller ethnic groups range from Tartars and Mongols to Chinese, and include a few whose lifestyle is still nomadic. Extensive Slav migration to the non-Russian areas has been officially encouraged, especially to the mineral-rich but underpopulated areas of Siberia and the Far East. In some national republics (e.g. Kazakhstan), the Slavs actually now outnumber the natives.

Although the *lingua franca* of the Soviet Union is Russian, it is the first language for only 58% of the population. Some of the other languages, such as Ukrainian, are very similar to Russian; others (like the Central Asian tongues and Azeri) are unrelated, but have been transcribed into a version of the Russian Cyrillic alphabet. The Latin alphabet is used in the Baltic languages, one of which (Estonian) is part of the Finno-Ugric group, although the others are Indo-European. Some nationalities, notably the Georgians and the Armenians, have managed to retain their own alphabets.

In total, 112 different languages are recognized in official Soviet censuses and there are many more minority tongues and local dialects. In some regions (e.g. the North Caucasus) three or more languages may be in everyday use. However, a good working knowledge of Russian is still essential for career advancement throughout the U.S.S.R., although several national republics are now making the native tongue the first language in official use. Many Soviet citizens speak some English, but most do not get much chance to practice it.

A GUIDE TO PRONUNCIATION

Living Language Traveltalk ™*: Russian* presents each word or phrase first in English, then in Russian. The phonetic transcription that follows helps you pronounce each Russian word correctly. All you have to do is read the transcription as you would read English and you will be speaking fairly comprehensible Russian. However, there are differences between many English and Russian sounds, so the phonetics are only an approximate guide. You can learn more accurate pronunciation by repeating after the native speakers on the *Traveltalk* ™ *Russian* cassette.

THE RUSSIAN ALPHABET
Russian uses the Cyrillic alphabet, which derives from the Greek, whereas English is written with the Latin alphabet. However, there are a few letters that are shared by both languages. Still other letters may be familiar to you from basic mathematics and the names of college fraternities and sororities. As you use this book, you may become more familiar with the different letters and sounds to the point where you no longer need the phonetics to read each word. It's not as hard as it first seems.

In the charts below, and throughout the book, the syllable stressed in a word appears in capital letters in the phonetic transcription and is indicated by an accent mark (') in the actual Cyrillic word.

RUSSIAN PRONUNCIATION CHART
Vowels
The location of a vowel within a word will determine its pronunciation. There is only one stressed syllable in any given Russian word and the pronunciation of a vowel will change depending on its position within a word in relation to the stressed syllable.

11

Russian Letters	Approximate Sound in English	Phonetic Symbol	Example– Transcription
A a (in the first syllable of a word, in the syllable before the stressed syllable, or in the stressed syllable)	(calm)	ah	ба́нк (bahnk) такси́ (tahk-SEE) познако́мить (pah-znah-KAW-meet')
A a (in any syllable following the stressed syllable)	(but)	uh	ко́шка (KAWSH-kuh)
A a (after a soft consonant)	(meet)	ee	чаевы́е (chee-yee-VY-yeh)
Э э (stressed)	(set)	eh	э́то (EH-tuh)
Э э (after a soft consonant or at beginning of word)	(meet)	ee	экску́рсия (eek-SKOOR-see-yuh)
Ы ы*	(sympathy)*	y	сы́н (syn)
О о (stressed)	(law)	aw	ко́шка (KAWSH-kuh)
О о (in the first syllable of a word or the syllable before the stressed syllable)	(calm)	ah	оди́н (ah-DEEN) голова́ (gah-lah-VAH)

*No equivalent in English. **Ы** is pronounced somewhere between the short i sound of sym- and the long ee sound of -thy in sympathy.

12

О о (in any syllable after the stressed syllable)	(b<u>u</u>t)	uh	**мя́со** (MYAH-s<u>uh</u>)
У у	(c<u>oo</u>)	oo	**у́мка** (<u>OO</u>T-kuh)
Я я (stressed)	(<u>yo</u>nder)	yah	**я́сно** (<u>YAH</u>-snuh)
Я я (unstressed)	(b<u>ee</u>)	ee	**ме́сяц** (MYEH-s<u>ee</u>ts)
Е е (stressed)	(<u>ye</u>t)	yeh	**ме́сто** (M<u>YEH</u>-stuh)
Е е (before stressed syllable)	(b<u>ee</u>)	ee	**метро́** (m<u>ee</u>-TRAW)
Е е (after stressed syllable)	(b<u>u</u>t)	uh	**мне́ние** (MNYEH-nee-<u>uh</u>)
И и	(b<u>ee</u>)	ee	**Ни́на** (N<u>EE</u>-nuh)
И и	(sympath<u>y</u>)	y	**саци́ви** (sah-TS<u>Y</u>-v<u>y</u>)
Ё ё	(<u>yaw</u>n)	yaw	**ёлка** (<u>YAW</u>L-kuh)
Ю ю	(<u>you</u>)	yoo	**ю́бка** (<u>YOO</u>P-kuh)

Consonants

Some consonants in Russian make more than one sound. This occurs most often when the consonant is located at the end of a word or syllable. The following list of consonants shows all of the variations in pronunciation.

Russian Letters	Approximate Sound in English	Phonetic Symbol	Example–Transcription
Б б	b (bear)	b	бóчка (BAWCH-kuh)
	p (part)	p	зýб (zoop)
В в	v (very)	v	вокзáл (vahg-ZAHL)
	f (full)	f	автóбус (ahf-TAW-boos)
Г г	g (go)	g	гáлстук (GAHL-stook)
	k (bake)	k	дóг (dawk)
Д д	d (dare)	d	дóктор (DAWK-tuhr)
	t (toll)	t	кóд (kawt)
Ж ж	zh (leisure)	zh	кóжа (KAW-zheh)
	sh (show)	sh	лóжка (LAWSH-kuh)
З з	z (zebra)	z	зáвтра (ZAHF-truh)
	s (sign)	s	рáз (rahs)
Й й	always silent	—	хорóший (khah-RAW-shee)
Ш ш	sh (show)	sh	шýм (SHOOM)
Щ щ	long sh	sh	ящик (YAH-shyk)

Hard and Soft Signs

Ъ ъ	silent hard sign (separates vowels and consonants, providing a syllable break)	—	объясня́ть (ahb-yee-SNYAHT')
Ь ь	silent soft sign (softens preceding consonant)		пла́тье (PLAHT'-yeh)

Vowels Combined with й

Although й does not make a sound on its own, it does affect the pronunciation of vowels, when placed directly after them.

Russian Letters	Approximate Sound in English	Phonetic Symbol	Example– Transcription
ой	oy (toy)	oy	мой (MOY)
ай	ie (tie)	ahy	Май (MAHY)
ей	yay (yea)	yay	друзей (droo-ZYAY)

Intonation

Russian intonation is quite different from English intonation. Here, we will briefly discuss the most common Russian intonational constructions. The first is IC-1, which is characteristic of the declarative sentence. In an IC-1 sentence, the words preceding the point of emphasis in the sentence are pronounced on a level, medium tone, smoothly and without pauses. Those words located after the point of emphasis in the sentence are pronounced on a lower pitch.

Я хочу́ есть.   (yah khah-CHOO yehst')   I want to eat.

The second intonational construction is IC-2, used in interrogative sentences that contain a question word. The stressed word in the sentence is pronounced with a slightly rising tone and strong emphasis. Those words which precede it are pronounced on a lower pitch, with a slight fall on the last syllable.

15

Кто́ говори́т?   (ktaw gah-vah-REET?)   Who is speaking?

IC-3 is used in interrogative sentences that do not contain a question word. As in IC-1, those words which precede the point of emphasis of the sentence are pronounced on a level, medium tone. The stressed part of the sentence is pronounced in a sharply higher tone and the rest of the sentence is pronounced on a low pitch with a slight fall at the last syllable, as in IC-1 and IC-2.

Вы́ бы́ли в Ленингра́де?   (vy BY-lee v lee-neen-GRAH-dee?)   Have you been to Leningrad?

1/ESSENTIAL EXPRESSIONS

COURTESY

Please.	pah-ZHAHL-stuh	Пожа́луйста.
Thank you.	spah-SEE-buh	Спаси́бо.
You're welcome.	NYEH-zuh-shtuh	Не́ за что.
Excuse me.	ee-zvee-NEE-tyeh	Извини́те.
It doesn't matter.	nee-chee-VAW	Ничего́.

GREETINGS

Good morning.	DAW-bruh-yeh OO-truh	До́брое у́тро.
Good afternoon.	DAW-bry dyehn'*	До́брый де́нь.
Good day.*	DAW-bry dyehn'	До́брый де́нь.*
Hello. (formal)	ZDRAH-stvoo-ee-tyeh	Здра́вствуйте.
Hello. (informal)	pree-VYEHT	Приве́т.
Hello. (telephone)	ah-LAW	Алло́.
Good night.	spah-KOY-nee NAW-chee	Споко́йной но́чи.
Good-bye.	duh svee-DAH-nee-yuh	До свида́ния.
See you soon.	dah FSTRYEH-chee	До встре́чи.
See you tomorrow.	dah ZAHF-trah	До за́втра.
Let's go.	pah-SHLEE	Пошли́.

*In Russian, до́брый де́нь is used generally throughout the day.

APPROACHING SOMEONE FOR HELP

Excuse me,	ee-zvee-NEE-tyeh, pah-ZHAHL-stuh	Извини́те, пожа́луйста
• sir (young man).*	• muh-lah-DOY cheh-lah-VYEHK	• молодо́й челове́к.
• madam (young woman).*	• DYEH-voosh-kuh	• де́вушка.
Do you speak English?	vy guh-vah-REE-tyeh puh ahn-GLEE-skee?	Вы говори́те по-англи́йски?

*There are no formal terms of address such as sir and madam in the Russian language. The most common terms used are literally translated as young man and girl.

Do you understand English?	vy puh-nee-MAH-yeh-tyeh ahn-GLEE-skee yee-ZYCK?	**Вы понима́ете англи́йский язы́к?**
Yes./No.	dah/nyeht	**Да́./Не́т.**
I'm sorry.	prah-STEE-tyeh, pah-ZHAHL-stuh	**Прости́те, пожа́луйста.**
I'm a tourist.	yah too-REEST/ too-REEST-kuh	**Я тури́ст./ тури́стка*.**
I speak very little Russian.	yah AW-cheen' PLOKH-uh guh-vah-RYOO pah ROO-skee	**Я о́чень пло́хо говорю́ по-ру́сски.**
I don't speak Russian.	yah nee guh-vah-RYOO pah ROO-skee	**Я не говорю́ по-ру́сски.**
I don't understand.	yah nee puh-nee-MAH-yoo	**Я не понима́ю.**
I understand a little.	yah puh-nee-MAH-yoo nee-MNAWSH-kuh	**Я понима́ю немно́жко.**
Please speak more slowly.	guh-vah-REE-tyeh pah-MYEH-dlee-nyeh-yeh, pah-ZHAHL-stuh	**Говори́те поме́дленнее, пожа́луйста.**
Please repeat that.	puhf-tah-REE-tyeh ee-SHAW rahs, pah-ZHAHL-stuh	**Повтори́те ещё ра́з, пожа́луйста.**
May I ask a question?	MAWZH-nuh zah-DAHT' vah-PRAWS?	**Мо́жно зада́ть вопро́с?**
Could you please help me?	nee mah-GLEE by vy mnyeh pah-MAWCH'?	**Не могли́ бы вы́ мне помо́чь?**
Okay.	LAH-dnuh	**Ла́дно.**

*In Russian, although there are some exceptions, most nouns end in a consonant for males and an **a** for females. Plurals for both sexes are **ы** or **и**. Feminine adjectives end in **ая** or **яя** and male end in **ой, ый** or **ий**. The plural adjectival ending for both is **ие** or **ые**.

So, if you're an American male you would say, "yah ah-mee-ree-KAHN-eets" (**Я америка́нец**). If you're an American female, you would say, "yah ah-mee-ree-KAHN-kuh" (**Я америка́нка**). A group of Americans of either sex would say, "my ah-mee-ree-KAHN-tsee (**Мы́ америка́нцы**).

18

Of course.	kah-NYEHSH-nuh	Конéчно.
Where is . . . ?	gdyeh . . . ?	Где . . . ?
Where is the bathroom?	gdyeh zdyehs' too-ah-LYEHT?	Где здесь туалéт?
Thank you.	spah-SEE-buh	Спасúбо.

QUESTION WORDS

Who?	ktaw?	Ктó?
What?	shtaw?	Чтó?
Why?	puh-chee-MOO?	Почемý?
When?	kahg-DAH?	Когдá?
Where?	gdyeh?	Где?
Where to?	koo-DAH?	Кудá?
Where from?	aht-KOO-duh?	Откýда?
How?	kahk?	Кáк?
How much is it?	SKAW'L-kuh STAW-eet?	Скóлько стóит?

NUMBERS

zero	nawl'	нóль
one*	ah-DEEN, ah-DNAH, ah-DNAW	одúн, однá, однó
two*	dvah, dvyeh, dvah	двá, двé, двá
three	tree	трú
four	chee-TY-ree	четúре
five	pyaht'	пять
six	shehst'	шéсть
seven	syehm'	сéмь
eight	VAW-seem'	вóсемь
nine	DYEH-veet'	дéвять
ten	DYEH-seet'	дéсять
eleven	ah-DEEN-uht-seet'	одúннадцать
twelve	dvee-NAHT-seet'	двенáдцать
thirteen	tree-NAHT-seet'	тринáдцать
fourteen	chee-TYR-nuht-seet'	четúрнадцать

*Numbers one and two are given in masculine, feminine, and neuter forms. When beginning to count, the word rahs is used to indicate one. When referring to one object, the word ah-DEEN is used. The other numbers appear here only in the masculine form.

fifteen	peet-NAHT-seet'	пятна́дцать
sixteen	shyst-NAHT-seet'	шестна́дцать
seventeen	seem-NAHT-seet'	семна́дцать
eighteen	vuh-seem-NAHT-seet'	восемна́дцать
nineteen	dee-veet-NAHT-seet'	девятна́дцать
twenty	DVAHT-seet'	два́дцать
twenty-one	DVAHT-seet' ah-DEEN	два́дцать оди́н
twenty-two	DVAHT-seet' dvah	два́дцать два́
twenty-three . . .	DVAHT-seet' tree . . .	два́дцать три́ . . .
thirty	TREET-seet'	три́дцать
forty	SAW-ruhk	со́рок
fifty	pee-dee-SYAHT	пятьдеся́т
sixty	shys'-dee-SYAHT	шестьдеся́т
seventy	SYEHM'-dee-seet	се́мьдесят
eighty	VAW-seem'-dee-seet	во́семьдесят
ninety	dee-vee-NAW-stuh	девяно́сто
one hundred	staw	сто́
one hundred one	staw ah-DEEN	сто́ оди́н
one hundred two . . .	staw dvah . . .	сто́ два́ . . .
one hundred twenty . . .	staw DVAHT-seet' . . .	сто́ два́дцать . . .
one hundred thirty . . .	staw TREET-seet' . . .	сто́ три́дцать . . .
two hundred	DVYEH-stee	две́сти
three hundred	TREE-stuh	три́ста
four hundred	chee-TY-ree-stuh	четы́реста
five hundred	peet'-SAWT	пятьсо́т
six hundred	shyst'-SAWT	шестьсо́т
seven hundred	seem'-SAWT	семьсо́т
eight hundred	vuh-seem'-SAWT	восемьсо́т
nine hundred	dee-veet'-SAWT	девятьсо́т
one thousand	TY-seech-uh	ты́сяча
two thousand	dvyeh TY-seech-ee	две́ ты́сячи
three thousand	tree TY-seech-ee	три́ ты́сячи
one million	mee-LYAWN	миллио́н
two million . . .	dvah mee-LYAWN-uh . . .	два́ миллио́на . . .

20

Ordinal Numbers*

first	PYEHR-vy, PYEHR-vuh-yuh, PYEHR-vuh-yeh	пе́рвый, пе́рвая, пе́рвое
second	ftah-ROY, ftah-RAH-yuh, ftah-RAW-yeh	второ́й, втора́я, второ́е
third	TRYEH-tee, TRYEH-t'yuh, TRYEH-t'yeh	тре́тий, тре́тья, тре́тье
fourth	cheet-VYAWR-ty, cheet-VYAWR-tuh-yuh, cheet-VYAWR-tuh-yeh	четвёртый, четвёртая, четвёртое
fifth	PYAH-ty, PYAH-tuh-yuh, PYAH-tuh-yeh	пя́тый, пя́тая, пя́тое
sixth	shys-TOY, shys-TAH-yuh, shys-TAW-yeh	шесто́й, шеста́я, шесто́е
seventh	seed'-MOY, seed'-MAH-yuh, seed'-MAW-yeh	седьмо́й, седьма́я, седьмо́е
eighth	vahs'-MOY, vahs'-MAH-yuh, vahs'-MAW-yeh	восьмо́й, восьма́я, восьмо́е
ninth	dee-VYAH-ty, dee-VYAH-tuh-yuh, dee-VYAH-tuh-yeh	девя́тый, девя́тая, девя́тое
tenth	dee-SYAH-ty, dee-SYAH-tuh-yuh, dee-SYAH-tuh-yeh	деся́тый, деся́тая, деся́тое
twentieth	dvah-TSAH-ty, dvah-TSAH-tuh-yuh, dvah-TSAH-tuh-yeh	двадца́тый, двадца́тая, двадца́тое
hundredth	SAW-ty, SAW-tuh-yuh, SAW-tuh-yeh	со́тый, со́тая, со́тое

*Ordinal numbers are given in their masculine, feminine, and neuter forms.

Other Terms of Quantity

a half	puh-lah-VEE-nuh	полови́на
a half hour	pawl-chee-SAH	полчаса́
a third	treht'	треть
a quarter	CHEHT-veert'	че́тверть
two-thirds	dvyeh TRYEH-tee	две́ тре́ти
3 percent	tree prah-TSEHNT-uh	три́ проце́нта
a lot of/many	MNAW-guh	мно́го

21

a little of	MAH-luh	ма́ло
a dozen	DYOO-zhy-nuh	дю́жина
half a kilo	pawl-kee-LAW	полкило́
a few	NYEH-skuhl'-kuh	не́сколько
enough	dah-STAH-tuhch-nuh	доста́точно
too little	SLEESH-kuhm MAH-luh	сли́шком ма́ло
too much	SLEESH-kuhm MNAW-guh	сли́шком мно́го
a kilo	kee-lah-GRAHM, (kee-LAW)	килогра́мм, (кило́)
a glass	stah-KAHN	стака́н
a cup	CHAHSH-kuh	ча́шка
once	ah-DEEN rahs	оди́н ра́з
twice	dvah RAH-zuh	два́ ра́за
last	pah-SLYEHD-nee, pah-SLYEHD-nuh-yuh, pah-SLYEHD-nuh-yeh	после́дний, после́дняя, после́днее

ABOUT THE CURRENCY

In all of the Soviet republics—Estonia, Latvia, Lithuania, Byelo-russia, Russia, the Ukraine, Georgia, Armenia, Moldavia, Azer-baijan, Kazakhstan, Turkmenistan, Uzbekistan, Tadzhikistan, and Kirghizia—the monetary unit is the *ruble* (ROO-bl), divided into 100 *kopeks* (kah-PYE-ek). Of course the value of the ruble relative to the dollar is in constant flux (exchange rates are posted daily in hotels and banks where money is exchanged). It is illegal to bring rubles into or out of the Soviet Union so you must change money there. You will be given a customs document on which banks will record the amount of money you have exchanged and you will be asked to give this up when you leave the country.

22

DIALOGUE: В БАНКЕ (AT THE BANK)

Клиéнтка:	Разменя́йте, пожáлуйста, стó дóлларов.	ruhz-meen-YAHY-tyeh, pah-ZHAHL-stuh, staw DAW-lahr-uhf.
Касси́р:	Конéчно.	kah-NYEHSH-nuh.
Клиéнтка:	Вóт мой чéки.	vawt mah-YEE CHEH-kee.
Касси́р:	Подпиши́те и́х, пожáлуйста.	puht-pee-SHY-tyeh eekh, pah-ZHAHL-stuh.
Клиéнтка:	Конéчно.	kah-NYEHSH-nuh.
Касси́р:	Вáшу деклара́цию, пожáлуйста.	VAH-shoo dee-klah-RAH-tsee-yoo, pah-ZHAHL-stuh.
Клиéнтка:	Пожáлуйста.	pah-ZHAHL-stuh.

. . . .

Customer:	Could you change $100 for me?
Teller:	Certainly.
Customer:	Great. Here are my checks.
Teller:	Please sign them.
Customer:	Of course.
Teller:	May I have your declaration form, please?
Customer:	Here it is.

CHANGING MONEY

Banks that change foreign currency are generally located in hotels, although in bigger cities some special exchange banks may also offer this service. There will also be a bank at the airport when you arrive. Banks are open in the morning and the afternoon. Check when the lunch break is if you think you might need to change money. You can only change your rubles back into dollars at the airport, which can be quite time-consuming, so try not to change more than you're sure you'll need. When you go to change money you will need your customs declaration. The current exchange rate is always posted. Although higher denominations exist, foreigners are never given bills larger than ten rubles. You may be approached on the street by people who would like to exchange money with you on the black market. The rate they offer will be much higher than that of official exchange. We do not advise becoming involved in any black market transactions as this is against the law and punishable by imprisonment.

Where can I change money?	gdyeh MAWZH-nuh ruhz-mee-NYAHT' DYEHN'-gee?	Где мо́жно разменя́ть де́ньги?
Is the bank open now?	bahnk aht-KRYT see-CHAHS?	Ба́нк откры́т сейча́с?
No, it's closed.	nyeht, zah-KRYT	Не́т, закры́т.
Where do I sign?	gdyeh NAH-duh puht-pee-SAHT'?	Где на́до подписа́ть?
May I have some coins?	DAHY-tyeh, pah-ZHAHL-stuh MYEH-luhch'.	Да́йте, пожа́луйста, ме́лочь.

CREDIT CARDS

At the moment, *Access, American Express, Diners Club, Eurocard, JCB, MasterCard,* and *Visa* credit cards are accepted in most Intourist offices and at most Intourist hotels and restaurants. Many joint-venture and co-operative restaurants also accept credit cards. In fact, in some it's the only form of payment accepted; it's best to inquire first. Credit cards can also be used —at least in major tourist centers—to book theater tickets and additional tours and excursions and to pay for goods bought in "Beriozka" shops.

TIPPING

A service charge of 5 percent is included in restaurant bills in the Soviet Union, but since it is unclear whether the waiter or waitress will ever receive this money you might want to leave a little extra on the table.

Cab drivers should get a 10 or 15 percent tip. They often refuse to give back change, so it's a good idea to have lots of one-ruble notes if you plan to take taxis.

Airport and railway porters charge a posted fee. Fifty kopeks or a ruble more is enough. You don't need to tip the bellman who delivers your luggage to your room, the concierge, the doorman, or the maid; in fact, giving them money would probably be perceived as an insult. You might consider bringing small gifts such as souvenirs from your hometown to give instead of a tip. This is also true for your tour guides.

PAYING THE BILL

The bill, please.	shawt, pah-ZHAHL-stuh	Счёт, пожалуйста.
How much is it?	SKAWL'-kuh EH-tuh STAW-eet?	Сколько это стоит?
Is service included?	chee-yee-VY-yeh vklyoo-CHAH-yoot-suh?	Чаевые включаются?
This is for you.	EH-tuh vahm	Это вам.

TIME AND TIME EXPRESSIONS

Telling Time*

What time is it?	kah-TAW-ry chahs?	Который час?
It's	see-CHAHS	Сейчас
• three o'clock.	• tree chee-SAH	• три часа.
• 3:15.	• peet-NAHT-seet' mee-NOOT cheet-VYOHRT-uh-vuh	• пятнадцать минут четвёртого.

*In Russian, 3:05 is translated as "five minutes into the fourth hour." After the half hour on the clock, minutes are subtracted from the next hour. The literal translation of 3:50 is "minus ten of four."

25

• 3:30.	• pawl-cheet-VYOHRT-uh-vuh	• по́лчетвёртого.
• 2:45.	• bees CHYEHT-veer-tee tree	• бе́з че́тверти три́.
• 3:10.	• DYEH-seet' mee-NOOT cheet-VYOHRT-uh-vuh	• де́сять ми́нут четвёртого.
• 2:50.	• bees dee-see-TEE tree	• бе́з десяти́ три́.
• one o'clock.	• chahs	• ча́с.
• two o'clock.	• dvah chee-SAH	• два́ часа́.
• four o'clock.	• chee-TY-ree chee-SAH	• четы́ре часа́.
• five o'clock.	• pyaht' chee-SAWF	• пять часо́в.
• six o'clock.	• shehst' chee-SAWF	• ше́сть часо́в.
• seven o'clock.	• syehm' chee-SAWF	• се́мь часо́в.
• eight o'clock.	• VAW-seem' chee-SAWF	• во́семь часо́в.
• nine o'clock.	• DYEH-veet' chee-SAWF	• де́вять часо́в.
• ten o'clock.	• DYEH-seet' chee-SAWF	• де́сять часо́в.
• eleven o'clock.	• ah-DEEN-uht-seet' chee-SAWF	• оди́ннадцать часо́в.
• twelve o'clock.	• dvee-NAHT-seet' chee-SAWF	• двена́дцать часо́в.
• midnight.	• PAWL-nuhch'	• по́лночь.
• noon.	• PAWL-dyeen'	• по́лдень.
five minutes ago	pyaht' mee-NOOT tah-MOO nah-ZAHT	пять мину́т тому́ наза́д
in a half hour	CHEH-rees puhl-chee-SAH	че́рез полчаса́
after 8	PAW-slee vahs'-MEE	по́сле восьми́
before 9	duh dee-vee-TEE	до девяти́
When does it begin?	kahg-DAH nah-CHAH-luh?	когда́ нача́ло?
He came	awn pree-SHAWL	Он пришёл
• on time.	• VAW-vree-myuh	• во́время.
• early.	• RAH-nuh	• ра́но.
• late.	• PAWZ-nuh	• по́здно.

26

The 24-Hour System

In the Soviet Union, the 24-hour system, known in the United States as "military time," is often used in official listings, such as transportation schedules and theater times. It is really quite easy to master, based as it is on the 24 hours of the day—after 12:00 noon one simply keeps on counting. Hence, 3:00 P.M. is 12 plus 3, or 15:00 and so on, until 24:00, which is midnight. Midnight is also expressed as 00:00, and minutes past midnight are expressed as 00:01, and so forth, until 01:00.

The following chart will help you for quick reference.

1 A.M.	01:00	chahs	час
2 A.M.	02:00	dvah chee-SAH	два часа́
3 A.M.	03:00	tree chee-SAH	три часа́
4 A.M.	04:00	chee-TY-ree chee-SAH	четы́ре часа́
5 A.M.	05:00	pyaht' chee-SAWF	пять часо́в
6 A.M.	06:00	shehst' chee-SAWF	шесть часо́в
7 A.M.	07:00	syehm' chee-SAWF	семь часо́в
8 A.M.	08:00	VAW-seem' chee-SAWF	во́семь часо́в
9 A.M.	09:00	DYEH-veet' chee-SAWF	де́вять часо́в
10 A.M.	10:00	DYEH-seet' chee-SAWF	де́сять часо́в
11 A.M.	11:00	ah-DEEN-uht-seet' chee-SAWF	оди́ннадцать часо́в
12 NOON	12:00	dvee-NAHT-seet' chee-SAWF	двена́дцать часо́в
1 P.M.	13:00	tree-NAHT-seet' chee-SAWF	трина́дцать часо́в
2 P.M.	14:00	chee-TYR-nuht-seet' chee-SAWF	четы́рнадцать часо́в
3 P.M.	15:00	peet-NAHT-seet' chee-SAWF	пятна́дцать часо́в

27

4 P.M.	16:00	shys-NAHT-seet' chee-SAWF	шестна́дцать часо́в
5 P.M.	17:00	seem-NAHT-seet' chee-SAWF	семна́дцать часо́в
6 P.M.	18:00	vuh-seem-NAHT-seet' chee-SAWF	восемна́дцать часо́в
7 P.M.	19:00	dyeh-veet-NAHT-seet' chee-SAWF	девятна́дцать часо́в
8 P.M.	20:00	DVAH-tseet' chee-SAWF	два́дцать часо́в
9 P.M.	21:00	DVAH-tseet' ah-DEEN chahs	два́дцать оди́н ча́с
10 P.M.	22:00	DVAH-tseet' dvah chee-SAH	два́дцать два́ часа́
11 P.M.	23:00	DVAH-tseet' tree chee-SAH	два́дцать три́ часа́
12 MIDNIGHT	24:00 (or) 00:00	DVAH-tseet' chee-TY-ree chee-SAH	два́дцать четы́ре часа́

28

2/AT THE AIRPORT

Welcome to the Soviet Union! Going through customs at the airport can be a lengthy process but should not present any problems. Before entering the country, you will be asked to fill out a declaration form on which you will list all your money and traveler's checks. You will also be asked to list all valuable items you are bringing into the Soviet Union, such as watches, jewelry, cameras, and any electrical appliances. You will need this declaration to exchange money at the bank. Each time you exchange money, a receipt will be attached to your declaration to show that you have legally made the exchange. When you leave the country you will have to return these forms. There are certain items you may want to avoid carrying into the Soviet Union as they might be construed as anti-Soviet propaganda. These would include articles written about the Soviet Union in the West, books by Soviet dissidents that are not published in the Soviet Union, and certain religious articles. Entering the country by land may sometimes be more involved in terms of customs and immigration procedures. Here's a typical dialogue you may encounter.

DIALOGUE: ПА́СПОРМНИЦ КОНМРО́ЛБ (PASSPORT CONTROL)

Тамо́женник:	Здра́вствуйте. Да́йте, пожа́луйста, ваш па́спорт.	ZDRAH-stvooy-tyeh. DAHY-tyeh, pah-ZHAHL-stuh, vahsh PAHS-puhrt.
Тури́стка:	Вот он.	vawt awn.
Тамо́женник:	Вы Америка́нка?	vy ah-mee-ree-KAHN-kuh?
Тури́стка:	Да.	dah.
Тамо́женник:	Ско́лько вре́мени вы собира́етесь быть в Сове́тском Сою́зе?	SKAWL'-kuh VREH-mee-nee vy suh-bee-RAH-yeh-tyehs' byt' v sah-VYEHT-skuhm sah-YOOZ-yeh?

29

Туристка:	Я бу́ду здесь три неде́ли.	yah BOO-doo zdyehs' tree nee-DYEH-lee.

. . . .

Officer:	Hello. Give me your passport, please.
Tourist:	Here it is.
Officer:	Are you an American?
Tourist:	Yes.
Officer:	How long do you plan to be in the Soviet Union?
Tourist:	I will be here for three weeks.

AIRPORT ARRIVAL

What nationality are you?	kah-KAH-yuh oo vahs nuh-tsyaw-NAHL'-nuhst'?	Кака́я у ва́с национа́льность?
I'm	yah	Я
• American.	• ah-mee-ree-KAHN-yehts/ah-mee-ree-KAHN-kuh	• америка́нец. /америка́нка.*
• Canadian.	• kah-NAH-dyehts/kah-NAHD-kuh	• кана́дец./ кана́дка.*
• English.	• ahn-glee-CHAHN-in/ahn-glee-CHAH-N-kuh	• англича́нин. /англича́нка.*
What's your name?	kahk vahs zah-VOOT?	Ка́к ва́с зову́т?
My name is . . .	mee-NYAH zah-VOOT . . .	Меня́ зову́т . . .
Where will you be staying?	gdyeh vy ah-stah-NAH-vlee-vah-yeh-tyehs'?	Где́ вы остана́вли-ваетесь?

*These are the feminine variations for the nationality given.

30

I am staying at the Intourist hotel.	yah ah-stah-NAH-vlee-vah-yoos' v gah-STEE-nee-tseh een-too-REE-ST	Я остана́вливаюсь в гости́нице Интури́ст.
Are you here on vacation?	vy zdyehs' v AWT-poosk-yeh?	Вы здесь в о́тпуске?
I'm just passing through.	yah TAWL'kuh prah-YEHZD-uhm	Я то́лько прое́здом.
I'm here on a business trip.	yah f kuh-muhn-dee-RAWF-kyeh	Я в командиро́вке.
I'll be here for	yah prah-BOO-doo zdyehs'	Я пробу́ду здесь
• a few days.	• NYEH-skul'-kuh dnyehy	• не́сколько дне́й.
• a week.	• nee-DYEH-lyoo	• неде́лю.
• several weeks.	• NYEH-skul'-kuh nee-DYEHL'	• не́сколько неде́ль.
• a month.	• MYEH-seets	• ме́сяц.
Your passport, please.	vahsh PAHS-puhrt, pah-ZHAHL-stuh	Ваш па́спорт, пожа́луйста.
Do you have anything to declare?	oo vahs yehst' SHTAW-nee-boot' deh-klah-REE-ruh-vuht'?	У вас есть что́-нибудь деклари́ровать?
No, I have nothing to declare.	nyeht, oo mee-NYAH NYEH-chee-vuh deh-klah-REE-ruh-v-uht'	Нет, у меня́ не́чего деклари́ровать.
Open your bag.	aht-KROY-tyeh, pah-ZHAHL-stuh, vahsh chee-mah-DAHN	Откро́йте, пожа́луйста, ваш чемода́н.
Of course.	kah-NYEHSH-nuh	Коне́чно.
What are these?	shtaw EH-tuh tah-KAW-yeh?	Что́ э́то тако́е?
They are gifts.	EH-tuh pah-DAHR-kee	Э́то пода́рки.
Do I have to pay duty?	mnyeh pree-DYAWT-suh zuh-plah-TEET' PAWSH-lee-noo?	Мне придётся заплати́ть по́шлину?
Yes./No.	dah/nyeht	Да́./Нет.

| Have a nice stay. | zhy-LAH-yoo vahm pree-YAHT-nuh pruh-vees-TEE VREH-myuh v sah- VYEHT-skuhm sah- YOOZ-yeh | Жела́ю вам прия́тно провести́ вре́мя в Сове́тском Сою́зе. |

LUGGAGE AND PORTERS

Although you may occasionally encounter a porter in a Soviet airport, this is not something you should count on. Baggage carts are also rarely available, although they can now be rented in some international airports. We recommend taking luggage with wheels that you can easily handle on your own.

I need a porter.	mnyeh NOO-zhehn nah-SEEL'-sheek	Мне́ ну́жен носи́льщик.
I need a baggage cart.	mnyeh noozh-NAH tee-LYEHSH-kuh	Мне́ нужна́ теле́жка.
Here is my luggage.	vawt mah-YEE chee-mah-DAHN-y	Вот мои́ чемода́ны.
Take my bags	duh-neh-SEE-tyeh mah-YEE chee-mah-DAHN-y	Донеси́те мои́ чемода́ны
• to the taxi.	• duh tahk-SEE	• до такси́.
• to the bus.	• duh ahf-TAW-boos-uh	• до авто́буса.
• to the sidewalk.	• duh trah-too-AHR-uh	• до тротуа́ра.
Please be careful.	ah-stah-RAWZH-nuh, pah-ZHAHL-stuh	Осторо́жно, пожа́луйста.
How much is it?	SKAWL'-kuh STAW-eet?	Ско́лько этосто́ит?

AT THE AIRLINE COUNTER

Where can I find	Gdyeh nah-KHAW-dit-suh	Где нахо́дится
• Pan Am?	• puh-nah-MYEHR-ee-kuhn?	• Пан Аме́рикан?
• Aeroflot?	• ah-ehr-ah-FLAWT?	• Аэрофло́т?

- an Intourist
  representative?
- the information
  booth?
- check-in?

- preed-stah-VEE-
  tyehl' een-too-REE-
  stuh?
- SPRAHF-kee?
- ree-gee-STRAH-tsy-
  yuh?

- представитель
  Интуриста?
- справки?
- регистрация?

COMMON AIRPORT TERMS AND SIGNS

прямой рейс	pree-MOY ryehys	direct flight (nonstop)
рейс с посадкой	ryehys s pah-SAHT-kuhy	direct flight (with stops)
номер рейса	NAW-meer RYEHYS-uh	flight number
рейс в один конец	ryehys v ah-DEEN kah-NYEHTS	one-way flight
туда и обратно	too-DAH ee ah-BRAHT-nuh	round-trip
первый класс	PYEHR-vy klahs	first class
туристический класс	too-ree-STEE-chees-kee klahs	tourist class
место у окна	MYEH-stuh OO ah-KNAH	window seat
место около прохода	MYEH-stuh AW-kuh-luh prah-KHAW-duh	aisle seat
номер места	NAW-meer MYEH-stuh	seat number
курящее место	koo-RYAH-shuh-yeh MYEH-stuh	seat in the smoking section
ручная кладь	rooch-NAH-yuh klaht'	carry-on luggage
бирка	BEER-kuh	luggage tag
ВЫЛЕТЫ	VY-leet-y	DEPARTURES
ПРИЛЁТЫ	pree-LYAWT-ee	ARRIVALS
НЕ КУРИТЬ	nee koo-REET'	NO SMOKING

AIRPORT SERVICES AND TRANSPORTATION

From every airport there are public buses that take you into the center of town. Taxis are also available, but you may have to wait a long time for your turn. If you are traveling with a group you will be met at the airport by a bus that will take you directly to your hotel.

Where is	gdyeh nah-KHAW-deet-suh	Где нахо́дится
• the lost-baggage office?	• RAWZ-ysk bah-gah-ZHAH?	• ро́зыск багажа́?
• the duty-free shop?	• muh-gah-ZEEN byehs-PAWSH-ly-nykh tah-VAH-ruhf?	• магази́н беспо́шлин-ных това́ров?
• the bank?	• ahb-MYEHN vah-LYOOT-uh?	• обме́н валю́ты?
• the bus stop?	• stah-YAHN-kuh ahf-TAW-boos-uh?	• стоя́нка авто́буса?
• the taxi stand?	• stah-YAHN-kuh tah-KSEE?	• стоя́нка такси́?

3/FINDING YOUR WAY

GETTING AROUND MOSCOW

Coins are no longer in use on public transportation in Moscow; you have to buy a booklet of tickets and punch them as you go.

By Metro (Subway)

There are nine subway lines with over 200 kilometers of track and 132 stations. The Metro (marked with a large illuminated *M* sign) runs from 6 A.M. to 1 A.M.; on Sundays, half an hour longer. It is the fastest and most convenient mode of transport; during the rush hours, trains leave the stations every 50 seconds. 12 million passengers use it daily and it celebrated its 50th anniversary in 1985.

Pocket maps are available from stations or Intourist offices. Plan your route beforehand and have your destination with you written down *in Russian* to help you spot the station. Each station is announced over the train's public address system as you approach it, and the name of the next one is given before the train moves off. Reminders of interchanges/transfers are also given, so if you understand Russian, keep your ears peeled. Be prepared for a lot of elbowing and pushing. Escalators run fast—be warned! Every station has a doctor in case of accidents.

Passengers on the Metro rarely speak when traveling and when they do they keep their voices down, foreign visitors can be recognized by their talking. Don't drop any litter on the floor; the Russians are determined to keep the Metro trains and stations clean!

By Trolley-Bus, Bus, Tram, and Minibus

In Moscow, these carry more than 8 million passengers daily. The stops are sometimes announced by the driver. The 320 bus and 75 trolley-bus services start at 6 A.M. and the final runs begin at 1 A.M. The trams start at 5.30 A.M. on 52 routes, mostly in the suburbs, finishing at 1.30 A.M. "Microbuses" link points difficult to reach by other means, providing a service on 60 routes every 10 minutes, with intermediate request stops.

River-Boats

River-boats provide a pleasant, if leisurely way of getting about Moscow. Small boats ply the Moskva River within city limits, from May–June until September–October, depending on the weather. Two of the 13 routes run through the city center. The first runs from the Kiev Terminal via the Lenin Hills–Gorky Park–Krymsky Bridge–Bolshoi Kamenny Bridge–Bolshoi Ustyinsky Bridge–Krasnokholmsky Bridge–Novospassky Bridge, passing the Novodevichy Convent, the Lenin Stadium, Moscow University, the Moskva swimming pool, the Kremlin and other Moscow landmarks. This cruise takes an hour and 20 minutes. The second route also begins at the Kiev Terminal via the Krasnopresensky Park to Kuntsevo-Krylatskoye. It takes you to the Fili-Kuntsevo Park and the river beach, lasting one hour.

By Taxi

There are more than 11,000 taxis in Moscow, available at 300 taxi stands marked by a special sign. They can be distinguished by a checkered line on their doors and a green light on the windshield. If this light is on, the taxi is free. You can also hail a taxi in the street by raising your hand. Outside the hotel they have usually been booked by Intourist, so you may have to ask at your hotel desk and pay an extra service charge. You pay according to the meter, irrespective of the number of passengers or the amount of luggage. Do not be alarmed if the driver picks up another passenger; if they are going in your direction the fare will be split between you. Russian-speakers may order by telephone. The best numbers are reported to be: 225-0000, 227-0040 or 256-9003 (for freight).

On Foot

For the pedestrian, the following traffic rules are prescribed:

Traffic moves on the right. Some central streets have one-way traffic. Cross the street only where crossings are indicated by zebra stripes or arrows and at a green light. Use the underpasses where available. If caught in the middle when traffic starts moving, stay put, do not run. Special markings in mid-street

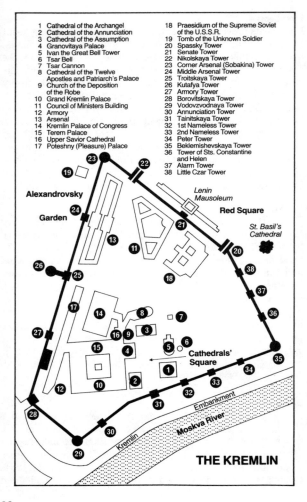

1 Cathedral of the Archangel
2 Cathedral of the Annunciation
3 Cathedral of the Assumption
4 Granovitaya Palace
5 Ivan the Great Bell Tower
6 Tsar Bell
7 Tsar Cannon
8 Cathedral of the Twelve
  Apostles and Patriarch's Palace
9 Church of the Deposition
  of the Robe
10 Grand Kremlin Palace
11 Council of Ministers Building
12 Armory
13 Arsenal
14 Kremlin Palace of Congress
15 Terem Palace
16 Upper Savior Cathedral
17 Poteshny (Pleasure) Palace

18 Praesidium of the Supreme Soviet
   of the U.S.S.R.
19 Tomb of the Unknown Soldier
20 Spassky Tower
21 Senate Tower
22 Nikolskaya Tower
23 Corner Arsenal (Sobakina) Tower
24 Middle Arsenal Tower
25 Troitskaya Tower
26 Kutafya Tower
27 Armory Tower
28 Borovitskaya Tower
29 Vodovzvodnaya Tower
30 Annunciation Tower
31 Tainitskaya Tower
32 1st Nameless Tower
33 2nd Nameless Tower
34 Peter Tower
35 Beklemishevskaya Tower
36 Tower of Sts. Constantine
   and Helen
37 Alarm Tower
38 Little Czar Tower

Alexandrovsky

Garden

Lenin
Mausoleum

Red Square

St. Basil's
Cathedral

Cathedrals'
Square

Embankment

Kremlin

Moskva River

THE KREMLIN

FINDING YOUR WAY

38

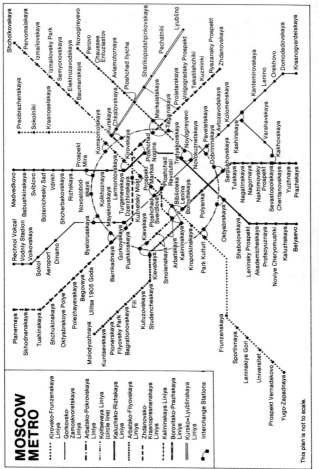

MOSCOW METRO

········ Kirovsko-Frunzenskaya Liniya

———— Gorkovsko-Zamoskvoretskaya Liniya

-·-·-· Arbatsko-Pokrovskaya Liniya

·········· Koltsevaya Liniya (circle line)

-··-··- Kaluzhsko-Rizhskaya Liniya

·········· Arbatsko-Filyovskaya Liniya

═══════ Zhdanovsko-Krasnopresnenskaya Liniya

═══════ Kalininskaya Liniya

═══════ Borovitsko-Prazhskaya Liniya

━━━━━━ Kursko-Lyublinskaya Liniya

◤ Interchange Stations

This plan is not to scale.

Planernaya
Skhodnenskaya
Tushinskaya
Shchukinskaya
Oktyabrskoye Polye
Polezhayevskaya
Begovaya
Ulitsa 1905 Goda

Rechnoi Vokzal
Vodniy Stadion
Volkovskaya
Sokol
Aeroport
Dinamo
Byelorusskaya

Medvedkovo
Babushkinskaya
Sviblovo
Botanichesky Sad
Vdnkh
Rizhskaya
Shcherbakovskaya
Prospekt Mira
Novoslobod-skaya
Kolkhoznaya
Lermontovskaya
Turgenevskaya
Dzerzhinskaya
Kuznetsky Most
Ploshchad Sverdlova
Ploshchad Revolutsii
Prospekt Marksa Nogina

Shcholkovskaya
Pervomaiskaya
Izmailovskaya
Izmailovsky Park
Semyonovskaya
Elektrozavodskaya
Baumanskaya
Chkalovskaya
Kurskaya
Marksistskaya
Taganskaya
Proletarskaya
Volgogradsky Prospekt
Tekstilshchiki
Kuzminki
Ryazansky Prospekt
Zhdanovskaya

Preobrazhenskaya
Sokolniki
Krasnoselskaya
Komsomolskaya
Kirovskaya

Novogireyevo
Perovo
Chaussee Entuziastov
Ploshchad Ilyicha
Aviamotornaya
Sharikopodshipnikovskaya
Pechatniki

Lyublino
Kantemirovskaya
Lenino
Orekhovo
Domodedovskaya
Krasnogvardeiskaya

Serpukhovskaya
Tulskaya
Nagatinskaya
Nagornaya
Nakhimovsky Prospekt
Sevastopolskaya
Chertanovskaya
Yuzhnaya
Prazhskaya

Varshavskaya
Kakhovskaya

Kolomenskaya
Avtozavodskaya
Paveletskaya
Dobrininskaya
Novokuznetskaya

Oktyabrskaya
Shabolovskaya
Leninsky Prospekt
Akademicheskaya
Profsoyuznaya
Noviye Cheryomushki
Kaluzhskaya
Belyaevo

Frunzenskaya
Sportivnaya
Leninskiye Gori
Universitet
Prospekt Vernadskovo
Yugo-Zapadnaya

Kuntsevskaya
Molodyozhnaya
Kutuzovskaya
Pionerskaya
Filyovsky Park
Bagrationovskaya
Fili
Studencheskaya
Kievskaya
Smolenskaya
Arbatskaya
Kalininskaya
Kropotkinskaya
Park Kulturi
Biblioteka Lenina
Borovitskaya
Polyanka

Barrikadnaya
Gorkovskaya
Pushkinskaya
Mayakovskaya

Tretyakovskaya
NovoYasenevo

indicate where you should stand if caught; traffic will pass *around* the spot, not over you! Cross *behind* parked buses and trolley-buses; only *in front* of stationary trams. As drivers are not allowed to hoot there may be no audible warning.

DIALOGUE: НА УЛИЦЕ (ON THE STREET)

Туристка:	Извините, пожалуйста. Как пройти к Эрмитажу?	ee-zvee-NEE-tyeh, pah-ZHAHL-stuh. kahk pruh-ee-TEE k eer-mee-TAHZH-oo?
Гражданин:	Да это не далеко отсюда. Идите прямо, и музей будет слева от вас.	dah EH-tuh nee duh-lee-KAW aht SYOO-duh. ee-DEE-tyeh PRYAH-muh ee moo-ZYEHY BOO-dyeht SLYEH-vuh aht vahs.
Туристка:	Спасибо. Можно пройти пешком?	spah-SEE-buh. MAWZH-nuh pruh-ee-TEE peesh-KAWM?
Гражданин:	Да, конечно! Но музей закрыт сегодня. Он закрыт по понедельникам.	dah, kah-NYEHSH-nuh! naw moo-ZYEHY zah-KRYT see-VAWD-nyuh. awn zah-KRYT puh puh-nee-DYEHL'-nee-kuhm.
Туристка:	Жаль. Тогда пойду завтра.	ZHAHL'. tahg-DAH puh-ee-DOO ZAHF-trah.
Гражданин:	Желаю вам приятно провести время в Ленинграде.	zheh-LAH-yoo vahm pree-YAHT-nuh pruh-vehs-TEE VRYEH-myuh v lee-neen-GRAH-dyeh.

Tourist:	Excuse me, how can I get to the Hermitage?
Citizen:	It's not far from here. Go straight ahead and the museum will be on the left.
Tourist:	Thanks. So I can walk there?
Citizen:	Yes, of course! But the museum is closed today. It's closed on Mondays.
Tourist:	Too bad. Then I'll go tomorrow.
Citizen:	Have a pleasant stay in Leningrad.

WALKING AROUND

It is hard to dispute the old adage that the best way to get to know a new city is to explore it on foot. If you are staying in one of the big Soviet cities for any length of time and plan to go anywhere on your own, you might do well to purchase a map from your hotel kiosk or from one of the many kiosks that sell newspapers and souvenirs on the street. The following section is designed to help you orient yourself and get directions from natives as you move around a city.

Excuse me, sir./madam.	ee-zvee-NEE-tyeh, muh-lah-DOY chee-lah-VYEHK/ DYEH-voosh-kuh	Извините, молодой человек/ девушка.
Where is the . . .	gdyeh nah-KHAW-deet-suh . . .	Где находится . . .
Do you have a map of the city?	oo vahs yehst' KAHR-tuh GAW-ruh-duh?	У вас есть карта города?
Could you show me on my map, please?	puh-kah-ZHY-tyeh, pah-ZHAHL-stuh nah mah-YEH KAHR-tyeh	Покажите, пожалуйста, на моей карте.
Can I get there on foot?	MAWZH-nuh too-DAH dah-BRAHT-suh peesh-KAWM?	Можно туда добраться пешком?

41

How far is it?	kahk duh-lee-KAW EH-tuh nah-KHAW-deet-suh?	Как далеко́ э́то нахо́дится?
I think I'm lost.	pah-MAW-yee-moo, yah zuh-bloo-DEEL-suh (-luhs).*	По-мо́ему, я заблуди́лся (-лась).*
Where can I find this address?	KAHK nuh-ee-TEE EH-tuht AH-drees?	Как найти́ э́тот а́дрес?
How long does it take on foot?	SKOL'-kuh VREH-mee-nee ee-TEE peesh-KAWM?	Ско́лько вре́мени идти́ пешко́м?
How can I get to	kahk pruh-ee-TEE	Как пройти́
• the Intourist Hotel?	• v gah-STEE-nee-tsoo een-too-REEST?	• в гости́ницу Интури́ст?
• . . . Street?	• nah OO-lee-tsoo . . . ?	• на у́лицу . . . ?
• . . . Avenue?	• nah prah-SPYEHKT . . . ?	• на проспе́кт . . . ?
• the train station?	• nah vahg-ZAHL?	• на вокза́л?
• the bus stop?	• nah uh-stah-NAWF-koo ahf-TAW-boo-suh?	• на́ остано́вку авто́буса?
• the ticket office?	• FKAH-soo?	• в ка́ссу?
• the subway?	• nah mee-TRAW?	• на метро́?
straight ahead	PRYAH-muh	пря́мо
to the right	na-PRAH-vuh	напра́во
to the left	na-LYEH-vuh	нале́во
a block away	CHYEH-reez ah-DEEN kvahr-TAHL	че́рез оди́н кварта́л
on the corner	nah oo-GLOO	на углу́
opposite	nah-PRAW-teef	напро́тив
across	CHYEH-reez	че́рез
next to	AW-kuh-luh	о́коло
near	RYAH-duhm	ря́дом
far	duh-lee-KAW	далеко́

*Заблуди́лась is the feminine form of lost.

42

PUBLIC TRANSPORTATION

Moscow and Leningrad are endowed with two of the most beautiful and most efficient public transportation systems in the world (see "Getting Around Moscow" above). Descending into the depths of the Moscow and Leningrad subway systems is like entering an underground museum complete with stained glass windows, marble pillars, and statues of important figures in Soviet history. Besides the subway, there are buses, tramways, trolleys, and taxi vans that follow a fixed route in these and other cities. Since most people don't own cars and public transportation is cheap, be prepared to fight the crowds on whatever form of public transportation you choose. But no trip to the Soviet Union is complete without braving a subway or trolley car.

As of this writing all forms of public transportation in every Soviet city cost 5 kopeks. You must pay extra for any baggage you carry on above-ground transportation. Occasionally an inspector does check to see that everyone has a ticket. In cities other than Moscow and Leningrad, you must buy your ticket directly from the driver. Wait till the vehicle has stopped, knock on the glass panel where the driver sits, and buy however many tickets you need. On these sorts of vehicles you'll need to stamp your ticket with stampers located throughout the vehicle. These tickets can also be bought at street kiosks and in your hotel.

To enter the subway, you must pass through a turnstile. You can get change from machines at the entrance to the subway station. If you are going to be in a city for an extended period of time you can buy a general monthly public transportation ticket, which can be used on all forms of transport. The ticket costs 6 rubles as of this writing. You flash it at the driver or turnstile attendant and pass through without paying the usual fare.

The public taxi vans make fewer, more extended stops than other forms of transportation.

USING THE METRO

Where's the nearest subway station?	gdyeh nah-KHAW-deet-suh blee-ZHAHY-shuh-yuh STAHN-tsee-yuh mee-TRAW?	Где находится ближайшая станция метро?
What line goes to . . . ?	kah-KAH-yuh LEE-nee-yuh ee-DYAWT nah/k . . .?	Какая линия идёт на/к . . . ?
Is this the train for . . . ?	EH-tuh mee-TRAW ee-DYAWT nah/k . . . ?	Это метро идёт на/к . . . ?
Where do I change to go to . . . ?	gdyeh MAWZH-nuh ZDYEH-luht' pee-ree-SAHD-koo nah . . . ?	Где можно сделать пересадку на . . . ?
Do I get off here to go to . . . ?	NAH-duh zdyehs' VY-ee-tee SHTAW-by pah-PAHST' nah . . . ?	Надо здесь выйти, чтобы попасть на . . . ?
Where can I get change?	gdyeh MAWZH-nuh ruhz-meen-YAHT' DYEHN'-gee?	Где можно разменять деньги?
Where is the map of the subway?	gdyeh zdyehs' nah-KHAW-deet-suh KAHR-tuh mee-TRAW?	Где здесь находится карта метро?

ON THE BUS

What bus do I take to go to . . . ?	kah-KOY ahf-TAW-boos ee-DYAWT duh . . . ?	Какой автобус идёт до . . . ?
Where is the nearest bus stop?	gdyeh nah-KHAW-deet-suh blee-ZHAHY-shuh-yuh ah-stah-NAWF-kuh ahf-TAW-boos-uh?	Где находится ближайшая остановка автобуса?

44

Does this bus go to . . . ?	ee-DYAWT lee EH-tuht ahf-TAW-boos duh . . . ?	Идёт ли э́тот авто́бус до . . . ?
When is the next bus to . . . ?	kahg-DAH aht-KHAW-deet SLYEH-doo-yoo-shee ahf-TAW-boos duh . . . ?	Когда́ отхо́дит сле́дующий авто́бус до . . . ?
What is the fare to . . . ?	SKAWL'-kuh STAW-eet prah-YEHZT duh . . . ?	Ско́лько сто́ит прое́зд до . . . ?
I want to get off at . . .	yah khah-CHOO VY-ee-tee nah . . .	Я хочу́ вы́йти на . .
Please tell me when to get off.	skah-ZHY-tyeh mnyeh, pah-ZHAHL-stuh, kahg-DAH mnyeh skhah-DEET'.	Скажи́те мне́, пожа́луйста, когда́ мне́ сходи́ть.
Do I need to change buses?	mnyeh NOOZH-nuh DYEH-luht' pee-ree-SAHD-koo?	Мне́ ну́жно де́лать переса́дку?
How many stops until the Hermitage?	SKAWL'-kuh ah-stah-NAW-vuhk duh eer-mee-TAHZH-uh?	Ско́лько остано́вок до Эрмита́жа?

TAKING A TAXI

Taxis in the Soviet Union are supposed to pick up passengers only at taxi stands. These are located near all the hotels and on most major streets and are marked with a big *T*. If taxis are free they have a green light in their front window. Also written on a sign in the front window is the time when the taxi goes off duty. Taxi drivers usually want to know where you are going before they decide to take you on as a passenger. Private citizens also pick up rides to make a little money on the side. Make sure you agree on the fee before taking off. If you don't feel comfortable doing this you can always order a taxi through your hotel.

DIALOGUE: НА ТАКСИ (IN A TAXI)

Тури́стка:	Здра́вствуйте. Вы свобо́дны?	ZDRAH-strooy-tyeh. vy svah-BAW-dny?
Води́тель:	Да́. Куда́ ва́м?	dah. koo-DAH vahm?
Тури́стка:	На́ автовокза́л.	nah ahf-tuh-vahg-ZAHL.
Води́тель:	Хорошо́.	khuh-rah-SHAW.
Тури́стка:	Ско́лько е́хать туда́?	SKOL'-kuh YEH-khuht' too-DAH?
Води́тель:	Два́дцать мину́т.	DVAHT-seet' mee-NOOT.
Тури́стка:	Прекра́сно. Спаси́бо.	pree-KRAH-snuh. spah-SEE-buh.

. . . .

Tourist:	Hello. Is this taxi free?
Driver:	Yes. Where are you going?
Tourist:	To the bus station.
Driver:	Fine.
Tourist:	How long does it take?
Driver:	Twenty minutes.
Tourist:	Great. Thank you.

Is this taxi	EH-tuh tah-KSEE	Это такси́
• free?	• svah-BAW-dnuh?	• свобо́дно?
• occupied?	• ZAHN-yeht-uh?	• за́нято?
Do you know this address?	vy ZNAH-yeh-tyeh EH-tuht AH-drehs?	Вы зна́ете э́тот а́дрес?
Please take me	uht-vee-ZEE-tyeh mee-NYAH pah-ZHAHL-stuh	Отвези́те меня́, пожа́луйста

46

• to the Intourist Hotel.	• v gah-STEE-nee-tsoo een-too-REEST	• в гости́ницу Интури́ст
• to the train station.	• nah vahg-ZAHL	• на вокза́л.
• to the center (of town).	• f TSEHN-tuhr	• в це́нтр.
• to Gorky Prospekt.	• nah prah-SPYEHKT GAWR'-kuh-vuh	• на проспе́кт Го́рького.
• to Lenin Street.	• nah OO-lee-tsoo LYEH-neen-uh.	• на у́лицу Ле́нина.
Slower, please.	puh-yeh-ZHAHY-tyeh MYEHD-leh-nyeh-y-eh, pah-ZHAHL-stuh	Поезжа́йте ме́дленнее, пожа́луйста.
Stop over here.	ah-stuh-nah-VEE-tyes' zdyehs'	Останови́тесь здесь.
meter	SHAWT-cheek	счётчик
fare	prah-YEHZD-nuh-yuh PLAH-tuh	проездна́я пла́та
tip	chee-yee-VY-yeh	чаевы́е
Where is the nearest taxi stand?	gdyeh blee-ZHAHY-shuh-yuh stah-YAHN-kuh tah-KSEE?	Где ближа́йшая стоя́нка такси́?
I'm in a hurry!	yah spee-SHOO!	Я спешу́!
How much is it to . . . ?	SKOL'-kuh STAW-eet dah-YEH-khuht' dah . . .?	Ско́лько сто́ит дое́хать до . . . ?
How much do I owe you?	SKOL'-kuh yah vahm DAWL-zhyn/dahl-ZHNAH?	Ско́лько я ва́м до́лжен/ должна́?

GOING BY TRAIN

As a foreigner in the Soviet Union you are not allowed to travel without a visa more than 40 kilometers out of the city where you are registered. Therefore if you wish to travel to another town by train you will probably have to organize this through the travel bureau in your hotel. Travel by train is a wonderful way to see the countryside.

There are four classes on Soviet trains, of which the *deluxe* (**международный вагóн** [mezhdunaródnyi vagón]) offers soft seats and private washrooms; the other classes have washrooms at the end of the cars. The *first-class* service is called "soft seat" (**мягкий вагóн** [miághii vagón]), with spring-cushioned berths; there are two or four berths in each compartment. There is no segregation of the sexes and you might find yourself sharing a two-berth compartment with someone of the opposite sex. The *second* or "hard-seat" class (**жесткий вагóн** [zhëstkii vagón]), has a cushion on wooden berths, available in two-, three- and four-berth compartments. The *third class* (**плацкáрм-ный вагóн** [platskártnyi vagón]), wooden berths without compartments, is used mostly in local service and rarely sold to foreigners. Most compartments have a small table, limited room for baggage (including under the seats) and usually a loudspeaker which can be cut off other than for arrival announcements on the rare occasions when these are made. In soft class there is also a table lamp.

As a foreigner, you may not have any choice but to travel first class, as that is all the travel agent in your hotel will sell you. The cars are divided into little cabins, which seat people during the day. At night the seats are converted into beds and the attendant brings fresh sheets and blankets. Smoking is not allowed in them and people go out to one end of the car, which is a designated smoking area. There are two bathrooms in each car and an attendant who will sell you tea and cookies. It's best to bring something to eat on an overnight trip, as not all trains are equipped with dining cars.

There is plenty of room to bring luggage with you on to the train. In the sleeper cars there is a big space above the beds to put suitcases.

Where is/are	Gdyeh	Где
• the train station?	• vahg-ZAHL?	• вокзáл?
• the ticket window?	• KAH-suh?	• кáсса?

• the first-class compartments?	• vah-GAW-ny PYEHR-vuh-vuh KLAH-suh?	• вагóны пéрвого клáсса?
• the sleeping cars?	• SPAHL'-ny-yeh vah-GAW-ny?	• спáльные вагóны?
• the baggage lockers?	• KAH-mee-ruh khrah-NYEH-nee-yuh?	• кáмера хранéния?
• the lost and found?	• KAWM-nuh-tuh pah-TYEHR-ee-nyx vee-SHEHY?	• кóмната потéрянных вещéй?
• the platform?	• pee-RAWN?	• перрóн?
I'd like a ticket to Minsk	mnyeh NOO-zhyn bee-LYEHT dah MEENSK-uh	Мнé нýжен билéт до Мúнска
• first class.	• v PYEHR-vuhm KLAH-syeh	• в пéрвом клáссе.
• second class.	• vuh ftah-RAWM KLAH-syeh	• во вторóм клáссе.
• one way.	• v ah-DEEN kah-NYEHTS.	• в одúн конéц.
• round trip.	• too-DAH ee ah-BRAHT-nuh.	• тудá и обрáтно.
• on the next train.	• nah SLYEH-doo-yoo-shee PAW-yeest	• на слéдующий пóезд.
I'd like to reserve	yah khah-CHOO zuh-kah-ZAHT'	Я хочý заказáть
• a bunk on top.	• VYEHRKH-nyeh-yeh MYEH-stuh	• вéрхнее мéсто.
• a bunk on the bottom.	• NEEZH-nyeh-yeh MYEH-stuh	• нúжнее мéсто.
• a bed in the sleeping car.	• MYEH-stuh f SPAHL'-nuhm vah-GAWN-yeh	• мéсто в спáльном вагóне.
Does this train stop in . . . ?	EH-tuht PAW-yeest uh-stah-NAH-vlee-vuh-yeht-suh v . . . ?	Этот пóезд останá-вливается в . . . ?
From which platform does it leave?	aht kah-KAW-vuh peh-RAWN-uh awn aht-KHOD-eet?	От какóго перрóна óн отхóдит?

Is the train on time?	PAW-yeest oo-KHAW-deet VAW-vree-myuh?	Поезд ухо́дит во́время?
Is there a change of trains in . . . ?	NOOZH-nuh DYEH-luht' pee-ree-SAHD-koo v . . . ?	Ну́жно де́лать переса́дку в . . . ?
I'm going to Riga; do I need to change trains?	yah YEH-doo v REE-goo; mnyeh NOOZH-nuh DYEH-luht' pee-ree-SAHD-koo?	Я е́ду в Ри́гу; мне́ ну́жно де́лать переса́дку?
Is this seat free?	EH-tuh MYEH-stuh svah-BAWD-nuh?	Это ме́сто свобо́дно?
This seat is occupied.	EH-tuh MYEH-stuh ZAHN-yuh-tuh	Это ме́сто за́нято.
Could you tell me when we get to Volgograd?	vy nee SKAH-ZHY-tyeh, kahg-DAH my pree-YEH-deem v vuhl-gah-GRAHD?	Вы́ не ска́жете, когда́ мы́ прие́дем в Волгогра́д?
When does the train arrive in Odessa?	vah SKOL'-kuh PAW-yeest pree-KHAW-deet vah-DYEH-soo?	Во ско́лько по́езд прихо́дит в Оде́ссу?
What time does it arrive?	vah SKOL'-kuh awn pree-KHAW-deet?	Во ско́лько о́н прихо́дит?
Is there a dining car?	yehst' vah-GAWN reh-stah-RAHN?	Есть ваго́н-рестора́н?
Is there a sleeping car?	yehst' SPAHL'-ny vah-GAWN?	Есть спа́льный ваго́н?
Excuse me, I believe this is my seat.	eez-vee-NEE-tyeh, pah-MAW-yee-moo EH-tuh mah-YAW MYEH-stuh	Извини́те, по-мо́ему э́то моё ме́сто.

COMMON PUBLIC SIGNS

Вхо́д	fkhawt	ENTRANCE
Вы́ход	VY-khuht	EXIT
Остано́вка	ah-stah-NAWV-kuh	(BUS) STOP
Откры́то	aht-KRY-tuh	OPEN
Закры́то	zah-KRY-tuh	CLOSED

50

Вниз	vnees	DOWN
Вверх	vyehrkh	UP
Нажмите	nahzh-MEE-tyeh	PUSH
Остановитесь	ah-stuh-nah-VEE-tyehs'	STOP
Осторожно	ah-stah-RAW-zhnuh	DANGER
Не входите	nee fkhah-DEE-tyeh	DO NOT ENTER
Туалет	too-ah-LYEHT	TOILET
Не курить	nee koo-REET'	NO SMOKING
Нельзя фотогра- фировать	neel'-ZYAH fuh-tuh- grah-FEER-uh-vuht'	NO PHOTOGRAPHS
Запасной выход	zuh-pahs-NOY VY- khuht	EMERGENCY EXIT
от себя	aht see-BYAH	PUSH (DOOR)
к себе	ksee-BYEH	PULL (DOOR)

4/ACCOMMODATIONS

Soviet hotels come in two basic categories: those for foreign tourists (Intourist hotels) and those for Soviet citizens. Most cities you will visit have an Intourist hotel, which is considerably more comfortable than regular hotels and offers a wide array of shops and services. Hotels are selected for you by Intourist and you are informed of the selection upon your arrival in the USSR.

Most every visitor, whether on business or pleasure, comes to the USSR with a travel package purchased through a licensed Intourist agent. In an age of increased joint ventures with the West, new options have become available for booking rooms upon arrival through travel services of such companies as Finnair and Pan American.

The Intourist hotel is a world unto itself; almost every service you could want may be found within: a foreign exchange bank; a post office; car rental and tour guide services; foreign-currency shops stocked with vodka, caviar, and souvenirs; restaurants; and bars. At every Intourist hotel there is a service bureau, where you may buy tickets to local performances of theater, ballet, opera, circus, and folkloric performances. Some hotels even have swimming pools, saunas, bowling alleys, bars, nightclubs, discotheques, and other entertainment, all available for hard currency through their service bureaus.

As with everything else in the Soviet Union, quality goods and services remain the object of healthy competition among visitors and residents alike. The glitter and hum of hotel restaurants and the bustling international atmosphere attract Soviet citizens, whose great desire to enter the hotel is equaled only by the hotel management's polite but firm request that they visit other establishments. Each guest is provided with a visitor's card, which is presented to the doorman when entering the hotel.

DIALOGUE В ПРИЁМНОЙ (AT THE FRONT DESK)

Клие́нт:	Здра́вствуйте! У ва́с е́сть двухме́стный но́мер?	ZDRAHST-vooy-tyeh! oo vahs yehst' dvookh-MYEHST-ny NAWM-eer?
Администра́тор:	Одну́ мину́точку. Та́к, у вас е́сть зака́з?	ahd-NOO mee-NOOT-uhch-koo. tahk, oo vahs yehst' zah-KAHS?
Клие́нт:	Да́, коне́чно. Во́т на́ше извеще́ние.	dah, kah-NYEHSH-nuh. vawt NAH-shuh eez-vee-SHEHN-yuh.
Администра́тор:	Да́йте ва́ш па́спорт, пожа́луйста. Вы его́ полу́чите в па́спортном столе́ за́втра.	DAHY-tyuh vahsh PAHS-puhrt, pah-ZHAHL-stuh. vy yee-VAW pah-LOO-chee-tyuh FPAHS-puhrt-nuhm stah-LYEH ZAHF-truh.
Клие́нт:	Где́ я получу́ клю́ч?	gdyeh yah puh-loo-CHOO klyooch?
Администра́тор:	Сда́йте визи́тную ка́рточку вон там. Когда́ бу́дете уходи́ть из гости́ницы, сдаёте клю́ч и берёте ка́рточку с собо́й.	ZDAHY-tyuh vee-ZEET-noo-yoo KAHRT-uhch-koo vawn tahm. kahg-DAH oo-KHAW-dee-tyuh ees gahs-TEE-nee-tsy, zdah-YAW-tyuh klyooch ee bee-RYAW-tyuh KAHR-tuhch-koo sah-BOY.
Клие́нт:	Спаси́бо большо́е.	spah-SEE-buh bahl'-SHOY-uh.

. . . .

53

Customer:	Hello. Do you have a room for two people?
Manager:	One moment, please. Do you have a reservation?
Customer:	Yes, of course. Here's our voucher.
Manager:	May I have your passport, please? You may pick it up tomorrow at the passport desk.
Customer:	Where do I get the key?
Manager:	Hand in your hotel pass over there. When you leave the hotel, drop off your key and take the pass with you.
Customer:	Thank you very much.

HOTEL ARRANGEMENTS

I have a reservation.	oo mee-NYAH zah-KAH-zuhn NAWM-eer	У меня́ зака́зан но́мер.
It's in the name of . . .	eh-tuh nah EE-myuh . . .	Это на и́мя . . .
I'd like a room	Yah by khah-TYEHL(-uh) NAWM-eer	Я бы хоте́л(-а)* но́мер
• for tonight.	• nah see-VAW-dnyuh	• на сего́дня.
• with one bed.	• ahd-nah-MYEHS-ny	• одноме́стный.
• with two beds.	• dvookh-MYEHS-ny	• двухме́стный.
• with a double bed.	• dvookh-SPAHL'-ny	• двухспа́льный.
• with a shower.	• ZDOOSH-uhm	• с ду́шем.

*Note male-female agreement with subjects.

• with air-conditioning.	• skahn-dee-tsy-ahn-EHR-uhm	• с кондиционе́ром.
• with hot water.	• zgah-RYAHCH-ee vah-DOY	• с горя́чей водо́й.
• with a private bath.	• ss VAHN-noy	• с ва́нной
• with a television.	• stee-lee-VEEZ-uhr-uhm	• с телеви́зором.
• with a balcony.	• zbahl-KAWN-uhm	• с балко́ном.
• with a view facing the street.	• SVEED-uhm nah OO-lee-tsoo	• с ви́дом на у́лицу.
• with a view facing the sea.	• SVEED-uhm nah MAWR-yuh	• с ви́дом на мо́ре.
We're going to stay	my nah	Мы на
• one night.	• ahd-NOO nawch	• одну́ но́чь.
• a few days.	• NYEH-skawl'-kuh dnyay	• не́сколько дней.
• a week.	• ahd-NOO nee-DYEH-lyoo	• одну́ неде́лю.
I'd like to see the room.	yah by khah-TYEHL(-uh) puh-smah-TRYEHT' NAWM-eer	Я бы хоте́л(-а) посмотре́ть но́мер.
I'll take it.	yah vahz'-MOO yee-VAW	Я возьму́ его́.
I don't want this room.	yah nee khah-CHOO EHT-uht NAWM-eer	Я не хочу́ э́тот но́мер.
This room is very	EH-tuht NAWM-eer AW-cheen'	Э́тот но́мер о́чень
• small.	• MAH-leen'-kee	• ма́ленький.
• cold.	• khah-LAWD-ny	• холо́дный.
• hot.	• TYAWP-ly	• тёплый.
• dark.	• TYAWM-ny	• тёмный.
• noisy.	• SHOOM-ny	• шу́мный.
How much is it	SKAWL'-kuh STAW-eet NAWM-eer	Ско́лько сто́ит но́мер
• per night?	• nah ahd-NOO nawch?	• на одну́ ночь?
• per week?	• nah ahd-NOO nee-DYEH-lyoo?	• на одну́ неде́лю?

55

• with all meals?	• SPAWL-nuhm pee-TAHN-yuhm?	• с по́лным пита́нием?
• with breakfast?	• ZAHF-truhk-uhm?	• с за́втраком?
• without meals?	• bees pee-TAHN-yuh?	• без пита́ния?
Does the price include	fklyoo-CHAHY-yuht lee tsy-NAH	Включа́ет ли цена́
• taxes?	• nah-LAWG-ee?	• нало́ги?
• service?	• oo-SLOO-gee?	• услу́ги?
Where can I park?	gdyeh MAWZH-nuh pah-STAHV-eet' mah-SHY-noo?	Где мо́жно поста́вить маши́ну?
Please have my bags sent up to my room.	aht-nee-SEE-tyuh pah-ZHAL-stuh, moy bah-GAHSH VNAWM-eer	Отнеси́те, пожа́луйста, мой бага́ж в но́мер.
This is for your safe.	EH-tuh nah khrah-NYEH-nee-yuh	Это на хране́ние.

HOTEL SERVICES

I'd like to speak with	yah by khah-TYEHL(-uh) puh-guh-vah-REET'	Я бы хоте́л(-а) поговори́ть
• the manager.	• sahd-mee-nee-STRAHT-uhr-uhm	• с администра́тором.
• the hall porter.	• snah-SEEL'-sheek-uhm	• с носи́льщиком.
• the maid.	• ZGAWR-neesh-noy	• с го́рничной.
Please bring me	pree-nee-SEE-tyuh pah-ZHAHL-stuh	Принеси́те, пожа́луйста,
• a blanket.	• ah-dee-YAH-luh	• одея́ло.
• hangers.	• VYEHSH-uhl-kee	• ве́шалки.
• some ice.	• l'dah	• льда́.
• a pillow.	• pah-DOO-shkoo	• поду́шку.
• some stationery.	• boo-MAHG-oo ee kahn-VYEHRT	• бума́гу и конве́рт.
• some soap.	• MYL-uh	• мы́ло.
• a towel.	• puh-lah-TYEHN-tsuh	• полоте́нце.

56

- toilet paper.

Is there
- an elevator?

- a garage?
- a laundry?

- a beauty salon?

- a swimming pool?
- an Intourist representative?

- an exchange bank?

- a restaurant?
- a Beriozka store?

- a bar?
- a newsstand?

My . . . doesn't work.
- lock
- light
- outlet
- television
- heat
- fan
- air conditioner

May I change to another room?

I have no hot water.

- too-ah-LYEHT-noo-yoo boo-MAHG-oo yehst' lee oo vahs
- leeft?

- gahr-AHSH?
- PRAH-cheech-nuh-yuh?

- puh-reekh-MAHKH-eer-skuh-yuh?

- bah-SYEHY-uhn?

- preet-stah-VEE-teel-'-stvuh een-too-REEST-uh?
- bahnk ahb-MYEHN-uh vah-LYOOT-y?

- rees-tah-RAHN?
- muh-gah-ZEEN beer-YAWS-kuh?

- bahr?
- kee-AWSK?

oo mee-NYAH nee rah-BAW-tuh-yeht
- zah-MAWK
- svyeht
- rah-ZYEHT-kuh
- tee-lee-VEEZ-uhr.
- ah-tah-PLYEH-nyuh.
- veen-tee-LYAH-tuhr.
- kahn-dee-tsyahn-EHR.

MAW-zhnuh pee-ree-YEHKH-uht' vdroo-GOY NAW-meer?

OO mee-NYAH nyeht gah-RYAH-chee vah-DEE

- туалéтную бумáгу.

Есть ли у вас
- лифт?

- гарáж?
- прáчечная?

- парикмá-херская?

- бассéйн?

- представи́-тельство Интури́ста?

- банк обмéна валю́ты?

- рестора́н?
- магази́н «Берёзка»?

- ба́р?
- кио́ск?

У меня́ не рабо́тает
- замо́к.
- свет.
- розéтка
- телеви́зор.
- отоплéние.
- вентиля́тор.
- кондиционéр.

Мо́жно переéхамь в другóй нóмер?

у меня́ нет горя́чей воды.

57

Could you make up the room now?	vy nee mahg-LEE by oo-BRAHT' NAWM-eer syehy-CHAHS	Вы не могли́ бы убра́ть но́мер сейча́с?
I'm in room . . .	yah FKAWM-nuh-tyuh NAWM-eer . . .	Я в ко́мнате но́мер . . .
Do you have a child care center?	NYEHT lee oo vahs KAWM-nuh-ty MAH-tee-ree ee ree-BYAWN-kuh?	Нет ли у вас ко́мнаты ма́тери и ребёнка?
We're leaving tomorrow. Please prepare the bill.	my oo-yee-ZHAHY-uhm ZAHF-truh; pree-gah-TAWF'-tyuh pah-ZHAHL-stuh, shawt	Мы уезжа́ем за́втра. Пригото́вьте, пожа́луйста, счёт.
We're leaving at 10:00 A.M.	my oo-yee-ZHAHY-eem VDYEH-seet chee-SAWF	Мы уезжа́ем в де́сять часо́в утра́.
Could you please call me a taxi?	vy nee mahg-LEE by VY-zvuht' mnyeh tahk-SEE?	Вы не могли́ бы вы́звать мне такси́?
Please have my baggage brought downstairs.	aht-nee-SEE-tyuh pah-ZHAL-stuh, moy bah-GAHSH vnees.	Омеси́те, пожа́луйста, мой бага́ж вниз.

USING THE TELEPHONE

At most hotels you must order long distance calls up to an hour ahead of time. You will find a list of telephone numbers for placing these orders in your room.

operator	tee-lee-fawn-EEST-kuh	телефони́стка
I'd like to make a call in the city.	yah khah-CHOO puh-zvah-NEET' VGAWR-uht	Я хочу́ позвони́ть в го́род.
I would like to order a call	yah by khah-TYEHL(-uh) zuh-kah-ZAHT'	Я бы хоте́л(-а) заказа́ть
• to another city.	• meezh-doo-gah-R-AWD-ny	• междугоро́дный.
• to another country.	• meezh-doo-nah-R-AWD-ny	• междунаро́дный.

• to the U.S.A.	• sshAH	• США.
• to England.	• VAHN-glee-yoo	• Англию.
• to Canada.	• fkah-NAH-doo	• Кана́ду.
Please connect me	suh-yeed-een-EE-tyuh mee-NYAH, pah-ZHAHL-stuh	Соедини́те меня́, пожа́луйста,
• with reception.	• spree-YOHM-nuhy	• с приёмной.
• with the restaurant.	• srees-tah-RAHN-uhm	• с рестора́ном.
• with room 203.	• SNAWM-eer-uhm DVYEH-stee tree	• с но́мером 203.

5/SOCIALIZING

Meeting people and making friends is perhaps one of the most exciting aspects of traveling abroad. Interpersonal relationships are especially important when visiting a socialist country because of the political and cultural stereotypes that have built up over many years when travel was less frequent. These encounters provide unique opportunities to learn about Russian culture, and to understand how Russians behave in social situations. An open mind, curiosity, and sensitivity to their culture will certainly help you create good relationships, and your interest will be matched by the Russians' enthusiasm to learn about your culture and interests.

You will notice that when Russian people meet or part, they always shake hands. Close friends often embrace, and it is not unusual for both men and women to kiss each other (traditionally, three times). Russians are very polite, and often wish each other a good appetite before a meal or safe journey before a trip and congratulate one another on special holidays and occasions. In everyday life, though, when people see each other twice or more in the course of a day, they usually greet each other only once.

You may notice that Russians stand closer to people than do North Americans and Northern Europeans. This subtle difference in the sense of "personal space" can be disconcerting at first, until you get used to it. But this is balanced by a slight Russian reserve in impersonal and public encounters; while friendship is very highly valued, Russians do not always smile at strangers. But once you are introduced you will find Russians to be extremely hospitable, warm, and generous.

The foreign guest may hope to maintain contact with his new friends after he returns home. Do not be too downcast if this proves impossible. Your letters, if they reach their destination, will probably not receive a reply, and you will find it very difficult to telephone a Soviet home from abroad. Partly this is the result of postal censorship, and partly the trouble of old habits of caution, which die hard.

DIALOGUE: ЗНАКОМСТВО (INTRODUCTIONS)

Джейн Браун:	Добрый день! Разрешите представиться. Меня зовут Джейн Браун.	DAW-bry dyehyn'! ruhz-ree-SHY-tyeh preet-STAH-veet-suh. mee-NYAH zah-VOOT Jane Brown.
Иван Семёнов:	Очень приятно с вами познакомиться. Меня зовут Иван Семёнов.	AW-cheen' pree-YAHT-nuh SVAH-mee puh-znah-KAWM-eet-suh. mee-NYAH zah-VOOT ee-VAHN see-MYAWN-uhf.
Джейн Браун:	Очень приятно.	AW-cheen' pree-YAHT-nuh.
Иван Семёнов:	Вы здесь в отпуске?	vy zdyehys VAWT-poosk-yeh?
Джейн Браун:	Да. Я буду в Москве ещё четыре дня.	dah. yah BOO-doo vmahsk-VYEH ee-SHAW chee-TYR-ee DNYAH.
Иван Семёнов:	Желаю вам приятно провести время!	zhy-LAH-yoo vahm pree-YAHT-nuh pruh-vees-TEE VRYEHY-myuh!

. . . .

Jane Brown:	Hello! Allow me to introduce myself. My name is Jane Brown.
Ivan Semyonov:	Pleased to meet you. My name is Ivan Semyonov.
Jane Brown:	Pleased to meet you.
Ivan Semyonov:	Are you here on vacation?

61

| Jane Brown: | Yes. I'll be here in Moscow another four days. |
| Ivan Semyonov: | Have a pleasant time! |

INTRODUCTIONS AND GREETINGS

I'd like to introduce you to	yah khah-TYEHL(-uh) by preet-STAH-veet' vahs	Я хоте́л(-а)* бы предста́вить вас
• Igor.	• EE-guhr-yoo	• Игорю.
• Tatyana.	• tah-TYAH-nyeh	• Татья́не.
• Mikhail Petrovich.	• mee-khah-EEL-oo pee-TRAW-vee-choo	• Михаи́лу Петро́вичу.
• Marina Ivanovna.	• mah-REE-nyeh ee-VAHN-uhv-nyeh	• Мари́не Ива́новне.
Pleased to meet you.	AW-cheen' pree-YAHT-nuh	Очень прия́тно.
Allow me to introduce myself.	ruhz-ree-SHY-tyeh preet-STAHV-eet-suh	Разреши́те предста́виться.
What's your name?	kahk vahs zah-VOOT?	Ка́к вас зову́т?
My name is	mee-NYAH zah-VOOT	Меня́ зову́т
• John.	• ee-VAHN	• Ива́н.
• Mary.	• mah-REE-yuh	• Мари́я.
I am . . .	yah . . .	Я . . .
This is	EH-tuh	Это
• my husband.	• moy MOOSH	• мой му́ж.
• my wife.	• mah-YAH zhy-NAH	• моя́ жена́.
• my colleague.	• moy kah-LYEHG-uh	• мой колле́га.
• my friend.	• moy DROOK	• мой дру́г.
How are you?*	kahk vy puh-zhy-VAH-yee-tyeh?	Ка́к вы пожива́ете?

*One can expect a long or detailed answer to this question in the Soviet Union, because the question is more than a formality.

Fine, thanks, and you?	spah-SEE-buh, khuh-rah-SHAW, ah vy?	Спаси́бо, хорошо́, а вы?
How's it going?	kahk dyee-LAH?	Ка́к дела́?
Everything's fine.	VSYAW fpah-RYAHT-kyeh	Всё в поря́дке.
Where are you from?	aht-KOO-duh vy?	Отку́да вы?
I live	yah zhy-VOO sshAH	Я живу́
• in the United States.		• в США.
• in England.	VAHN-glee-ee	• в А́нглии.
• in Canada.	fkah-NAH-dyeh	• в Кана́де.
• in New York.	vnyoo-YAWR-kyeh	• в Нью-Йо́рке.
• in California.	fkah-lee-FAWR-nee-ee	• в Калифо́рнии.
That's in the	EH-tuh	Э́то
• north.	• nah SYEH-vee-ryeh	• на се́вере.
• south.	• nah YOO-gyeh	• на ю́ге.
• east.	• nuh vahs-TAWK-yeh	• на восто́ке.
• west.	• nah ZAH-puh-dyeh	• на за́паде.
That's near	EH-tuh nee-duh-lee-KAW uht	Э́то недалеко́ от
• the coast.	• puh-bee-RYEHZH-yuh	• побере́жья.
• Canada.	• kah-NAH-dy	• Кана́ды.
• the border.	• grah-NEE-tsy	• грани́цы.
• the ocean.	• ah-kee-AHN-uh	• океа́на.
• the mountains.	• gawr	• гор.
I'm from New York.	yah ees nyoo-YAWRK-uh	Я из Нью-Йо́рка.
How long will you be here?	SKAWL'-kuh VRYEH-mee-nee vy zdyehys' prah-BOO-dee-tyeh?	Ско́лько вре́мени вы здесь пробу́дете?
I'll be here for	yah prah-BOO-doo zdyehys'	Я пробу́ду здесь
• a week.	• nee-DYEH-lyoo	• неде́лю.
• another week.	• yee-SHAW ahd-NOO nee-DYEH-lyoo	• ещё одну́ неде́лю.

• three weeks.	• tree nee-DYEH-lee.	• три неде́ли.
• a short while.	• nee-DAWL-guh	• недо́лго.
• a long while.	• DAWL-guh	• до́лго.
What hotel are you staying at?	fkah-KOY gahs-TEEN-ee-tsyeh vy zhy-VYAW-tyeh?	В како́й гости́нице вы живёте?
I am at the . . . hotel.	yah zhy-VOO vgahs-TEEN-ee-tsuh . . .	Я живу́ в гости́нице . . .
How do you like the Soviet Union?	kak vahm NRAH-vee-tsuh sah-VYEHT-skee sah-YOOS?	Как вам нра́вится Сове́тский Сою́з?
It's just the way I imagined it.	yah yee-VAW preet-stah-VLYAHL(-uh) EE-myeh-nuh tahk	Я его́ представля́л(-а)* и́менно та́к.
It's hard to say—I just arrived.	pah-KAH TROO-dnuh skah-ZAHT'. yah TAWL'-kuh shtaw pree-YEKH-uhl(-uh)	Пока́ тру́дно сказа́ть. Я то́лько что прие́хал(-а).*
It's wonderful!	pree-KRAHS-nuh!	Прекра́сно!
I like the people very much.	mnyeh AW-cheen' NRAH-vee-tsuh LYOO-dee	Мне о́чень нра́вятся лю́ди.
I like the countryside.	Mnyeh NRAHV-ee-tsuh dee-RYEHV-nyuh	Мне нра́вится дере́вня.
Everything is so . . . here.	VSYAW zdyehys' tahk	Всё здесь так
• interesting	• een-tee-RYEHS-nuh	• интере́сно.
• different	• puh-droog-AWM-oo	• по-друго́му.
• pretty	• krah-SEE-vuh	• краси́во.
That's	EH-tuh	Э́то
• strange.	• STRAHN-nuh	• стра́нно.
• silly.	• GLOO-puh	• глу́по.
• wonderful.	• pree-KRAHS-nuh	• прекра́сно.
• sad.	• pee-CHAHL'-nuh	• печа́льно.
• beautiful.	• krah-SEE-vuh	• краси́во.

*In the past tense, verbs agree in number and gender with the subject of the sentence. Masculine past-tense endings are -л, femine are -ла, neuter are -ло, and plural are -ли.

GETTING ACQUAINTED

What's your profession?	ktaw vy puh-prah-FYEHS-see-ee?	Кто́ вы по профе́ссии?
Where do you work?	gdyeh vy rah-BAW-tuh-yeh-tyeh?	Где вы рабо́таете?
I work	yah rah-BAW-tuh-yoo	Я рабо́таю
• in an office.	• fkahn-TAWR-yeh	• в конто́ре.
• in a factory.	• nuh zah-VAWD-yeh	• на заво́де.
I'm a	yah	Я
• businessman./ businesswoman.	• beez-nees-MYEHN (-kuh)	• бизнесме́н (-ка).
• doctor.	• vrahch	• вра́ч.
• lawyer.	• ahd-vah-KAHT	• адвока́т
• teacher.	• pree-puh-dah-VAH-teel'(-nee-tsuh)	• преподава́тель (-ница).
• artist.	• khoo-DAWZH-neek	• худо́жник.
• plumber.	• vuh-duh-prah-VAWT-cheek	• водопрово́дчик
I don't work.	yah nee rah-BAW-tuh-yoo.	Я не рабо́таю.
I'm retired.	Yah nah PYEHN-see-ee.	Я напе́нсии.
May I offer you a drink?	MAWZH-nuh preed-lah-ZHYT' vahm SHTAW-nee-boot' VY-peet'?	Мо́жно предложи́ть вам что-нибу́дь вы́пить?
Yes, please.	dah, pah-ZHAL-stuh	Да, пожа́луйста.
No, thanks.	nyeht, spah-SEE-buh	Нет, спаси́бо.
Let's drink	dah-VAHY-tyeh VY-peem	Дава́йте вы́пьем
• to our meeting.	• zah FSTRYEH-choo	• за встре́чу.
• to friendship.	• zah DROOZH-boo	• за дру́жбу.
• to your health.	• zah VAH-shuh zdah-RAWV-yeh	• за ва́ше здоро́вье.
• to our acquaintance.	• zuh znah-KAWMST-vuh	• за знако́мство.
Do you mind if I smoke?	Transcription to come	Вы не возража́ете, е́сли я закурю́?

65

Not at all, go ahead and smoke.	nee-chee-VAW, koo-REE-tyeh	Ничего, курите.
Yes, a bit. Please smoke on the balcony.	dah, neem-NAWZH-kuh. koo-REE-tyeh nuh-bahl-KAWN-y-eh, pah-ZHAHL-stuh	Да, немножко. Курите на балконе, пожалуйста.
Are you married?	vy zhy-NAHT-y-zAH-moozh-uhm?	Вы замужем?/ женаты?
No, but I have a boyfriend./ girlfriend.	nyeht, naw oo meen-yah yehst' pree-YAH-teel'(-nee-tsuh)	Нет, но у меня есть приятель (-ница).
I'm single.	yah ah-DEEN/ahd-NAH	Я не женат/не замужем.
I'm a widow(-er).	yah vdah-VAH/vdah-VYEHTS	Я вдова./вдовец.
I'm divorced.	yah vrahz-VAWD-yeh	Я в разводе.
I'm traveling with a friend.	yah-oo spree-YAH-teel'-yehm/spree-Y-AH-teel'-neet-sehy	Я путешествую с приятелем/с приятельницей.
May I telephone you?	MAWZH-nuh vahm pah-zvah-NEET'?	Можно вам позвонить?
What's your phone number?	kah-KOY vahsh NAWM-eer tee-lee-FAWN-uh?	Какой ваш номер телефона?
What is your address?	kah-KOY oo vahs AHD-rees?	Какой у вас адрес?
Can I give you a ride somewhere?	MAWZH-nuh vahs pahd-vees-TEE koo-DAH nee-BOOT'?	Можно вас подвезти куда-нибудь?
Don't bother, thank you.	spah-SEE-buh, nee NAH-duh	Спасибо, не надо.
I can take a taxi.	yah mah-GOO vzyaht' tahk-SEE	Я могу взять такси.

WITH FRIENDS

| Would you like to come with us | khah-TEE-tyeh pah-ee-TEE SNAHM-ee | Хотите пойти с нами |

• to a cafe?	• fkah-FEH?	• в кафе́?
• to a restaurant?	• vrees-tah-RAHN?	• в рестора́н?
• to the movies?	• fkee-NAW?	• в кино́?
• to someone's house?	• VGAWS-tee?	• в го́сти?
Gladly.	soo-dah-VAWL'ST-vee-yehm	С удово́ль-ствием.
May I bring a friend?	MAWZH-nuh mnyeh pree-glah-SEET' sah-BOY DROOG-uh?	Мо́жно мне пригласи́ть с собо́й дру́га?
Please come visit us at our house!	pree-khah-DEE-tyeh VGAWS-tee!	Приходи́те в го́сти!
You're so kind!	Transcription to come	Как э́то ми́ло с ва́шей стороны́!
Are you free	vy svah-BAWD-ny	Вы свобо́дны
• this evening?	• see-VAWD-nyuh VYEHCH-eer-uhm?	• сего́дня ве́чером?
• tomorrow?	• ZAHF-truh?	• за́втра?
I'll wait here.	yah puh-dah-ZHDOO zdyehys'.	Я подожду́ здесь.
I'll pick you up in the hotel lobby.	yah vahs FSTRYEH-choo vees-tee-BYOO-lyeh	Я вас встре́чу в вестибю́ле.
It's late.	PAWZ-nuh	По́здно.
It's time to go.	pah-RAH ee-TEE	Пора́ идти́.
We're leaving tomorrow.	my ZAHF-truh oo-yee-ZHAH-yehm	Мы за́втра уезжа́ем.
I had a very good time.	yah AW-cheen' khuh-rah-SHAW prah-VYAWL/prah-veel-AH VRYEH-myuh	Я о́чень хорошо́ провёл/ провела́ вре́мя.
We're going to miss you.	my BOOD-yehm skoo-CHAHT' beez vahs	Мы бу́дем скуча́ть без вас.
It was nice to have met you.	BYL-uh AW-cheen' pree-YAHT-nuh SVAHM-ee puh-znah-KAWM-eet-suh	Бы́ло о́чень прия́тно с ва́ми позна-ко́миться.

Give my best wishes to	pee-ree-DAHY-tyeh pree-VYEHT	Переда́йте приве́т
• your family.	• VAHSH-y seem-YEH	• ва́шей семье́.
• your friend.	• VAHSH-y-moo DROOG-oo	• ва́шему дру́гу.
• Nina.	• NEE-nyeh	• Ни́не.
• Volodya.	• vah-LAW-dyeh	• Воло́де.

TALKING ABOUT LANGUAGE

Do you speak*	vy guh-vah-REE-tyeh	Вы говори́те
• English?	• puh-ahn-GLEE-skee?	• по-англи́йски?
• French?	• puh-frahn-TSOO-skee?	• по-францу́зски?
• German?	• puh-nee-MYEHTS-kee?	• по-неме́цки?
• Russian?	• pah-ROOS-kee?	• по-ру́сски?
I only speak English.	yah guh-vahr-YOO TAWL'-kuh puh-ahn-GLEE-skee	Я говорю́ то́лько по-англи́йски.
I speak a little Russian.	yah guh-vahr-YOO nee-MNAW-guh pa-ROOS-skee	Я говорю́ немно́го по-ру́сски.
My Russian is so bad!	yah tahk PLAW-khuh gah-vah-RYOO pah-ROOS-kee	Я так пло́хо говорю́ по-ру́сски.
That is not true. Your Russian is excellent.	nee-PRAHV-duh. oo vahs aht-LEECH-nee ROO-skee yee-ZYK	Непра́вда. У вас отли́чный ру́сский язы́к.
I really want to learn Russian.	yah AW-cheen' khah-CHOO VY-oo-cheet' ROO-skee yee-ZYK	Я о́чень хочу́ вы́учить ру́сский язы́к.
Speak more slowly.	guh-vah-REE-tyeh MYEHD-leen-yeh-yeh	Говори́те ме́дленнее.

*For a more complete list of languages, see p. 196.

Could you repeat that?	puhf-tah-REE-tyeh, pah-ZHAHL-stuh?	Повтори́те, пожа́луйста.
How do you write that?	kahk EH-tuh PEE-shyt-suh?	Как э́то пи́шется?
How do you say . . . in Russian?	kahk skah-ZAHT' . . . pah-ROO-skee?	Как сказа́ть . . . по-ру́сски?
Is there anyone who speaks English here?	KTAW-nee-boot' zdyehys guh-vahr-EET puh-ahn-GLEE-skee?	Кто-нибу́дь здесь говори́т по-англи́йски?
Could you translate this for me?	nee mahg-LEE by vy pee-ree-vees-TEE EH-tuh dlyah mee-NYAH?	Не могли́ бы вы перевести́ э́то для меня́?
Can you understand me?	vy mee-NYAH puh-nee-MAH-yee-tyeh?	Вы меня́ понима́ете?
I understand.	yah puh-nee-MAH-yoo	Я понима́ю.
I don't understand.	yah nee puh-nee-MAH-yoo	Я не понима́ю.
Russian is a beautiful language.	ROOS-kee AW-cheen' krah-SEE-vy yee-ZYK	Ру́сский о́чень краси́вый язы́к.
I like Russian a lot.	ROOS-kee yee-ZYK mnyeh AW-cheen' NRAH-veet-suh	Ру́сский язы́к мне о́чень нра́вится.

THE FAMILY

I'm traveling	yah poo-tee-SHEHST-voo-yoo	Я путеше́ствую
• with my family.	• suh-svah-YEHY see-MYOY	• со свое́й семьёй.
• without my family.	• bees svah-YEHY see-MEE	• без свое́й семьи́.
My family lives in New York.	mah-YAH see-MYAH zhy-VYAWT vnyoo-YAWR-kyeh	Моя́ семья́ живёт в Нью-Йо́рке.
My family is spread out.	mah-YAH see-MYAH rahz-BRAWS-uhn-uh	Моя́ семья́ разбро́сана.

I have a . . . family.	oo mee-NYAH . . . see-MYAH	У меня́ . . . семья́.
• big	• bahl'-SHAH-yuh	• больша́я
• small	• MAH-leen'-kuh-yuh	• ма́ленькая
Do you have any children?	oo vahs yehyst DYEHY-tee?	У вас есть де́ти?
Yes, I have	dah, oo mee-NYAH yehyst'	Да́, у меня́ есть
• a child.	• ree-BYAWN-uhk	• ребёнок.
• two children.	• DVAW-yeh dee-TYEHY	• дво́е дете́й.
• three children.	• TRAW-yeh dee-TYEHY	• тро́е дете́й.
• four children.	• CHEHT-vee-ruh dee-TYEHY	• че́тверо дете́й.
• five children.	• PYAH-tee-ruh dee-TYEHY	• пя́теро дете́й.
• a daughter.	• dawch	• до́чь.
• a son.	• syn	• сы́н.
• two daughters.	• dvyeh DAWCH-eer-ee	• две́ до́чери.
• two sons.	• dvah SYN-uh	• два́ сы́на.
• a father.	• ah-TYEHTS	• оте́ц.
• a mother.	• maht'	• ма́ть.
• a grandfather.	• DYEHD-oosh-kuh	• де́душка.
• a grandmother.	• BAHB-oosh-kuh	• ба́бушка.
• a husband.	• moosh	• му́ж.
• a wife.	• zhy-NAH	• жена́.
• a grandson.	• vnook	• вну́к.
• a granddaughter.	• VNOOCH-kuh	• вну́чка.
• a cousin. (male)	• dvah-YOO-ruhd-nee braht	• двою́родный бра́т.
• a cousin. (female)	• dvah-YOO-ruhd-nuh-yuh sees-TRAH	• двою́родная сестра́.
• an aunt.	• TYAW-tyuh	• тётя.
• an uncle.	• DYAH-dyuh	• дя́дя.
• a sister.	• sees-TRAH	• сестра́.
• a brother.	• braht	• бра́т.
• in-laws.	• svuh-ee-KEE	• свояки́.

• a father-in-law. (wife's father/ husband's father)	• tyehyst'/SVYAW-kor	• тесть./свёкор.
• a mother-in-law. (wife's mother/ husband's mother)	• TYAW-shuh/svee-KRAWF'	• тёща./ свекро́вь.
Here are pictures of my family.	vawt fuh-tah-GRAH-fee-ee mah-YEHY see-MEE	Вот фотогра́фии мое́й семьи́.
my eldest son	moy STAHR-shy syn	мой ста́рший сын
my eldest daughter	mah-YAH STAHR-shuh-yuh dawch	моя́ ста́ршая дочь
my youngest son	moy MLAHT-shy syn	мой мла́дший сын
my youngest daughter	mah-yah MLAHT-shuh-uh dawch	моя́ мла́дшая дочь
How old are your children?	SKAWL'-kuh lyeht VAHSH-eem DYEHYT-yuhm?	Ско́лько лет ва́шим де́тям?
My children are	mah-YEE DYEHYT-ee	Мои́ де́ти
• very young.	• AW-cheen' MAH-leen-kee-yeh	• о́чень ма́ленькие.
• all grown up.	• vsyeh VY-ruhs-lee	• все вы́росли.
Ivan is three years older than Pavel.	ee-VAHN nah tree GAW-duh STAHR-shuh, chehm PAHV-eel	Ива́н на три го́да ста́рше, чем Па́вел.

IN THE HOME

Make yourself at home.	CHOOST-voo-yeh-tyeh see-BYAH kahk DAW-muh	Чу́вствуйте себя́ как до́ма.
You may sit here.	sah-DEE-tees' syoo-DAH	Сади́тесь сюда́.
What a pretty apartment!	kah-KAH-yuh krah-SEE-vuh-yuh kvahr-TEE-ruh!	Кака́я краси́вая кварти́ра!

71

I really like this neighborhood.	EH-tuht rah-YAWN mnyeh AW-cheen' NRAHV-eet-suh	Этот райо́н мне о́чень нра́вится.
at our house	oo nahs DAWM-uh	у нас до́ма
at your house	oo vahs DAWM-uh	у вас до́ма
at my house	oo mee-NYAH DAWM-uh	у меня́ до́ма
At home (i.e., in the U.S.) we like baseball.	oo nahs LYOO-beet byehys-BAWL	У нас лю́бят бейсбо́л.
Here (i.e., in the U.S.S.R.) people like soccer.	oo vahs LYOO-beet food-BAWL	У вас лю́бят футбо́л.
Here is	EH-tuh	Это
• the kitchen.	• KOOKH-nyuh	• ку́хня.
• the living room.	• gahs-TEEN-uh-yuh	• гости́ная.
• the dining room.	• stahl-AWW-uh-yuh	• столо́вая.
• the bedroom.	• SPAL'-nyuh	• спа́льня.
• the attic.	• cheer-DAHK	• черда́к.
• the cellar.	• pahd-VAHL	• подва́л.
• the closet.	• stee-NOY shkahf	• стенно́й шкаф.
• the couch.	• dee-VAHN	• дива́н.
• the rug.	• kah-VYAWR	• ковёр.
• the appliances.	• pree-spuh-sah-BLYEHN-ee-yuh	• приспо-собле́ния.
• the armchair.	• KRYEHS-luh	• кре́сло.
• the table.	• stawl	• стол.
• the ceiling.	• puh-tah-LAWK	• потоло́к.
• the floor.	• pawl	• пол.
It's	EH-tuh	Это
• a house.	• dawm	• дом.
• an apartment.	• kvahr-TEER-uh	• кварти́ра.
• a villa.	• VEEL-luh	• ви́лла.
• a country house.	• DAH-chuh	• да́ча.
Would you like something to drink?	khah-TEE-tyeh shtaw-nee-BOOT' pah-PEET'?	Хоти́те что-нибу́дь попи́ть?
Would you like something to eat?	khah-TEE-tyeh shtaw-nee-BOOT' pah-YEHYST'?	Хоти́те что-нибу́дь пое́сть?

Have you tried real Russian food?	vy PRAW-buh-vuh-lee nuhs-tah-YAHSH-o-o-yoo ROOSK-oo-yoo KOOKH-nyoo?	Вы про́бовали настоя́щую ру́сскую ку́хню?
Thanks for your hospitality.	spah-SEE-buh zah guhs-tee-pree-EEM-stvuh	Спаси́бо за гостепри- и́мство.
This is something for you to remember us by.	EH-tuh vahm nah PAHM-yuht' ah nahs	Это вам на па́мять о нас.
Come and visit us!	pree-yeh-ZHAHY-tyeh knahm VGAWST-ee!	Приезжа́йте к нам в го́сти!

6/DINING OUT

The visitor to the Soviet Union encounters a wide range of national and regional cuisines across the country's 15 republics. This cultural diversity is reflected as well in many of the new cooperative restaurants in Moscow. Discovering a charming restaurant or a new cuisine is always part of the adventure of visiting a foreign country. However, if you like, the service bureau at your hotel can recommend one, as it may be difficult to obtain a reservation on your own. The following is a partial list of categories of eating establishments:

ресторáн [rees-tah-RAHN]

Restaurants are the largest, most varied, and most expensive eating establishments in the Soviet Union. They are not simply for dropping in and eating. Restaurant meals are rarely casual or quick. Instead, Russians arrange leisurely parties or intimate dinners at restaurants. At the larger nightspots there is live music, dancing, and drinking, and occasionally toasts are exchanged with people at neighboring tables.

кафé [kah-FEH]

Cafés are also special places for social events and often match the festive atmosphere of restaurants. However they often offer special menus ranging from ice cream, (**морóженое**, mah-RAW-zhehn-nuh-yeh) to a standard local menu. As with all popular meeting places, admittance often requires waiting in line.

гриль-бáр
(greel'-BAHR)

These are small and warm restaurants featuring a menu of rotisserie-grilled food, usually chicken.

74

пельме́нная
(peel'-MYEHN-uh-yuh)

Cheap and fast, this is a self-serve cafeteria for Russian workers in a hurry. Very often it's standing room only. It offers the basic hearty Russian dumplings (**пельме́ни**, peel'-MYEH-nee), served with sour cream, mustard, or vinegar.

пивно́й бар
(peev-NOY bahr)

Bars serve beer only and occasionally seafood, such as **креве́тки** (kree-VYEHT-kee), shrimp, or dried fish snacks.

пиццери́я
(pee-TSEH-ree-yah)

Pizzerias appeared all across the USSR not long ago (along with Italian pop music), offering their own interpretation of pizza, as well as calzones.

столо́вая
[stah-LAW-vuh-yuh]

Springing from the belief that the working Soviet man and woman must be provided with inexpensive meals the **столо́вая** (stah-LAW-vuh-yuh)) (cafeteria) offers plain but filling food.

шашлы́чная
[shahsh-LYCH-nuh-yuh]

Either stand-up or sit-down style, you can get smoky Georgian shishkebab with tomato sauce, onion and a hunk of bread.

Eating hours are usually interrupted by a staff lunch break either from 1:00 to 2:00 or 2:00 to 3:00 in the afternoon. All restaurants close by 11:00 P.M., except for some hard-currency restaurants and bars in Intourist hotels, which may stay open as late as 2:00 A.M.

MEALS AND MEALTIMES

Breakfast (за́втрак, ZAHF-truhk), is traditionally a very solid meal in Russia. At the breakfast table you'll usually find one or more of the following: sausages (**соси́ски**, sah-SEES-

75

kee), bread and cheese, hearty pancakes made with farmer's cheese (**твóрог**, TVAW-ruhk), fried eggs, or a steaming bowl of cream of wheat (**мáнная кáша**, MAHN-uh-yuh KAH-shuh). Though fresh fruit juices are not drunk, the Russians drink a beverage of stewed fruit (**компóт**, kahm-PAWT) or a healthy yogurt drink (**кефúр**, kee-FEER), and the customary glass of hot tea. While coffee is available, don't be surprised if it is Turkish style (with thick grounds in the bottom of your cup), coffee with milk and sugar, or instant coffee, and is served after the food, as it is with lunch and dinner.

Lunch (**обéд**, ah-BYEHT) is traditionally the largest meal of the day and is served from 1:00 to 2:00 in the afternoon. Lunch always begins with a salad or appetizer—**закýска** (zah-KOOS-kuh)—then one of the hot soups the Russians love: the famous borscht (**борщ**, borsh), which may be either tart (**щи**, shi), or full of meat and vegetables (**солянка**, sah-LYAHN-kuh), or fish soup (**уха́**, oo-KHAH.) Soup is usually served with **пирожки** (pee-ransh-KEE), a pastry stuffed with a filling of rice, cabbage, or meat. Lunch also includes a hot main course, dessert, and tea or coffee.

Dinner (**ýжин**, OO-zhyn) is eaten later in the evening than is customary in the United States, usually around 8:00. In the Soviet Union eating at restaurants is not an everyday occurrence, so dinner most often is eaten at home and may be a simpler meal than lunch. It does not usually include a soup course.

DIALOGUE: В РЕСТОРАНЕ (AT THE RESTAURANT)

| Официáнт: | Чтó вы закáзываете? | shtaw vy zah-KAHZ-y-vahy-tyeh? |
| Гость: | Я не знáю. Какúе у вас специáльные блю́да? | yah nee ZNAH-yoo. kah-KEE-yeh oo vahs spee-TSYAL'-ny-yeh BLYOO-duh? |

76

Официа́нт:	Я рекоменду́ю бифште́кс.	yah ree-kuh-meen-DOO-yoo beef-SHTYEHKS.
Гость:	Хорошо́.	khuh-rah-SHAW.
Официа́нт:	А что́ вы бу́дете пи́ть?	ah shtaw vy BOO-dee-tyeh peet'?
Гость:	Принеси́те мне буты́лку минера́льной воды́.	pree-nee-SEE-tyeh mnyeh boo-TYL-koo mee-nee-RAHL'-nuhy vah-DY.

. . . .

Waiter:	May I take your order?
Customer:	I don't know. What are your specialties?
Waiter:	I recommend beefsteak.
Customer:	Fine.
Waiter:	Will you have something to drink?
Customer:	Please bring me a bottle of mineral water.

FINDING A RESTAURANT

Can you recommend a good restaurant?	nee puh-ree-kuh-meen-DOO-yeh-tyeh lee khah-RAW-shy rees-tah-RAHN?	Не пореко-менду́ете ли хоро́ший рестора́н?
I want a . . . restaurant.	yah khah-CHOO . . . rees-tah-RAHN	Я хочу́ . . . рестора́н.
• typical Russian	• tee-PEECH-nuh ROOS-kee	• типи́чно ру́сский
• national (i.e., ethnic)	• nah-tsyah-NAHL'-ny	• национа́льный
Is it far from here?	awn nah-KHAW-dee-tsuh duh-lee-KAW aht-SYOO-duh?	Он нахо́дится далеко́ отсю́да?

77

Is it expensive?	tahm DAW-ruh-guh?	Там до́рого?
No, it's inexpensive.	nyeht, tahm DYAW-shuh-vuh	Нет, там дёшево.
Do they accept foreign currency or credit cards?	ah-NEE pree-nee-MAH-yoot vah-LYOO-too EE-lee kree-DEET-ny-yeh KAHR-tuhch-kee?	Они́ принима́ют валю́ту и́ли креди́тные ка́рточки?
What's the name of the restaurant?	kahk nah-zy-VAHY-eet-suh rees-tah-RAHN?	Ка́к называ́ется рестора́н?
It's called Moskva.	awn nah-zy-VAH-eet-suh mahsk-VAH	Он называ́ется «Москва́».
Do you need to reserve a table?	NOOZH-nuh zuh-kah-ZAHT' STAWL-eek?	Ну́жно заказа́ть сто́лик?
I'd like to reserve a table	yah by khah-TYEHL(-uh) zuh-kah-ZAHT' STAWL-eek	Я бы хоте́л(-а) заказа́ть сто́лик
• for two people.	• nah dvah-EEKH	• на двои́х.
• for this afternoon.	• nah see-VAW-dnyuh dnyawm	• на сего́дня днём.
• for tomorrow evening.	• nah ZAHF-truh VYEHCH-uhr-uhm	• на за́втра ве́чером.
• for 8:00 P.M.	• nah VAW-seem' chee-SAWF	• на во́семь часо́в.
• near the orchestra.	• pah-BLEE-zheh kahr-KYEHS-troo	• побли́же к орке́стру.
• far from the orchestra.	• pah-DAHL-sheh aht-ahr-KYEHS-truh	• пода́льше от орке́стра.
• by the window.	• AWK-uh-luh ahk-NAH	• о́коло окна́.
• in the no-smoking section.	• dlyah nee-koo-RYAH-sheekh	• Для некуря́щих.

RESTAURANT EXPRESSIONS

| Waiter! | muh-lah-DOY chee-lah-VYEHK! | Молодо́й челове́к! |
| Waitress! | DYEH-voo-shkuh! | Де́вушка! |

78

The menu, please.	pree-nee-SEE-tyeh pah-ZHAHL-stuh, mee-NYOO	Принеси́те, пожа́луйста, меню́.
What are your specialties?	kah-KEE-yeh oo vahs FEER-meen-ny-yeh BLYOO-duh?	Каки́е у вас фи́рменные блю́да?
I'd like a light meal.	yah by khah-TYEHL (-uh) SHTAW-tuh LYAWKH-kuh-yuh	Я бы хоте́л(а) что-то лёгкое.
Do you have children's portions?	oo vahs yehyst' DYEHT-skee-yee PAWR-tsy-ee?	У ва́с есть де́тские по́рции?
I'm ready to order.	yah VY-bruhl(-ah)	Я вы́брал(-а).
To begin with . . . (for starters)	nah PYEHR-vuh-yuh yah vahz'-MOO . . .	На пе́рвое я возьму́ . . .
Next . . .	pah-TAWM . . .	Пото́м . . .
Finally . . .	nuh-kah-NYEHTS . . .	Наконе́ц . . .
That's all.	ee fsyaw	И всё.
Is the dish	EH-tuh BLYOO-duh	Э́то блю́до
• baked?	• zuh-pee-CHAWN-uh-yuh?	• запечённое?
• boiled?	• vah-RYAWN-uh-yu-h?	• варёное?
• broiled?	• ahb-ZHAHR-een-uh-yuh?	• обжа́реное?
• braised?	• too-SHAWN-uh-yuh?	• тушёное?
• fried?	• ZHAHR-een-uh-yuh?	• жа́реное?
• smoked?	• kahp-CHAWN-uh-yeh?	• копчёное?
I prefer the meat	yah preed-puh-chee-TAH-yoo MYAH-suh	Я предпочита́ю мя́со
• well-done.	• khuh-rah-SHAW prah-ZHAHR-een-uh-yuh	• хорошо́ прожа́ренное.
• medium.	• prah-ZHAHR-een-uh-yuh	• прожа́ренное.
• rare.	• SKRAWV-yoo	• с кро́вью.
The soup is cold.	soop ah-STYL	Суп осты́л.

79

I'd like another dish.	yah khah-CHOO droo-GOY-uh BLYOO-duh	Я хочу́ друго́е блю́до.
More water, please.	pree-nee-SEE-tyeh yee-SHAW vah-DY, pah-ZHAHL-stuh	Принеси́те ещё воды́, пожа́луйста.
I'm on a special diet.	yah nah dee-EH-tyeh	Я на дие́те.
I'm a vegetarian.	yah-vee-gee-tah-RYAHN-eets(-AHN-kuh)	Я вегетариа́нец (-а́нка).
Is it spicy? (hot)	EH-tuh AWS-truh-yuh?	Это о́строе?
I'm diabetic.	yah dee-ah-BYEHT-eek	Я диабе́тик.
I can't eat	mnyeh neel'-ZYAH	Мне нельзя́
• salt.	• sawl'	• соль.
• fat.	• zhyr	• жи́р.
• sugar.	• SAH-khuhr	• са́хар.
• flour.	• moo-KOO	• муку́.
I don't eat pork.	yah nee yehm svee-NEE-ny	Я не ем свини́ны.
I want to lose weight.	yah khah-CHOO puh-khoo-DYEHYT'	Я хочу́ похуде́ть.
Have you finished?	vy zah-KAWN-chee-lee?	Вы зако́нчили?
Could we have	pree-nee-SEE-tyeh, pah-ZHAHL-stuh,	Принеси́те, пожа́луйста,
• tap water?	• vah-DY	• воды́.
• silverware?	• pree-BAWR-y	• прибо́ры.
• a napkin?	• sahl-FYEHT-koo	• салфе́тку.
• a cup?	• CHAHSH-koo	• ча́шку.
• a glass?	• stah-KAHN	• стака́н.
• a fork?	• VEEL-koo	• ви́лку.
• a spoon?	• LAWSH-koo	• ло́жку.
• a knife?	• nawsh	• нож.
• an ashtray?	• PYEH-peel'-nee-tsoo	• пе́пельницу.
• a plate?	• tah-RYEHL-koo	• таре́лку.
• a toothpick?	• zoo-bah-CHEEST-koo	• зубочи́стку.
• a saucer?	• BLYOO-tseh	• блю́дце.

• some bread?	• KHLYEHB-uh	• хлеба.
• some butter?	• MAHS-luh	• масла.
• some salt?	• SAWL-ee	• соли.
• some pepper?	• PYEHR-tsuh	• перца.
• some mustard?	• gahr-CHEE-tsy	• горчицы.
• some lemon?	• lee-MAWN-uh	• лимона.
• some sugar?	• SAH-khuh-roo	• сахару.
• some ketchup?	• KYEHTCH-oop-uh	• кетчупа.
• some horseradish?	• KHRYEHN-uh	• хрена.
• some mayonnaise?	• muh-yah-NEHZ-uh	• майонеза.
• a little more . . . ?	• yee-SHAW neem-NAWSH-kuh . . .	• ещё немножко .
• some coffee?	• KAW-fyeh	• кофе.
• some tea?	• CHAH-yoo	• чаю.
Where is the bathroom?	gdyeh too-ah-LYEHT?	Где туалет?

PAYING THE BILL

May I have the check, please?	pree-nee-SEE-tyeh, pah-ZHAHL-stuh shawt	Принесите, пожалуйста, счёт.
Only one check, please.	ah-DEEN shawt	Один счёт.
Please give us separate checks.	rah-shee-TAHY-tyeh nahs pah-aht-DYEHL'-nym sheet-AHM, pah-ZHAHL-stuh	Рассчитайте нас по отдельным счетам, пожалуйста.
Is service included?	ahp-SLOO-zhy-vah-nyeh fklyoo-CHAHY-eet-suh?	Обслуживание включается?
I think there's a mistake.	yah DOO-muh-yoo, shtaw ah-SHYB-lees' FSHAWT-yeh	Я думаю, что ы ошиблись в счёте.
Do you accept	vy pree-nee-MAH-yeh-tyeh	Вы принимаете
• credit cards?	• kree-DEET-ny-yeh KAHR-tuhch-kee?	• кредитные карточки?

81

• traveler's checks?	• dah-RAWZH-ny-yeh CHEHY-kee?	• доро́жные че́ки?
• dollars?	• DAWL-uhr-y?	• до́ллары?
This is for you.	EH-tuh dlyah vahs	Это для вас.
Keep the change.	byehs ZDAH-chee	Без сда́чи.
The meal was excellent.	yee-DAH by-LAH pree-KRAHS-nuh-yuh.	Еда́ была́ прекра́сная.
And the service was also.	ee ahp-SLOO-zhy-vah-nyeh TAW-zhuh	И обслу́живание то́же.

ABOUT RUSSIAN FOOD

In the USSR, eating occupies a central part of daily life, and the kitchen is the principal gathering place in the Russian home for family and friends. The kettle on the stove boils constantly, providing hot water for tea—the fuel of conversation and friendships. Early influences on Russian cooking came from the Turks, the Vikings, the Mongols, and the Tatars (who introduced tea to Russia). Later culinary innovations and refinements were brought by the Dutch, the Swiss, and especially the French. Many of the dishes you will try bear the mark of one of these cuisines, though by now they have been thoroughly integrated into Russian cooking.

A Russian meal normally begins with many appetizers such as a salad of diced meat, potatoes, and pickles; smoked fish; pickled mushrooms; eggplant caviar; or chicken liver pâté. Pickled vegetables and milk products are staples of the Russian cuisine. Appetizers are often followed at lunchtime with a soup made from vegetables such as beets, cabbage, and potatoes, and served with stuffed pastries (пирожки́, pee-rahsh-KEE). Russians are partial to hearty main courses of beef, chicken, or fish served with potatoes and aromatic Russian black bread. They are particularly fond of sweets, which makes the occasional shortage of sugar all the more sharply felt. Dessert, served with tea, is very often ice cream, rich cakes, or sweets. Jam, preserves, or honey are served along with tea, and are eaten with a spoon from a small saucer.

Some typical Russian dishes are **котле́ты по-ки́евски** (kaht-LYEHT-y pah-KEE-ehf-skee; Chicken Kiev), **бефстро́ганоь** (beef-STROH-guhn-uhf; Beef Stroganoff), **цыплёнок табака́** (tsy-PLYOHN-uhk tuh-bah-KAH; grilled chicken), **голубцы́** (guh-loop-TSY; stuffed cabbage), and **пельме́ни** (peel'-MYEHY-ny; meat-filled dumplings served with sour cream). Even if you do not travel further than the major cities of the Russian republic, you will have ample opportunity to taste the national cuisines of the Caucasus, Central Asia, and the Baltic republics. Georgian, Armenian, and Azerbaijani cooking offer dishes somewhat spicier than Russian ones. Georgian restaurants are particularly plentiful in Russia and feature chicken in walnut sauce (**саци́ви**, sah-TSY-vy), peppery lamb-tomato soup, (**харчо́**, khahr-CHOH), and round cheese-filled pastry (**хачапу́ри**, khuh-chuh-POO-ree), served hot, and **шашлы́к** (shahsh-LYK), a dish like shish kebab served with delicious flat bread, **лава́ш**, lah-VAHSH). A Central Asian meal offers fried meat pastries (**чебуре́ки**, chee-boo-RYEH-kee), grilled lamb shish kebab, and the delicious rice dish **плов** (plohf), prepared with carrots, raisins, and either beef or lamb. As a rule, almost every republic has its own state-run restaurant in Moscow, and the appearance of numerous private (cooperative) and family-run establishments has added to the multinational variety of foods available in the Soviet Union.

Russians are legendary drinkers. Strong spirits—vodka, especially—can play a part in daily activities and situations: as a folk remedy for a cold, for good luck before departing on a trip or any new undertaking, and of course in social and family gatherings and events. While grapes for wine are grown in the Caucasus, Moldavia, and other regions, these are not usually as available in the quantity and quality of vodka, which you will also find with various added ingredients such as lemon juice and pepper. Georgian wines, though, are among the best available. Cognac produced in Armenia is often very fine (the more stars on the label, the better the cognac) and Soviet champagne (without vintage) comes in a variety of styles: semidry, semisweet, and sweet, the latter being the favorite in the Soviet Union. Other drinks include cordials flavored with fruits. Nonalcoholic beverages are also plentiful. At meals you will be served mineral water or light beverages flavored with red currant, strawberry, or cranberry juice. More familiar soft drinks such as Coca-Cola and Pepsi, as well as Fanta orange soda, are widely available. Every meal of the day is accompanied by and completed with tea.

To most people of average means living in the Soviet Union, restaurants are for special occasions, and considerable planning usually goes into making the events smooth and satisfying. Not surprisingly, the level of service, selection, and quality of the food is often in direct proportion to the cost of the meal. The criterion most people use for selecting an eating place is knowing someone who works there. This can make the difference between a lackluster, even frustrating evening out and a satisfying and memorable dining experience.

TYPICAL RUSSIAN DISHES

Закуска	zah-KOOS-kuh	Appetizers
салат из помидоров	sah-LAHT ees puh-mee-DAWR-uhf	tomato salad
салат из огурцов	sah-LAHT eez ah-goor-TSAWF	cucumber salad
винегрет	vee-nee-GRYEHT	beet salad
селёдка	see-LYAWT-kuh	herring
сёмга	SYAWM-guh	salmon (smoked)
лососина	luh-sah-SEE-nuh	salmon
шпроты	SHPRAW-ty	sprats
сардины	sahr-DEE-ny	sardines
миноги	mee-NAW-gee	lampreys
кильки	KEEL'-kee	spiced sprats
. . . икра	. . . ee-KRAH	. . . caviar
• паюсная	• PAH-yoos-nuh-yuh	• pressed
• зернистая	• zeer-NEEST-uh-yuh	• fresh black
• кётовая	• KYEHT-uh-vuh-yuh	• red
паштет	pahsh-TYEHT	pâté
студень	STOO-dyehyn'	aspic
холодец	khuh-lah-DYEHTS	jellied meat or fish

84

| масли́ны | mahs-LEE-ny | black olives |
| ассорти́ | ah-sahr-TEE | assortment |

Суп — soop — Soup

бульо́н	boo-LYAWN	bouillion
борщ	bawrsh	borscht
щи	shee	cabbage soup
рассо́льник	rahs-SAWL'-neek	sorrel and meat soup
соля́нка	sah-LYAHN-kuh	fish or meat soup with pickled cucumber
уха́	oo-KHUH	fish soup
окро́шка	ah-KRAWSH-kuh	cold vegetable soup made with *kvass*
суп-пюре́	soop-pyoo-REH	puree or cream soup
похлёбка	pah-KHLYAWP-kuh	meat and potato soup

Мя́со — MYAH-suh — Meat

говя́дина	gah-VYAH-dee-nuh	beef
теля́тина	tee-LYAH-tee-nuh	veal
бара́нина	bah-RAH-nee-nuh	lamb, mutton
свини́на	svee-NEE-nuh	pork
бифште́кс	beef-SHTYEHKS	steak
ланге́т	lahn-GYEHT	cut of lean beef
эскало́п	ee-skah-LAWP	escalope
рагу́	rah-GOO	ragout
гуля́ш	goo-LYAHSH	goulash
шни́цель	SHNEE-tsehl'	schnitzel
бито́чки	bee-TAWCH-kee	meatballs
котле́ты	kaht-LYEHT-y	ground-meat patties
шашлы́к	shahsh-LYK	shish kebab
люля́ кеба́б	Lyoo-LYAH kee-BAHP	ground-lamb patties
бастурма́	buh-stoor-MAH	grilled marinated meat
филе́	fee-LYEH	filet
руле́т	roo-LYEHT	roulade
антреко́т	ahn-tree-KAWT	entrecote
жарко́е	ZHAHR-kaw-yeh	stewed meat
колбаса́	kuhl-bah-SAH	sausage
соси́ски	sah-SEES-kee	wieners

85

поросёнок	puh-rah-SYAWN-uhk	suckling pig
ветчина́	vee-chee-NAH	ham
печёнка	pee-CHAWN-kuh	liver
по́чки	PAWCH-kee	kidneys
кро́лик	KRAW-leek	rabbit
за́яц	ZAH-yeets	hare
язы́к	yee-ZYK	tongue
каба́н	kah-BAHN	wild boar
медвежа́тина	meed-vee-ZHAHT-een-uh	bear meat
олени́на	ah-lee-NEE-nuh	venison
лося́тина	lah-SYAH-tee-nuh	elk

Пти́ца	PTEE-tsuh	Fowl
ку́рица	KOO-reet-suh	chicken
у́тка	OOT-kuh	duck
гусь	goos'	goose
инде́йка	een-DYEHY-kuh	turkey
куропа́тка	koo-rah-PAHT-kuh	partridge
фаза́н	fah-ZAHN	pheasant
ря́бчик	RYAHP-cheek	grouse

Ры́ба	RYB-uh	Fish
сельдь/селёдка	syehyl'd'/see-LYAWT-kuh	herring
севрю́га	see-VRYOOG-uh	sevruga (sturgeon)
белу́га	bee-LOOG-uh	beluga (white sturgeon)
сте́рлядь	STEER-lyaht	sterlet (Black Sea sturgeon)
осетри́на	ah-see-TREE-nuh	sturgeon
о́кунь	AW-koon'	perch
форе́ль	fah-RYEHYL'	trout
щу́ка	SHOOK-uh	pike
треска́	trees-KAH	cod
карп	kahrp	carp
у́горь	OO-guhr'	eel
креве́тки	kree-VYEHT-kee	shrimp

86

кра́бы	KRAHB-y	crabs
ра́ки	RAHK-ee	crayfish
ка́мбала	KAHM-buh-luh	flounder
лососи́на	luh-saw-SEE-nuh	salmon
туне́ц	too-NYEHTS	tuna
па́лтус	PAHL-toos	halibut
суда́к	soo-DAHK	zander (pike perch)

Хлеб, мучны́е блю́да	khlyehp, mooch-NY-yeh BLYOO-duh	Bread, Grains, Dumplings, Pancakes, etc.
бе́лый хлеб	BYEHL-y khlyehp	white bread
чёрный хлеб	CHAWRN-y khlyehp	black bread
бу́лочка	BOO-luhch-kuh	roll
сухари́	soo-khahr-EE	melba toast
бутербро́д	boo-tyeer-BRAWT	open sandwich
пиро́г	pee-RAWK	baked filled pastry
пирожо́к	pee-rah-ZHAWK	small baked or fried filled pastry
запека́нка	zuh-pee-KAHN-kuh	baked pudding
кулебя́ка	koo-lee-BYAH-kuh	baked filled pie
пельме́ни	peel'-MYEHYN-ee	boiled meat-filled dumplings
варе́ники	vah-RYEHN-ee-kee	cheese or fruit dumplings
чебуре́ки	chee-boo-RYEHK-ee	fried meat-filled pastries
ватру́шка	vah-TROOSH-kuh	curd-tart
расстега́й	ruh-stee-GAHY	oval meat- or fish-filled pastry
блины́	blee-NY	pancakes
бли́нчики	BLEEN-cheek-ee	blintzes
ола́дьи	ah-LAHD'-ee	fritters
рис	rees	rice
плов	plawf	rice pilaf
ка́ша	KAH-shuh`	hot cereal
ма́нная ка́ша	MAHN-nuh-yuh KAH-shuh	cream of wheat
гре́чневая ка́ша	GRYEHCH-nee-vuh-yuh KAH-shuh	buckwheat grits

87

ри́совая ка́ша	REES-uh-vuh-yuh KAH-shuh	rice cereal
лапша́	lahp-SHAH	noodles, spaghetti
макаро́ны	muh-kah-RAWN-y	noodles, macaroni

Моло́чные блю́да	mah-LAWCH-ny-yeh BLYOO-duh	Dairy Products
молоко́	muh-lah-KAW	milk
ма́сло	MAHS-luh	butter
сыр	syr	cheese
тво́рог	TVAWR-uhk	cottage cheese
сыро́к	syr-AWK	cream cheese with sugar and raisins
сы́рники	SYR-nee-kee	cheese pancakes
кефи́р	kee-FEER	buttermilk-like drink
ря́женка	RYAHZH-uhn-kuh	baked yogurt
сли́вки	SLEEF-kee	cream
смета́на	smee-TAHN-uh	sour cream
простоква́ша	pruhs-tah-KVAH-shuh	yogurt
яйцо́	yee-TSAW	egg
омле́т	ahm-LEHT	omelet
яи́чница	yee-EESH-nee-tsuh	fried egg/omelet
глазу́нья	glah-ZOO-nyuh	sunny-side up
яйцо́ всмя́тку	yee-TSAW FSMYAHT-koo	soft-boiled egg
яйцо́ вкруту́ю	yee-TSAW fkroo-TOO-yoo	hard-boiled egg

Овощи	AW-vuh-shee	Vegetables
помидо́ры	puh-mee-DAWR-y	tomatoes
огурцы́	ah-goor-TSY	cucumbers
солёные огурцы́	sah-LYAWN-y-yeh ah-goor-TSY	pickles
карто́фель	kahr-TAWF-eel'	potatoes
свёкла	SVYAWK-luh	beets
морко́вь	mahr-KAWF'	carrots
горо́шек	gah-RAWSH-uhk	peas

лук	look	onion
зелёный лук	zee-LYAWN-y look	scallions
грибы	gree-BY	mushrooms
капуста	kah-POOS-tuh	cabbage
редиска	ree-DEES-kuh	radish
кукуруза	koo-koo-ROOZ-uh	corn
баклажаны	buh-klah-ZHAHN-uh	eggplant
кабачки	kah-bahch-KEE	squash
тыква	TYK-vuh	pumpkin
перец	PYEHR-eets	bell pepper

Фрукты	FROOK-ty	Fruits
апельсины	ah-peel'-SEEN-y	oranges
мандарины	muhn-dah-REEN-y	mandarin oranges
абрикосы	ah-bree-KAWS-y	apricots
груши	GROO-shy	pears
персики	PYEHR-see-kee	peaches
яблоки	YAH-bluh-kee	apples
виноград	veen-ah-GRAHT	grapes
сливы	SLEEV-y	plums
лимон	lee-MAWN	lemon
дыня	DYN-yuh	melon
арбуз	ahr-BOOS	watermelon
ананас	ah-nah-NAHS	pineapple
бананы	bah-NAHN-y	bananas
гранат	grah-NAHT	pomegranate
изюм	ee-ZYOOM	raisins
земляника	zeem-lee-NEEK-uh	wild strawberry
клубника	kloob-NEEK-uh	strawberry
малина	mah-LEEN-uh	raspberry
чёрная смородина	CHAWRN-uh-yuh smah-RAWD-ee-nuh	black currants
красная смородина	KRAHS-nuh-yuh smah-RAWD-ee-nuh	red currants
крыжовник	kry-ZHAWV-neek	gooseberries
вишня	VEESH-nyuh	cherries
инжир	een-ZHYR	figs
финики	FEEN-eek-ee	dates
миндаль	meen-DAHL'	almonds
каштаны	kahsh-TAHN-y	chestnuts

89

гре́цкие оре́хи	GRYEHTS-kee-yuh ah-RYEH-khee	walnuts
се́мечки	SYEHYM-eech-kee	sunflower seeds

Спе́ции, пря́ности	SPYEH-tsy-ee, PRYAH-nuh-stee	Spices, Condiments
соль	sawl'	salt
пе́рец	PYEHR-eets	pepper
чесно́к	chees-NAWK	garlic
горчи́ца	gahr-CHEET-suh	mustard
са́хар	SAH-khuhr	sugar
укро́п	oo-KRAWP	dill
мак	mahk	poppy seed
со́ус	SAW-oos	gravy/sauce
гарни́р	gahr-NEER	garnish
майоне́з	muh-yah-NYEHS	mayonnaise
мёд	myawt	honey
варе́нье	vah-RYEHN-yuh	preserves
джем	dzhehm	jam

Десе́рт	dee-SYEHRT	Dessert
моро́женое	mah-RAWZH-uh-nuh-yuh	ice cream
пломби́р	plahm-BEER	thick ice cream with whipped cream
желе́	zhy-LYEH	flavored gelatin
мусс	moos	mousse
крем	kryehm	cream
кисе́ль	kee-SYEHL'	fruit jelly
компо́т	kahm-PAWT	compote
пу́динг	POOD-eenk	pudding
конфе́ты	kahn-FYEHT-y	candy
шокола́д	shuh-kah-LAHT	chocolate
халва́	khahl-VAH	halvah
мармела́д	mahr-mee-LAHT	candies with fruit jelly
пиро́жное	pee-RAWZH-nuh-yuh	small cake or cookie
кекс	kyehks	cupcake/sponge cake
ва́фли	VAHF-lee	dry cookies
бискви́т	beesk-VEET	sweet biscuit
торт	tawrt	cake

| бара́нки | bah-RAHN-kee | small round cookies |
| по́нчик | PAWN-cheek | plain doughnut |

Напи́тки	nah-PEET-kee	Beverages
вода́	vah-DAH	water
газиро́ванная вода́	guh-zee-RAW-vuhn-uh-yuh vah-DAH	soda water
минера́льная вода́	mee-nee-RAHL'-nuh-yuh vah-DAH	mineral water
лимона́д	lee-mah-NAHT	soft drink
квас	kvahs	kvass (fermented bread or fruit drink)
пи́во	PEE-vuh	beer
чай	chai	tea
• с лимо́ном	• slee-MAWN-uhm	• with lemon
• с са́харом	• SAH-khuh-ruhm	• with sugar
• с молоко́м	• smuh-lah-KAWM	• with milk
ко́фе	KAW-fyuh	coffee
• с молоко́м	• smuh-lah-KAWM	• with milk
• со сли́вками	• sah-SLEEF-kuh-mee	• with cream
• со льдо́м	• sahl'-DAWM	• iced
лёд	lyawt	ice
морс	mawrs	cranberry juice drink
со́ки	SAW-kee	juices
• тома́тный	• tah-MAHT-ny	• tomato
• виногра́дный	• vee-nah-GRAHD-ny	• grape
• я́блочный	• YAHB-luhch-ny	• apple
• абрико́совый	• ah-bree-KAWS-uh-vy	• apricot
• айво́вый	• ahy-VAW-vy	• quince
• вишнёвый	• veesh-NYAW-vy	• cherry
• апельси́новый	• ah-peel'-SEEN-uh-vy	• orange
• грана́товый	• grah-NAHT-uh-vy	• pomegranate
крюшо́н	kryoo-SHAWN	fruit punch
пунш	poonsh	punch
вино́	vee-NAW	wine

91

• кра́сное	• KRAHS-nuh-yuh	• red
• бе́лое	• BYEHL-uh-yuh	• white
• сухо́е	• soo-KHAW-yuh	• dry
• сла́дкое	• SLAHT-kuh-yuh	• sweet
• полусухо́е	• puh-loo-soo-KHAW-yuh	• semidry
• полусла́дкое	• puh-loo-SLAHT-kuh-yuh	• semisweet
• десе́ртное	• dee-SYEHRT-nuh-yuh	• dessert
• игри́стое шампа́нское	• ee-GREEST-uh-yuh shahm-PAHN-skuh-yuh	• sparkling champagne
портве́йн	pahrt-VYEHYN	fortified wine
во́дка	VAWT-kuh	vodka
конья́к	kahn-YAHK	cognac
ви́ски	VEES-kee	whiskey
ром	rawm	rum
нали́вка	nah-LEEF-kuh	fruit liqueur
кокте́йль	kahk-TYEHYL'	cocktail
моло́чный кокте́йль	mah-LAWCH-ny kahk-TYEHYL'	milk shake
шербе́т	shyr-BYEHT	fruit drink
ликёр	lee-KYAWR	liqueur
бальза́м	bahl'-ZAHM	herb liqueur

7/PERSONAL CARE

AT THE BARBER SHOP/BEAUTY PARLOR

Most hotels in the Soviet Union have their own barber shop and beauty parlor. You'll be able to make an appointment directly with them. If you want to go to a barber shop or beauty parlor outside your hotel you can either go there and make an appointment (it's very difficult to do this on the phone—even Soviet citizens tend to go themselves to make the appointment), or you can decide to wait there until a hairdresser is free. When you go into the waiting room, find out who is the last person on line. The attendant will periodically let those waiting know when the next hairdresser is available and you can simply wait your turn.

DIALOGUE: В ПАРИКМАХЕРСКОЙ (AT THE HAIRDRESSER)

Парикма́хер:	Кто́ сле́дующий?	ktaw SLYEH-doo-yoo-shee?
Клие́нтка:	Я. Я хочу́ стри́жку.	yah. yah khah-CHOO STREESH-koo.
Парикма́хер:	Каку́ю вы хоти́те?	kak-KOO-yoo vy khah-TEE-tyeh?
Клие́нтка:	Подлине́е сза́ди, но покоро́че спе́реди.	pah-dlee-NYEH-yeh ZAH-dee, naw puh-kah-RAW-cheh SPYEH-reh-dee.
Парикма́хер:	Хорошо́. Вы хоти́те вы́мыть го́лову?	khuh-rah-SHAW. vy khah-TEE-tyeh VY-myt' GAW-luh-voo?
Клие́нтка:	Нет. То́лько стри́жку, пожа́луйста.	nyeht. TAWL'-kuh STREESH-koo, pah-ZHAHL-stuh.
Парикма́хер:	Пожа́луйста.	pah-ZHAHL-stuh.

. . . .

93

Hairdresser:	Who's next?
Client:	I am. I'd like a haircut.
Hairdresser:	How would you like it?
Client:	Long in the back, but shorter in the front.
Hairdresser:	Fine. Do you want a shampoo as well?
Client:	No. Just a haircut, please.
Hairdresser:	Fine.

Is there a barber shop/beauty parlor nearby?	zdyehs' yehst' BLEES-kuh puh-reek-MAH-kheer-skuh-yuh?	Здесь есть близко парик-махерская?
Do I need an appointment?	mnyeh NOOZH-nuh nahz-NAH-cheet' VRYEH-myuh?	Мне нужно назначить время?
Can I get an appointment for today?	MAWZH-nuh ZDYEH-luht' preed-vah-REE-tehl'-ny zah-KAHS nah see-VAWD-nyuh?	Можно сделать предвари-тельный заказ на сегодня?
I need a haircut.	mnyeh NOOZH-nuh paht-STREECH'-suh	Мне нужно подстричься.
Please leave it long here.	pah-ZHAHL-stuh, ah-STAHV'-tyeh zdyehs' pah-dlee-NYEH-yeh	Пожалуйста, оставьте здесь подлиннее.
Please, cut it short.	pah-ZHAHL-stuh, puht-stree-GEE-tyeh KAW-ruht-kuh	Пожалуйста, подстригите коротко.
Not too short!	nee SLEESH-kuhm KAW-ruht-kuh!	Не слишком коротко!
Cut a bit more off	puht-stree-GEE-tyeh ee-SHAW nee-MNAWSH-kuh	Подстригите ещё немножко
• here.	• zdyehs'	• здесь.

94

• in front.	• SPYEH-ree-dee	• впереди.
• on the side.	• ZBAW-koo	• сбоку.
• the neck.	• nah SHEH-yeh	• на шее.
• the back.	• ZAH-dee	• сзади.
• the top.	• nuh-veer-KHOO	• наверху.
It's fine like that.	tahk khuh-rah-SHAW	Так хорошо.
I'd like a razor cut.	pah-BREY-tyeh mnyeh SHEY-oo	Побрейте мне шею.
I'd like a shampoo.	VY-muh-tyeh mnyeh GAW-luh-voo	Вымойте мне голову.
I'd like a set.	ZDYEH-luhy-tyeh oo-KLAHT-koo	Сделайте укладку.
I'd like a permanent.	ZDYEH-luhy-tyeh peer-mah-NYEHNT	Сделайте перманент.
I'd like a manicure.	ZDYEH-luhy-tyeh muh-nee-KYOOR	Сделайте маникюр.
I'd like a touch-up.	paht-KRAHS'-tyeh	Подкрасьте.
I'd like a facial.	yah khah-CHOO MAHS-koo dlyah lee-TSAH	Я хочу маску для лица.
I'd like a blow-dry.	puht-soo-SHY-tyeh	Подсушите.
I'd like to have my hair dyed . . .	puh-KRAHS'-tyeh VAW-luh-sy v . . . tsvyeht	Покрасьте волосы в . . . цвет.
Make the part	ZDYEH-luhy-tyeh prah-BAWR	Сделайте пробор
• on the right.	• SPRAH-vuh	• справа.
• on the left.	• SLYEH-vuh	• слева.
• down the middle.	• puh-see-ree-DEE-nyeh	• посередине.
No hairspray, please.	bees LAH-kuh, pah-ZHAHL-stuh	Без лака, пожалуйста.
I prefer	yah preed-puh-chee-TAH-yoo	Я предпочитаю
• a lighter shade.	• sveht-LEH-yeh aht-TYEH-nuhk.	• светлее оттенок.
• a darker shade.	• tehm-NYEH-yeh aht-TYEH-nuhk.	• темнее оттенок.
• light blond.	• byee-lah-KOO-ry	• белокурый.
I'd like a shave.	yah khah-CHOO pah-BREET-suh	Я хочу побриться.

Trim my	puht-stree-GEE-tyeh mnyeh	Подстригите мне
• mustache.	• oo-SY	• усы.
• beard.	• BAW-ruh-doo	• бороду.
• sideburns.	• buh-keen-BAHR-dy	• бакенбарды.

LAUNDRY AND DRY CLEANING

I need	mnyeh noozh-NAH	Мне нужна
• a laundry.	• PRAH-cheech-nuh-yuh	• прачечная.
• a dry cleaner.	• kheem-CHEEST-kuh	• химчистка.
I have a dress to be	mnyeh NOOZH-nuh PLAHT'-yeh	Мне нужно платье
• washed.	• puh-stee-RAHT'	• постирать.
• ironed.	• pah-GLAH-deet'	• погладить.
• dry-cleaned.	• pah-CHEES-teet'	• почистить.
• mended.	• zah-SHIT'-puht'	• зашить.
I need it	mnyeh EH-tuh NOOZH-nuh	Мне это нужно
• tomorrow.	• ZAHF-truh	• завтра.
• the day after tomorrow.	• puh-slee-ZAHF-truh	• послезавтра.
• in a week.	• nah SLYEH-doo-yoo-shehy nee-DYEH-lee	• на следующей неделе.
When will it be ready?	kahg-DAH ah-NAW BOO-dyeht gah-TAW-vuh?	Когда оно будет готово?
I'm leaving tomorrow.	yah oo-yeh-ZHAH-yoo ZAHF-truh	Я уезжаю завтра.
This isn't mine.	EH-tuh nee mah-YAW	Это не моё.
There is a shirt missing.	ah-DNOY roo-BAHSH-kee nee khvah-TAH-yeet	Одной рубашки не хватает.
Can you get this stain out?	vy MAW-zheht-yeh VY-vehs-tee EH-tuh pit-NAW?	Вы можете вывести это пятно?
Can you sew on this button?	vy MAW-zheht-yeh pree-SHEET' EH-too POO-guh-vee-tsoo?	Вы можете пришить эту пуговицу?

96

I have	oo meen-YAH yehst'	У меня́ есть
• two shirts.	• dvyeh roo-BAHSH-kee	• две руба́шки.
• five underpants.	• pyaht' troo-SAWF	• пять трусо́в.
• a suit.	• ah-DEEN kah-STYOOM	• оди́н костю́м.
• eight pairs of socks.	• VAW-seem' pahr nah-SKAWF	• во́семь пар носко́в.
• several handkerchiefs.	• NYEH-skul'-kuh plaht-KAWF	• не́сколько платко́в.
• two ties.	• dvah GAHL-stoo-kuh	• два́ га́лстука.
• a sweater.	• ah-DEEN SVEE-tehr	• оди́н сви́тер.
• two pairs of pants.	• dvyeh PAH-ry bryook	• две́ па́ры брюк.
• a bathing suit.	• koo-PAHL'-neek	• купа́льник.
• three blouses.	• tree BLOOS-kee	• три́ блу́зки.

8/HEALTH CARE SERVICES

DOCTORS AND MEDICAL SERVICES

Before traveling abroad it's always wise to check with your health insurance company to find out which accident and illness expenses are covered under your current policy. Some companies offer comprehensive travel, accident, and life insurance policies for those visiting Eastern Europe. American International Assistance Services, Inc., sells a policy through travel agents and offers a policy valid in the Soviet Union. For information, contact American International Assistance Services, Inc., (INTERCLAIM), P.O. Box 515095, Dallas, TX 75251; tel. 800-252-7799 or 214-680-6400. The number of the U.S. embassy in Moscow is 252-2451.

Be sure to bring with you all over-the-counter and prescription medicines you usually use—it will be practically impossible to find them while traveling in the Soviet Union.

Water is usually safe. There is no risk in the major cities, but if you have any doubts you can stick to the ever-present bottled, canned, or mineral water or coffee, tea and beer. Leningrad's water supply has had occasional problems (see below), and tourist hotels will not warn you when their water is affected.

Food is as safe as it looks or as you see it handled. Greasy-spoon restaurants are a hazard anywhere in the world, so be certain that dairy products—including cheese and ice cream—have been carefully processed and handled, that fresh-vegetable salads are clean, and so on. Generally speaking, only independent travelers going off into the remoter, non-European parts of Russia—Central Asia, for instance—need worry about the food, and then only outside hotel restaurants. *You should, however, be warned that some visitors to Russia, especially in past years to Leningrad, have returned home with a specific form of diarrhea called giardiasis, caused by an intestinal parasite. It can be effectively treated, but needs slightly different drugs from the normal ones for diarrhea. If you find yourself suffering from such an illness after you return home, consult your physician.*

If you need to see a doctor, you may be brought to a clinic or hospital with a bilingual staff. For less serious cases, house calls, made by doctors in the emergency medical service, **Скорая помощь** (SKAW-ruh-yuh PAW-mush), are still common.

There is a **special clinic** in Moscow that cares for foreign visitors. Its address is 12 Herzen Street, the telephone numbers 229-7323 and 229-0382. Its staff includes qualified doctors and nurses, and there are X-ray, physiotherapy, dental and other departments. A new **International Health Care** clinic, 3 Gruzinsky Pereulok, Korpus 2 (tel. 253-0703, 253-0704) offers a full range of medical services to foreigners traveling in the Soviet Union.

There is a **Diplomatic polyclinic** at 3 Sverchkov Per. (tel. 221-5992 and 221-4911, day and night). It has a **children's section** (228-0725) and the director can be reached at 223-5515. The **Botkin Hospital,** 5, 2nd Botkinsky Proyezd, tel. 255-0015, ext. 268, has a Diplomatic Block (Korpus 5).

First Aid and Ambulance: dial 03; people in hospital, dial 294-3152.

DIALOGUE: У ВРАЧА (AT THE DOCTOR'S)

Врач:	Что с вами?	shtaw SVAH-mee?
Турист:	Я не знаю точно . . . Я плохо себя чувствую. У меня болит голова.	yah ne ZNAH-yoo TAWCH-nuh . . . yah PLAW-khuh see-BYAH CHOOST-voo-yoo. oo mee-NYAH bahl-EET guh-lah-VAH.
Врач:	Вас тошнит?	vahs tahsh-NEET?
Турист:	Да. Сегодня утром меня вырвало.	dah. see-VAW-dnyuh OO-trahm mee-NYAH VYR-vuh-luh.
Врач:	Сколько вы болеете?	SKAWL'-kuh vy bah-LYEHY-yeh-tyeh?

99

Турист:	С воскресéнья, то есть три дня.	svuhs-kree-SYAYN'-yuh, taw yehyst tree dnyah.

. . . .

Doctor:	What's the matter?
Tourist:	I don't know exactly . . . I'm not feeling well. I have a headache.
Doctor:	Are you nauseated?
Tourist:	Yes. I threw up this morning.
Doctor:	How long have you been ill?
Tourist:	Since Sunday, that is, for three days.

PATIENT/DOCTOR EXPRESSIONS

Before the Visit

Could you please call me a doctor?	VY-zuh-vee-tyeh, pah-ZHAHL-stuh vrah-CHAH	Вы́зовите, пожа́луйста, врача́.
Where's the doctor's office?	gdyeh kuh-bee-NYEHT vrah-CHAH?	Где́ кабине́т врача́?
I need a doctor who speaks English.	mnyeh NOOZH-uhn vrahch, kah-TAWR-y guh-vah-REET puh-ahn-GLEE-skee	Мне́ ну́жен вра́ч, кото́рый говори́т по-англи́йски.
Could the doctor see me here?	MAWZH-yt lee vrahch ah-smah-TRYEHT' mee-NYAH zdyehys'?	Мо́жет ли вра́ч осмотре́ть меня́ здесь?
Can I have an appointment	MOZH-nuh puh-vee-DAHT'-suh zvrah-CHAWM	Мо́жно повида́ться с врачо́м
• for 2 o'clock?	• vdvah chah-SAH?	• в два́ часа́?
• for today?	• see-VAW-dnyuh?	• сего́дня?

• for tomorrow?	• ZAHF-truh?	• за́втра?
• as soon as possible?	• kahk MAWZH-nuh skah-RYEHY-yuh?	• ка́к мо́жно скоре́е?
What are the doctor's visiting hours?	fkah-KEE-yeh chee-SEE pree-YAWM?	В каки́е часы́ приём?
I need	mnyeh NOO-zhyhn	Мне́ ну́жен
• a general practioner.	• vrahch	• вра́ч.
• a pediatrician.	• pee-dee-AHTR	• педиа́тр.
• a gynecologist.	• gee-nee-KAWL-uhk	• гинеко́лог.
• an eye doctor.	• glahz-NOY vrahch	• глазно́й вра́ч.

TALKING TO THE DOCTOR

I don't feel well.	mnyeh nee-zdah-RAWV-eet-suh	Мне́ нездоро́вится.
I'm sick.	yah BAWL-ehn/bahl'-NAH	Я бо́лен./больна́.
I don't know what I've got.	yah nee-ZNAH-yoo shtaw sah mnoy	Я не зна́ю, что́ со мно́й.
I have a chill.	oo mee-NYAH ah-ZNAWP	У меня́ озно́б.
I have a fever.	oo mee-NYAH zhahr	У меня́ жа́р.
I don't have a fever.	oo mee-NYAH ZHAR-ah nyeht	У меня́ жа́ра нет.
I'm nauseated.	mee-NYAH tahsh-NEET	Меня́ тошни́т.
I feel weak.	yah CHOOST-voo-yoo SLAH-buhst'	Я чу́вствую сла́бость.
I feel dizzy.	oo mee-NYAH KROO-zheet-suh gah-lah-VAH	У меня́ кру́жится голова́.
I can't sleep.	oo mee-NYAH bees-SAWN-eet-suh	У меня́ бессо́нница.
I threw up.	mee-NYAH VYR-vuh-luh	Меня́ вы́рвало.
I'm constipated.	oo mee-NYAH zah-PAWR	У меня́ запо́р.
I have	oo mee-NYAH	У меня́

101

- asthma.
- a bite.
- bruises.
- a burn.
- something in my eye.
- a cold.
- a cough.
- cramps.
- a cut.
- diarrhea.
- a headache.

- a lump.
- rheumatism.

- a sore throat.

- a stomachache.

- sunstroke.

- a swelling.
- an upset stomach.

My . . . hurt(s).
- head

- stomach

- neck

- feet

I'm allergic to

- penicillin.

- certain medicines.

- AHST-muh
- oo-KOOS
- see-nee-KEE
- ah-ZHAWK
- SHTAW-tuh pah-PAHL-uh vglahs
- prah-STOO-duh
- KAHSH-eel'
- SKHVAHT-kee
- pah-RYEHS
- pah-NAWS
- bah-LEET guh-lah-VAH
- AW-poo-khul'
- reev-mah-TEEZ-uhm
- bah-LEET GAWR-luh
- bah-LEET zhy-LOO-duhk
- SAWL-neech-ny oo-DAHR
- AW-poo-khul'
- nee-svah-RYEHN-yeh zhy-LOOT-kuh
oo mee-NYAH
- bah-LEET guh-lah-VAH
- bah-LEET zhy-LOO-duhk
- bah-LEET SHEHY-yuh
- bah-LYAHT NAW-gee
oo mee-NYAH ah-leer-GEE-yuh
- kpeen-ee-tsy-LEEN-oo
- KNYEH-kuh-tuhr-ym lee-KAHRST-vuhm

- áстма.
- укýс.
- синякú.
- ожóг.
- чтó-то попáло в глаз.
- простýда.
- кáшель.
- схвáтки.
- порéз.
- понóс.
- болúт головá.

- óпухоль.
- ревматúзм.

- болúт гóрло.

- болúтд желýдок.

- сóлнечный удáр.

- óпухоль.
- несварéние желýдка.

У меня́
- болúт головá.

- болúт желýдок.
- болúт шéя.

- боля́т нóги.

У меня́ аллергúя

- к пенициллúну.
- к нéкоторым лекáрствам.

Here is the medicine I take.	VAWT lee-KAHRST-vuh kah-TAW-ruh-yuh yah pree-nee-MAH-yoo	Вот лека́рство, кото́рое я принима́ю.
I've had this pain for two days.	EH-tee BAW-lee oo mee-NYAH dvah dnyah	Э́ти бо́ли у меня́ два дня.
I had a heart attack four years ago.	oo mee-NYAH byl een-FAHRKT chee-TY-ree GAW-duh nah-ZAHT	У меня́ был инфа́ркт четы́ре го́да наза́д.
I'm four months pregnant.	yah bee-RYEHM-eh-nuh cheet-VYOR-ty MYEHS-eets	Я бере́менна четвёртый ме́сяц.
I have menstrual cramps.	oo mee-NYAH MYEHS-eech-ny-yeh SKHVAHT-kee	У меня́ ме́сячные схва́тки.

Parts of the Body

ankle (left/right)	SHEE-kuh-luht-kuh (LYEHV-uh-yuh/PRAH-vuh-yuh)	щи́колотка (ле́вая/пра́вая)
appendix	ahp-PYEHN-deeks	аппе́ндикс
arm	roo-KAH	рука́
artery	ahr-TYEHR-ee-yuh	арте́рия
back	spee-NAH	спина́
bladder	muh-chee-VOY-poo-ZYR'	мочево́й пузы́рь
bone	kawst'	ко́сть
bowels	kee-SHEHCH-neek	кише́чник
breast	grood'	гру́дь
buttocks	YAH-guh-dee-tsuh	я́годицы
calf	ee-KRAH nawk	икра́ ног
chest	groot'	гру́дь
ear, ears	OO-khuh, OO-shy	у́хо, у́ши
an eye/eyes	glahs/glah-ZAH	гла́з/глаза́
face	lee-TSAW	лицо́
finger	PAHL-eets	па́лец
foot	nah-GAH	нога́

forehead	lawp	лоб
gland	zhy-lee-ZAH	железа́
hair	VAW-luhs-y	во́лосы
hand	roo-KAH	рука́
head	guh-lah-VAH	голова́
heart	SYEHR-tsuh	се́рдце
hip	bee-DRAW	бедро́
jaw	CHEHL-yoost'	че́люсть
joint	soos-TAHF	суста́в
kidneys	PAWCH-kee	по́чки
knee	kah-LYEHN-uh	коле́но
leg	nah-GAH	нога́
lip	goo-BAH	губа́
liver	PYEHY-cheen'	пе́чень
lungs	LYOKH-kee-yeh	лёгкие
mouth	rawt	рот
muscle	MYSH-tsuh	мы́шца
nail	NAWG-uht'	но́готь
neck	SHEY-yuh	ше́я
nose	naws	нос
penis	moosh-SKOY puh-lah-VOY chlyehn	мужско́й половой член
ribs	RYAWB-ruh	рёбра
shoulder	plee-CHAW	плечо́
skin	KAW-zhuh	ко́жа
spine	puh-zvah-NAWCH-neek	позвоно́чник
stomach	zhy-LOOD-uhk	желу́док
teeth	ZOO-by	зу́бы
thigh	bee-DRAW	бедро́
throat	GAWR-luh	го́рло
thumb	bahl'-SHOY PAHL-eets	большо́й па́лец
toe	PAHL-eets nah-GEE	па́лец ноги́
tongue	yee-ZYK	язы́к
tonsils	meen-DAH-lee-nuh	минда́лина
vagina	vlah-GAH-leeshch-uh	влага́лище
vein	VYEHN-uh	ве́на
wrist	zah-PYAHS-tyeh	запя́стье

What the Doctor Says

На чтó вы жáлуетесь?	nah shtaw vy ZHAH-loo-yoo-tyehs'?	What is your complaint?
Какие у вáс симптóмы?	kah-KEE-yeh oo vahs seemp-TAWM-y?	What are your symptoms?
Раздéньтесь, пожáлуйста.	rahz-DYEHN-tyehys', pah-ZHAL-stuh	Undress, please.
Раздевáйтесь, пожáлуйста, до пóяса.	rahz-dee-VAHY-tyehys', pah-ZHAL-stuh, dah PAW-yuh-suh	Please undress to the waist.
Ложитесь, пожáлуйста, на кушéтку.	lah-ZHY-tyehys' pah-ZHAHL-stuh nah koo-SHEHT-koo	Lie down on the couch, please.
Открóйте рот.	aht-KROY-tyeh rawt.	Open your mouth.
Покáшляйте, пожáлуйста.	puh-KAHSH-lee-tyeh, pah-ZHAHL-stuh	Cough, please.
Вдохните.	vdakh-NEE-tyeh	Breathe deeply.
Укажите, гдé бóльно.	oo-kah-ZHY-tyeh, gdyeh BAWL'-nuh	Show me where it hurts.
Покажите, пожáлуйста, язык.	puh-kah-ZHY-tyeh, pah-ZHAHL-stuh, yee-ZYK	Stick out your tongue, please.
Одевáйтесь.	ah-dee-VAHY-tyehys'	Get dressed.
Эти бóли у вáс давнó?	EH-tee BAWL-ee oo vahz dahv-NAW?	How long have you had these pains?

У вáс	oo vahs	It's
• выIвих.	• VY-veekh	• dislocated.
• перелóм.	• pee-ree-LAWM	• broken.
• растяжéние.	• rahs-tye-ZHEH-nyeh	• sprained.
• серьёзно.	• see-RYAWZ-nuh	• serious.
• несерьёзно.	• nee-see-RYAWZ-nuh	• not serious.
• инфéкция	• en-FYEHKS-ty-uh	• infected.
Вáм	vahm	You'll need to get
• нýжен рентгéн.	• NOO-zhuhn reent-GYEHN	• an X ray.
• нýжен укóл.	• NOOZH-ehn oo-KAWL	• an injection.

HEALTH CARE

105

Я вам дам болеутоляющее средство.	yah vahm dahm buh-lee-oo-tah-LYAH-yoo-shcheh-yeh SREHT-stvuh	I'm going to give you a painkiller.
Вам нужно	vahm NOOZH-nuh	You need to
• **лечь в больницу.**	• lyehych vbahl'-NEE-tsoo	• go to the hospital.
• **проконсуль-тироваться со специалистом.**	• pruh-kuhn-sool'-TEER-uh-vuht-suh suh-spee-tsyahl-EEST-uhm	• see a specialist.
Я буду измерять	yah BOO-doo eez-meer-YAHT'	I'm going to take your
• **вашу температуру.**	• VAH-shuh teem-peer-ah-TOO-roo	• temperature.
• **ваше давление.**	• VAH-shuh dah-VLYEH-nyuh	• blood pressure.
У вас	oo vahs	You have
• **аппендицит.**	• ah-peen-dee-TSYT	• appendicitis.
• **переломанная кость.**	• pee-ree-LAWM-uh-n-uh-yuh kawst'	• a broken bone.
• **гастрит.**	• gahs-TREET	• gastritis.
• **грипп.**	• greep	• the flu.
• **отравление.**	• ah-trahv-LYAY-nyuh	• food poisoning.
• **венерическая болезнь.**	• vee-neer-EE-chees-kuh-yuh bah-LYAYZN'	• venereal disease.
• **кистатит.**	• kees-tah-TEET	• cystitis.
• **пневмония.**	• pneev-nah-MEE-yuh	• pneumonia.
• **корь.**	• kawr'	• measles.
• **СПИД.**	• speet	• AIDS.
Нужно сдать анализ	NOOZH-nuh zdaht' ah-NAH-lees	I need a sample of
• **крови.**	• KRAW-vee	• your blood.
• **кала.**	• KAH-luh	• your stool.
• **мочи.**	• mah-CHEE	• your urine.

106

PATIENT QUESTIONS

Is it serious?	EH-tuh see-RYAWZ-nuh?	Это серьёзно?
Is it contagious?	EH-tuh een-feeks-tsy-AWN-nuh?	Это инфекцио́нно?
When can I get out of bed?	kahg-DAH yah smah-GOO fstaht' spahs-TYEHYL'-ee?	Когда́ я смогу́ встать с посте́ли?
What exactly is wrong with me?	shtaw EE-meen-nuh sah mnoy?	Что́ и́менно со мно́й?
How do I use this medication?	kahk oo-puh-tree-BLYAH-ee-tsuh EH-tuh lee-KAHRST-vuh?	Ка́к употребля́ется э́то лека́рство?
Do I need to see you again?	NOOZH-nuh lee VEE-deet' vahs yee-SHAW rahs?	Ну́жно ли ви́деть ва́с ещё ра́з?
Can I get this medicine without a prescription?	mah-GOO lee yah puh-loo-CHEET' EH-tuh lee-KAHRST-vuh beez ree-TSEHPT-uh?	Могу́ ли я получи́ть э́то лека́рство бе́з реце́пта?
When can I start traveling again?	kahg-DAH yah mah-GOO prah-DAWL-zheet' pah-YEHST-koo?	Когда́ я могу́ продо́лжить пое́здку?
Can you give me a prescription for	MAWZH-uh-tyuh lee vy VY-pee-suht' mnyeh ree-TSEHPT nah	Мо́жете ли вы вы́писать мне реце́пт на
• a painkiller?	• buhl-ee-oo-tah-LYAH-yoo-shlyeh-yeh SRYEHTST-vuh?	• болеутоля́ющее сре́дство?
• a tranquilizer?	• truhn-kvee-lee-ZAH-tuhr?	• транквили-за́тор?
• a sleeping pill?	• snah-TVAWR-nuh-yuh?	• снотво́рное?
Are these pills or suppositories?	EH-tuh tah-BLYEHT-kee EE-lee SVYEHCH-kee?	Это табле́тки и́ли све́чки?

Can I have a bill for my insurance company?	MAWZH-nuh puh-loo-CHEET' kvee-TAHN-tsy-yoo dlyah mah-YEHY struh-khah-VOY kahm-PAHN-ee-ee?	Мо́жно получи́ть квита́нцию для мое́й страхово́й компа́нии?
Could you fill out this medical form?	MAWZH-uh-tyuh lee vy zah-PAWL-neet' EH-too myehd-ee-TSYN-skoo-yoo ahn-KYEHT-oo?	Мо́жете ли вы запо́лнить э́ту медици́нскую анке́ту?

AT THE HOSPITAL

Where is the nearest hospital?	gdyeh blee-ZHAY-shuh-yuh bahl'-NEE-tsuh?	Где ближа́йшая больни́ца?
Call an ambulance!	VY-zuh-vee-tyeh SKAWR-oo-yoo PAWM-uhshch!	Вы́зовите ско́рую по́мощь!
Help me!	puh-mah-GEE-tyeh mnyeh!	Помоги́те мне!
Get me to a hospital!	aht-vee-ZEE-tyeh mee-NYAH vbahl'-NEE-tsoo!	Отвези́те меня́ в больни́цу!
I need first aid fast!	mnyeh SRAWCH-nuh noozh-NAH PYEHR-vuh-yuh PAWM-uhsh!	Мне́ сро́чно нужна́ пе́рвая по́мощь!
I was in an accident!	yah pah-PAHL(-uh) vah-VAHR-ee-yoo!	Я попа́л(-а) в ава́рию!
I cut	yah pah-RYEHZ-uhl (-uh) see-BYEH	Я поре́зал(-а) себе́
• my hand.	• ROOK-oo	• ру́ку.
• my leg.	• NAWG-oo	• но́гу.
• my face.	• lee-TSAW	• лицо́.
I can't move	yah nee mah-GOO DVEE-guht'	Я не могу́ дви́гать
• my finger.	• PAHL'-tsuhm	• па́льцем.
• my leg.	• nahg-OY	• ного́й.
• my neck.	• SHEHY-ay	• ше́ей.

108

He/she hurt his/her head.	awn/ah-NAH puh-vree-DEEL(-ah) see-BYEH GAW-luh-voo	Он/Она́ повреди́л(-а) себе́ го́лову.
His/Her ankle is	yee-VAW/yee-YAW SHEE-kuh-luht-kuh	Его́/Её щи́колотка
• broken.	• pee-ree-LAWM-uhn-nuh	• перело́мана.
• twisted.	• rahs-TYAHN-oo-tuh	• растя́нута.
• swollen.	• ah-POOKH-luh	• опу́хла.
She's/He's bleeding heavily.	oo nee-YAW/oo-nee-VAW krawf' SEEL'-nuh tee-CHAWT	У неё/У него́ си́льно кро́вь течёт.
He's unconscious.	awn puh-teer-YAHL sah-ZNAHN-yuh	Он потеря́л созна́ние.
He burned himself.	awn ahb-ZHAWK-suh	Он обжёгся.
She burned herself.	ah-NAH ahb-ahzh-GLAHS'	Она́ обожгла́сь.
I ate something poisonous./I got food poisoning.	yah ah-trah-VEEL-syuh/ah-trah-VEEL-uhs'	Я отрави́лся./ отрави́лась.
When can I leave?	kahg-DAH yah smah-GOO VY-tee nah OO-lee-tsoo?	Когда́ я смогу́ вы́йти на у́лицу?
When will the doctor come?	kahg-DAH pree-DYAWT vrahch?	Когда́ придёт врач?
I can't	yah nee mah-GOO	Я не могу́
• eat.	• yehyst'	• есть.
• drink.	• peet'	• пить.
• sleep.	• spaht'	• спать.
Where's the nurse?	gdyeh meet-sees-TRAH?	Где медсестра́?
What are the visiting hours?	kahg-DAH puh-see-SHAH-yoot bahl'-NYKH?	Когда́ посеща́ют больны́х?

THE DENTIST

| Do you know a dentist? | nee MAWZH-uh-tyeh lee vy puh-ree-kuh-meen-dah-VAHT' zoob-NAW-vuh vrah-CHAH? | Не мо́жете ли вы пореко-мендова́ть зубно́го врача́? |

It's an emergency.	EH-tuh KRAY-nyuh-yuh nee-uhb-khah-DEEM-uhst'	Это крáйная необхо-дúмость.
I'm in a lot of pain.	mnyeh AW-cheen' BAWL'-nuh	Мне óчень бóльно.
My gums are bleeding.	oo mee-NYAH ees DYAWS-uhn tee-CHAWT krawf'	У меня из дёсен течёт крóвь.
I've lost a filling.	oo mee-NYAH VY-puh-luh PLAWM-buh	У меня вы́пала плóмба.
I broke a tooth.	oo mee-NYAH ees-PAWR-chuhn zoop	У меня испóрчен зуб.
This tooth hurts.	bahl-EET EH-tuht zoop	Болúт э́тот зуб.
I don't want to have it extracted.	yah nee khah-CHOO, SHTAW-by zoop oo-dah-LEE-lee	Я не хочý, чтобы зуб удалúли.
Can you fill it	vy MAWZH-uh-tyuh mnyeh yee-VAW zuh-plahm-BEER-uh-vuht'	Вы мóжете мне его заплом-бúровать
• with gold?	• ZAWL-uh-tuhm?	• зóлотом?
• with silver?	• see-ree-BRAWM?	• серебрóм?
• temporarily?	• VRYEH-meen-nuh?	• врéменно?
I want a local anesthetic.	yah khah-CHOO, SHTAW-by vy zuh-mah-RAWZ-ee-lee mnyeh dees-NOO	Я хочý, чтобы вы заморóзили мне деснý.
I want a general anesthetic.	yah kha-CHOO AWB-shee nahr-KAWS	Я хочý óбщий наркóз.
My . . . is broken.	moy/mah-YAH . . . ees-PAWRCH-uhn(-uh)	Мой/Моя́ . . . испóрчен(-а)
• denture	• prah-TYEHS	• протéз.
• bridge	• mawst	• мост.
• crown	• kah-RAWN-kuh	• корóнка.
Can you fix it?	SMAWZH-uh-tyuh lee vy yee-VAW/yee-YAW puh-chee-NEET'?	Смóжете ли вы егó/её починúть?

110

| How much do I owe? | SKAWL'-kuh yah vahm DAWLZH-uhn/dahlzh-NAH zah fsyaw? | Ско́лько я вам до́лжен/должна́ за всё? |

What the Dentist Says

У вас	oo vahs	You have
• инфе́кция.	• een-FYEHKS-tsy-yuh	• an infection.
• испо́рчен зуб.	• ees-PAWR-chuhn zoop	• a cavity.

Это бо́льно?	EH-tuh BAWL'-nuh?	Does that hurt?
Придётся удали́ть зуб.	pree-DYAWT-suh oo-dahl-EET' zoop	That tooth must come out.
Вам сле́дует верну́ться	vahm SLYEHD-oo-yeht veer-NOOT'-suh	You'll need to come back
• за́втра.	• ZAHF-truh	• tomorrow.
• че́рез не́сколько дней.	• CHEH-rees NYEH-skuhl'-kuh dnyehy	• in a few days.
• на сле́дующей неде́ле.	• nah SLYEHD-oo-yoo-shee nee-DYEHL-yee	• next week.

THE OPTICIAN

If you wear glasses or contact lenses, it's a good idea to bring an extra pair and to have your prescription with you in case of loss. Contact lenses, frames, and glass lenses for eyeglasses may not be readily available.

I broke	yah slah-MAHL(-uh)	Я слома́л(-а)
• a lens.	• LEENZ-oo	• ли́нзу.
• the frame.	• ah-PRAHV-oo	• опра́ву.
I lost	yah puh-teer-YAHL (-uh)	Я потеря́л(-а)
• my glasses.	• mah-YEE ach-KEE	• мои́ очки́.
• a contact lens.	• kahn-TAHKT-noo-yoo LEENZ-oo	• конта́ктную ли́нзу.

111

Can they be replaced right away?	eekh MOZH-nuh SRAHZ-oo zah-meen-EET'?	Их мо́жно сра́зу замени́ть?
I'd like soft/hard lenses.	yah by khah-TYEHL (-uh) MYAKH-kee-yeh/TVYAWR-dee-yeh LEENZ-ee	Я бы хоте́л(-а) мя́гкие/твёрдые ли́нзы.
Here's the prescription.	vawt ree-TSEHPT	Вот реце́пт.
When can I come and get them?	kahg-DAH MAWZH-nuh eekh puh-loo-CHEET'?	Когда́ мо́жно их получи́ть?
I need sunglasses.	mnyeh noozh-NY SAWL-neech-ny-yeh ahch-KEE	Мне нужны́ со́лнечные очки́.

AT THE PHARMACY

You can recognize a pharmacy by the sign, **апте́ка** (ahp-TYEHK-uh) and the international medical symbol of the serpents entwined around a staff (caduceus). In most sections of every city there are pharmacies that are open on weekends, late at night, and all night. The address of the nearest 24-hour pharmacy, **дежу́рная апте́ка** (dee-ZHOOR-nuh-yuh ahp-TYEHK-uh), is usually posted on the door of the regular pharmacy.

Is there an all-night pharmacy near here?	yehyst pah-BLEEZ-uhst-ee dee-ZHOOR-nuh-yuh ahp-TYEHK-uh kah-TAWR-uh-yuh rah-BAWT-uh-yeht KROOG-ly-uh SOOT-kee?	Есть побли́зости дежу́рная апте́ка, кото́рая рабо́тает кру́глые су́тки?
I need something for	mnyeh NOOZH-nuh shtuh-nee-BOOT' aht	Мне ну́жно что-нибу́дь от
• a cold.	• prah-STOOD-y	• просту́ды.
• constipation.	• zah-PAWR-uh	• запо́ра.
• a cough.	• KAHSH-lyuh	• ка́шля.

112

• diarrhea.	• pah-NAWS-uh	• поноса.
• fever.	• ZHAHR-uh	• жара.
• hay fever.	• ah-leer-GEE-ee nah ZAH-pukh SYEHN-uh	• аллергии на запах сена.
• headache.	• guh-lahv-NOY BAWL-ee	• головной боли.
• a mosquito bite.	• kuh-mah-REEN-uh-vuh oo-KOOS-uh	• комариного укуса.
• sunburn.	• zah-GAHR-uh	• солнца.
• motion sickness.	• mahr-SKOY bah-LYEHZ-nee	• морской болезни.
• an upset stomach.	• nee-svah-RYEHN-yuh zhy-LOOT-kuh	• несварения желудка.
I'd like to buy	yah by khah-TYEHL (-uh) koo-PEET'	Я бы хотел(-а) купить
• some alcohol.	• ahl-kah-GAWL-yuh	• спирма.
• an analgesic.	• buh-lee-oo-tah-LYAH-yoo-shchehy-yeh SREHTS-vuh	• болеутоляющее средство.
• an antiseptic.	• ahn-tee-seep-TEE-chees-kuh-yuh SREHTS-vuh	• антисептическое средство.
• some aspirin.	• ahs-pee-REEN	• аспирин.
• a bandage.	• pah-VYAHS-koo	• повязку.
• some contact lens solution.	• ZHYD-kuhst' dlyah kahn-TAHKT-nykh LEENS	• жидкость для контактных линз.
• some contraceptives.	• pree-seer-vah-TEEV-y.	• презервативы.
• some cotton.	• VAHT-y	• ваты.
• some cough drops.	• tah-BLYEHT-kee aht KAHSH-lyuh	• капли от кашля.
• a disinfectant.	• deez-een-fee-TSYR-oo-yoo-sheh-yeh SRYEHTST-vuh	• дезинфици-рующее средство.
• some ear drops.	• oosh-NY-yeh KAHP-lee	• ушные капли.
• some eye drops.	• glahz-NY-yeh KAHP-lee	• глазные капли.
• some gauze.	• MAHR-lee	• марли.

- some insect spray.
- some iodine.
- a laxative.

- some nose drops.
- some pills.
- some sanitary napkins.
- some suppositories.

- some tampons.
- a thermometer.
- some vitamins.

It's urgent!

- ZHYT-kuhst' aht kuh-mahr-AWF
- yawt
- slah-BEE-teel'-nuh-yuh

- KAHP-lee aht NAHS-muhr-kuh
- tah-BLYEHT-kee
- been-TY

- SVYEHCH-ee

- tahm-PAWN-y
- teer-MAW-mee-tuhr
- vee-tah-MEEN-uhf

EH-tuh SRAWCH-nuh!

- жи́дкость от комаро́в.
- йод.
- слаби́тельное.

- ка́пли от на́сморка.
- табле́тки.
- бинты́.

- све́чи.

- тампо́ны.
- термо́метр.
- витами́нов.

Это сро́чно!

114

9/ON THE ROAD

RENTING A CAR

It is possible to organize renting a car in advance through your travel agent or you can do this with the travel bureau in your hotel. It is best to make arrangements in advance because you will have to get visas for the various cities you will be visiting and check in with the police department in each place. You will not be able simply to wander aimlessly on your own itinerary.

Speed limits, parking regulations, and all highway rules should be strictly obeyed. Traffic officers can often be found at every corner and often stop cars for seemingly no reason at all, so always have all your papers in order. You must wear your seat belt in the Soviet Union.

DIALOGUE: ВЗЯТЬ МАШИНУ НАПРОКАТ (AT THE CAR RENTAL AGENCY)

Клиентка:	Здравствуйте. Я хочу взять машину на-прокат.	ZDRAHST-voo-ee-tyeh. yah khah-CHOO vzyaht' mah-SHY-noo nah-prah-KAHT.
Продавец:	Хорошо. У нас есть прекрасная Лада.	khuh-rah-SHAW. oo nahs yehst' pree-KRAH-snuh-yuh LAH-duh.
Клиентка:	Можно её взять на три дня?	MAWZH-nuh yeh-YAW vzyaht' nah tree dnyah?
Продавец:	Конечно. Скажите нам ваш маршрут и мы получим ваши визы.	kah-NYEHSH-nuh. skah-ZHY-tyeh nahm vahsh mahr-SHROOT ee my pah-LOO-cheem VAH-shy VEE-zy.
Клиентка:	Я хочу поехать из Ленинграда в Новгород. Сколько это будет стоить?	yah khah-CHOO pah-YEH-khuht' eez lee-neen-GRAH-duh v NAWV-guh-ruht. SKOL'-kuh EH-tuh BOO-dyeht STAW-eet'?

115

Продавец:	Это будет стоить тысячу двести рублей.	EH-tuh BOO-dyeht STAW-eet' TY-seech-oo DVYEH-stee roo-BLEHY.
Клиентка:	Хорошо.	khuh-rah-SHAW.
Продавец:	Дайте ваш паспорт и водительские права и всё будет готово через несколько дней.	DAHY-tyeh vahsh PAHS-puhrt ee vah-DEE-teel'-skee-yeh prah-VAH ee vsyaw BOO-dyeht gah-TAW-vuh CHEH-rees NYEH-skuhl'-kuh dnyehy.

. . . .

Customer:	Hello. I'd like to rent a car.
Salesperson:	Fine. We have a wonderful Lada.
Customer:	Could I have it for three days?
Salesperson:	Certainly. Give us your itinerary and we will take care of getting your visas.
Customer:	I'd like to drive from Leningrad to Novgorod. How much will this cost?
Salesperson:	It will cost 1,200 rubles.
Customer:	Okay.
Salesperson:	Give us your passport and driver's license and everything will be arranged in a few days.

I'd like to rent	yah khah-CHOO vzyaht' nah prah-KAHT	Я хочу взять на-прокат
• a small car.	• MAH-leen'-koo-yoo mah-SHY-noo	• маленькую машину.
• a large car.	• bahl'-SHOO-yoo mah-SHY-noo	• большую машину.

• the least expensive car.	• SAH-moo-yoo dee-SHAW-voo-yoo mah-SHY-noo	• са́мую дешёвую маши́ну.
• a car with automatic transmission.	• s uhf-tuh-mah-TEE-chees-kuhy kah-RAWP-kuhy pee-ree-DAHCH	• с автомати́ческой коро́бкой переда́ч.
Do you have unlimited mileage?	oo vahs yehst' nee-uh-gruh-nee-CHEH-nyeh kee-luh-mee-TRAH-zhuh?	У ва́с есть неограни́ченный километра́ж?
I'd like insurance coverage.	yah khah-TYEHL/TYEH-luh by strah-KHAWF-koo	Я хоте́л(-а) бы страхо́вку.
How much will it cost	SKAWL'-kuh STAW-eet	Ско́лько сто́ит
• per day?	• nuh dyehn'?	• на де́нь?
• per week?	• nuh nee-DYEHL-yoo?	• на неде́лю?
• per kilometer?	• zuh kee-lah-MYEH-tuhr	• за киломе́тр?
Do you accept credit cards?	vy pree-nee-MAHY-yeh-tyeh kree-DEET-ny-yeh KAHR-tuhch-kee?	Вы принима́ете креди́тные ка́рточки?
Do you need my driver's license?	vahm NOOZH-ny mah-YEE vah-DEE-tehl'-skee-yeh prah-VAH?	Ва́м нужны́ мои́ води́тельские права́?
Can I rent it here and return it in . . . ?	mnyeh MAWZH-nuh yeh-YAW vzyaht' nah prah-KAHT zdyehs' ee veer-NOOT' yeh-YAW v . . . ?	Мне́ мо́жно её взя́ть напрока́т здесь и верну́ть её в . . . ?

DISTANCES AND LIQUID MEASURES

Distances in the Soviet Union are expressed in kilometers and liquid measures (gas and oil, for example) in liters. Unless you

117

are a whiz at mental calculations, the switch from one system to another can be hard to get used to. The following conversion formulas and charts should help.

MILES/KILOMETERS

| 1 kilometer (*km*) = .62 miles |
| 1 mile 1.51 km |
| (1,51 km) |

Kilometers	Miles
1	0.62
5	3.1
8	5.0
10	6.2
15	9.3
20	12.4
50	31.0
75	46.5
100	62.0

GALLONS/LITERS

| 1 liter(/) = .26 gallon |
| 1 gallon = 3.75 liters |
| (3.75 l) |

Liters	Gallons
10	2.6
15	3.9
20	5.2
30	7.8
40	10.4
50	13.0
60	15.6
70	18.2

AT THE GAS STATION

Gas stations in the Soviet Union are few and far between. They can be identified by a sign depicting a gas pump. You pay the cashier for the amount of gas you need and serve yourself. There are three kinds of gas: 72, 93, and diesel. The number represents the amount of octane in the gas. There is no unleaded gas. All forms of repair are done at special repair shops called **ста́нция техобслу́живания** (STAHN-tseyeh teekh-ahp-SLOO-zhy-vuh-nyeh). No repair work will be done at a gas station, although you may be able to buy certain basics like motor oil there.

I'd like 30 liters of	pah-ZHAHL-stuh, TREE-tseet' LEE-truhf	Пожа́луйста, три́дцать ли́тров
• 72	• SYEHM'-dee-seet ftah-RAW-vuh	• се́мьдесят второ́го.
• 93	• dee-vee-NAW-stuh TRYEHT'-yeh-vuh	• девяно́сто тре́тьего.
• diesel.	• DEE-zeel'-yuh	• ди́зельното.
I'd like 20 rubles of 72.	pah-ZHAHL-stuh nah DVAH-tseet' roo-BLEHY SYEM'-dyeh-seht ftah-RAW-vuh	Пожа́луйста, на два́дцать рубле́й се́мьдесят второ́го.

AT THE REPAIR SHOP

Please check	prah-VYEHR'-tyeh, pah-ZHAHL-stuh,	Прове́рьте, пожа́луйста,
• the battery.	• ah-koo-moo-LYAH-tuhr	• аккумуля́тор.
• the brake fluid.	• tuhr-mahz-NOO-yoo ZHEED-kuhst'	• тормозну́ю жи́дкость.
• the carburetor.	• kuhr-byoo-RAH-tuhr	• карбюра́тор.
• the tire pressure.	• dah-VLYEH-nyeh v SHY-nuhkh	• давле́ние в ши́нах.
• the water.	• VAW-doo	• во́ду.
• the spark plugs.	• zah-PAHL'-ny-yeh SVEH-chee	• запа́льные све́чи.
• the oil.	• MAH-sluh	• ма́сло.
The . . . needs to be changed.	NOOZH-nuh puh-mee-NYAHT' . . .	Ну́жно поменя́ть . . .
My car has broken down.	mah-YAH mah-SHY-nuh slah-MAH-luhs'	Моя́ маши́на слома́лась.
Can you repair it?	vy SMAW-zhy-tyeh yee-YAW puh-chee-NEET'?	Вы смо́жете её почини́ть?
Do you have the part?	oo vahs yehst' EH-tuh zahp-CHAHST'?	У ва́с есть э́та запча́сть?
I've run out of gas.	oo mee-NYAH KAWN-cheel-syuh been-ZEEN	У меня́ ко́нчился бензи́н.

It won't start.	mah-SHY-nuh nee zah-VAW-deet-suh	Маши́на не заво́дится.
I have a flat tire.	oo mee-NYAH SPOO-sheh-nuh SHY-nuh	У меня́ спу́щена ши́на.
Can you check the battery.	nee MAW-zhy-tyeh lee vy prah-VYEH-reet' ah-koo-moo-LYAH-tuhr	Не мо́жете ли вы прове́рить аккумуля́тор?
The battery's dead.	ah-koo-moo-LYAH-tuhr ruhz-ree-DEEL-suh	Аккумуля́тор разряди́лся.
It's overheating.	pee-ree-gree-VAH-yeht-suh	Перегрева́ется.
Can you tow me?	vy MAW-zhy-tyeh mee-NYAH aht-book-SEER-uh-vuht?	Вы мо́жете меня́ отбук-си́ровать?
I have a problem with	oo mee-NYAH prah-BLYEHM-uh	У меня́ пробле́ма
• the carburetor.	• kuhr-byoo-RAH-tuhr-uhm	• с карбюра́тором.
• the directional signal.	• s puh-vah-RAWT-nee-kuh-mee	• с поворо́т-никами.
• the gears.	• s pee-ree-klyoo-CHEH-nyehm	• с переключе́-нием.
• the brakes.	• s tuhr-mahz-AH-mee	• с тормоза́ми.
• the headlights.	• s FAHR-uh-mee	• с фа́рами.
• the ignition.	• z zuh-zhy-GAH-nee-yehm	• с зажига́нием.
• the radiator.	• s ruh-dee-AH-tuhr-uhm	• с радиа́тором.
• the starter.	• sah STAHR-teer-uhm	• со ста́ртером.
• the transmission.	• s kah-RAWP-kuhy pee-ree-DAHCH	• с коро́бкой переда́ч.
I have no tools.	oo mee-NYAH nyeht een-stryoo-MYEHN-tuhf	У меня́ нет инструме́нтов.
Do you have	oo vahs yehst'	У ва́с е́сть
• a flashlight?	• fah-NAHR'?	• фона́рь?
• a jack?	• dahm-KRAHT?	• домкра́т?

• pliers?	• pluhs-kah-GOOP-tsy?	• плоскогубцы?
• a screwdriver?	• aht-VYAWRT-kuh?	• отвёртка?
When will it be ready?	kahg-DAH BOO-dyeht gah-TAW-vuh?	Когда будет готово?
I need it today.	ah-NAH mnyeh BOO-dyeht noozh-nah see-VAWD-nyuh	Она мне будет нужна сегодня.

DRIVING ABOUT

If you haven't done it before, you may be hesitant to drive in a foreign country. You can reduce your anxiety by getting a good road map. When you have decided upon your itinerary with your travel agent or through your hotel, you will be provided with a map and detailed directions.

Most people in the Soviet Union still don't own a car, so you will share the road mostly with trucks and buses. Speed limits are clearly marked and strictly enforced. Traffic officers often pull cars over just to look at the registration papers, to make sure everything is in order, so don't be surprised or panic if this should happen to you. Roads in the Soviet Union are not kept up particularly well and potholes abound. If you are unfamiliar with such conditions you probably won't want to drive too fast, and it's a good idea to let other drivers pass.

Excuse me, how do I get to	ee-zvee-NEE-tyeh, pah-ZHAHL-stuh, kahk mnyeh prah-YEH-khuht' v	Извините, пожалуйста, как мне проехать в
• Leningrad?	• lee-neen-GRAHT?	• Ленинград?
• Moscow?	• mahsk-VOO?	• Москву?
Is this the road to	EH-tuh dah-RAW-guh	Это дорога
• the Intourist hotel?	• v gah-STEE-nee-tsoo een-too-REEST?	• в гостиницу Интурист?

121

• the next town?	• v blee-ZHAHY-shy GAW-ruht?	• в ближа́йший го́род?
• the highway?	• nah shah-SEH?	• к шоссе́?
• the center of town?	• v TSEHN-tuhr?	• в центр?
How far is it to . . . ?	kak duh-lee-KAW duh . . . ?	Ка́к далеко́ до . . . ?
Where can I buy a map?	gdyeh MAWZH-nuh koo-PEET' KAHR-too?	Где мо́жно купи́ть ка́рту?
Is there a better road?	yehst' dah-RAW-guh pah-LOO-cheh?	Есть доро́га полу́чше?
Is there a shortcut?	yehst' poot' kah-RAW-cheh?	Есть пу́ть коро́че?
I think we are	KAH-zhyt-suh my	Ка́жется, мы
• lost.	• zuh-bloo-DEE-lees'	• заблуди́лись.
• in the outskirts.	• nah uh-KRAH-ee-nyeh	• на окра́ине.
• in the wrong lane.	• nee f tawm ree-DOO	• не в то́м ряду́.
• in the wrong exit.	• nee nah tawm VY-khuhd-yeh	• не на то́м вы́ходе.
• in the center of town.	• v TSEHN-treh GAW-ruhd-uh	• в це́нтре го́рода.
• arriving at the next town.	• puhd-yee-ZHAH-yehm k SLYEH-doo-yoo-sheh-moo GAW-ruhd-oo	• подъезжа́ем к сле́дующему го́роду.
Do I	mnyeh	Мне
• go straight?	• YEH-khuht' PRYAH-muh?	• е́хать пря́мо?
• turn right?	• YEH-khuht' nah-PRAH-vuh?	• е́хать напра́во?
• turn left?	• YEH-khuht' nah-LYEH-vuh?	• е́хать нале́во?
• go two more blocks?	• YEH-khuht' ee-SHAW dvah kvahr-TAHL-uh?	• е́хать ещё два́ кварта́ла?
• make a U-turn?	• DYEH-luht' ruhz-vah-RAWT?	• де́лать разворо́т?

122

Is it	EH-tuh	Это
• nearby?	• BLEES-kuh?	• близко?
• far from here?	• duh-lee-KAW?	• далеко?
• far from the center?	• duh-lee-KAW aht TSEHN-truh?	• далеко от центра?
• close to the center?	• AW-kuh-luh TSEHN-truh?	• около центра?
Where can I park?	gdyeh MAWOZH-nuh zuh-puhr-kah-VAHT'-suh?	Где можно запарковаться?

ROAD SIGNS

НЕРОВНАЯ ДОРОГА	nee-RAWV-nuh-yuh dah-RAW-guh	BAD SURFACE
ОСТОРОЖНО: ВПЕРЕДИ КРУТОЙ ПОВОРОТ	uh-stah-RAWZH-nuh: vpeh-reh-DEE kroo-TOY puh-vah-RAWT	CAUTION: CURVES
КРУТОЙ ПОДЪЕМ	kroo-TOY pahd-YAWM	CAUTION: STEEP HILL
ДЕТИ	DYEH-tee	CHILDREN CROSSING
ТАМОЖНЯ	tah-MAWZH-nyuh	CUSTOMS
ТУПИК	too-PEEK	DEAD END
ОБЪЕЗД	ahb-YEHST	DETOUR
ЦЕНТР	TSEHN-tuhr	DOWNTOWN
ДОРОЖНЫЕ РАБОТЫ	dah-RAWZH-ny-yeh rah-BAW-ty	EMERGENCY ROAD REPAIRS
ПАДЕНИЕ КАМНЕЙ	pah-DEH-nee-yeh kahm-NYEHY	FALLING ROCKS
ВЫБРОС ГРАВИЯ	VY-bruhs GRAH-vee-yuh	GRAVEL
АВТОМА-ГИСТРАЛЬ	ahf-tuh-muh-gee-STRAHL'	HIGHWAY
ВЫЕЗД С АВТОМА-ГИСТРАЛИ	VY-yehst s uhf-tuh-muh-gee-STRAHL-y	HIGHWAY EXIT
ДЕРЖИТЕСЬ ПРАВОЙ СТОРОНЫ	dehr-ZHEE-tyehs' prah-VAWY stuh-rah-NEE	KEEP RIGHT

ЛЕВАЯ ЛИНИЯ	LYEH-vuh-yuh LEE-nee-yuh	LEFT LANE
СТОЯНКА ЗАПРЕЩЕНА	stah-YAHN-kuh zuh-preh-sheh-NAH	NO PARKING
ДВИЖЕНИЕ ПЕШЕХОДОВ ЗАПРЕЩЕНО	dvee-ZHEH-nee-yeh pee-shee-KHAWD-uhf zuh-pree-shee-NAW	NO PEDESTRIANS
ОСТАНОВКА ЗАПРЕЩЕНА	ah-stah-NAWF-kuh zuh-pree-shee-NAH	NO STOPPING
ДВИЖЕНИЕ ЗАПРЕЩЕНО	dvee-ZHEH-nee-yeh zuh-pree-shee-NAW	NO THROUGH TRAFFIC
ПРОЕЗД ЗАПРЕЩЕН	prah-YEHST zuh-PREH-shyn	NO TRESPASSING
ОДНОСТО- РОННЕЕ ДВИЖЕНИЕ	uhd-nuh-stah-RAWN-neh-yeh dvee-ZHEH-nee-yeh	ONE WAY
СТОЯНКА	stah-YAHN-kuh	PARKING LOT
СТОЯНКА НА ЭТОЙ СТОРОНЕ	stah-YAHN-kuh nah eh-TAWY stuh-rah-NYEH	PARKING THIS SIDE
ПЕРЕХОД	pee-ree-KHAWT	PEDESTRIAN CROSSING
НЕРОВНАЯ ДОРОГА	nee-RAWV-nuh-yuh dah-RAW-guh	POTHOLES
ЖЕЛЕЗНОДО- РОЖНЫЙ ПЕРЕЕЗД	zhee-lyehz-nuh-dah-RAWZH-ny pee-ree-YEHST	RAILROAD CROSSING
ОГРАНИЧЕНИЕ СКОРОСТИ 70 КМ/ЧАС	ah-gruh-nee-CHEH-nee-yeh SKAW-ruh-stee 70 kee-lah-MYEH-truhf fchahs	REMINDER: SPEED LIMIT IS 70 KM/H
ПРАВАЯ ЛИНИЯ	PRAH-vuh-yuh LEE-nee-yuh	RIGHT LANE
СУЖЕНИЕ ДОРОГИ	soo-ZHEH-nee-yeh dah-RAW-gee	ROAD NARROWS
СКОЛЬЗКАЯ ДОРОГА	SKAWL'S-kuh-yuh dah-RAW-guh	SLIPPERY ROAD

124

СВЕТОФОРНОЕ РЕГУЛИРО- ВАНИЕ ВПЕРЕДИ	sveh-tah-FAWR-nuh- yeh reh-goo-lee-rah -VAH-nee-yeh	TRAFFIC LIGHT AHEAD
ГРУЗОВОЕ ДВИЖЕНИЕ	fpee-ree-DEE groo- zah-VAW-yeh dvee- ZHEH-nee-yeh	TRUCKS
УСТУПИТЕ ДОРОГУ	oo-stoo-PEE-tyeh dah- RAW-goo	YIELD RIGHT OF WAY

ONE WAY

MAIN ROAD

PARKING

SUPERHIGHWAY

YIELD

GAS
(10 km ahead)

**DANGER
AHEAD**

**DANGEROUS
DESCENT**

BUMPS

**ROAD
NARROWS**

**LEVEL
(RAILROAD)
CROSSING**

**TWO-WAY
TRAFFIC**

**SLIPPERY
ROAD**

**CAUTION—SHARP
CURVES**

**PEDESTRIAN
CROSSING**

NO ENTRY FOR MOTOR VEHICLES

DANGEROUS INTERSECTION AHEAD

STOP

NO ENTRY

MINIMUM SPEED (km/hr)

SPEED LIMIT (km/hr)

DIRECTION TO BE FOLLOWED

OVERHEAD CLEARANCE (meters)

ROTARY

NO PASSING

END OF NO PASSING ZONE

END OF RESTRICTION

NO LEFT TURN

NO U-TURN

NO PARKING

10/COMMUNICATIONS

DIALOGUE: ПО ТЕЛЕФОНУ (ON THE TELEPHONE)

Таня:	Алло́.	ah-LAW.
Ива́н:	Здра́вствуйте.	ZDRAHST-voo-ee-tyeh.
Таня:	Позови́те, пожа́луйста, Са́шу.	pah-zah-VEE-tyeh, pah-ZHAHL-stuh, SAH-shoo.
Ива́н:	Подожди́те . . . Извини́те, но его́ сейча́с нет.	puh-dahzh-DEE-tyeh . . . ee-zvee-NEE-tyeh, naw yee-VAW see-CHAHS nyeht.
Таня:	Когда́ он бу́дет?	kahg-DAH awn BOO-dyeht?
Ива́н:	Около трёх.	AW-kuh-luh tryawkh.
Таня:	Переда́йте ему́, пожа́луйста, чтобы он мне́ перезвони́л.	pee-ree-DAHY-tyeh yee-MOO, pah-ZHAHL-stuh, SHTAW-by awn mnyeh pee-ree-zvah-NEEL.
Ива́н:	Хорошо́. Я ему́ скажу́.	khuh-rah-SHAW. yah yee-MOO skah-ZHOO.
Таня:	Спаси́бо. До свида́ния.	spah-SEE-buh. duh svee-DAH-nee-yuh.

. . . .

Tanya:	Hello.
Ivan:	Hello.
Tanya:	May I speak with Sasha?
Ivan:	Just a moment . . . He's not here right now.
Tanya:	When will he be in?

Ivan:	At around three.
Tanya:	Can you please ask him to call me back?
Ivan:	Okay, I'll tell him.
Tanya:	Thank you. Good-bye.

TELEPHONES

Telephones can be found in most public places (on main streets, in subway stations, and around department stores, hotels, and theaters). Sometimes it can be difficult to find a phone that actually works, but they are plentiful so don't be discouraged.

You can use public phones for local calls. This will cost you 2 kopeks. You can either use a 2-kopek coin or two 1-kopek coins. Put your coins in the slot at the top of the phone and dial the number. When the phone is picked up at the other end your coins will fall into the machine.

Long-distance and international calls must be made from the post office or from your hotel room. In the post office there are phone booths marked with the name of the city that can be called from that booth. Otherwise you must order your call and, if it is overseas, you may be told to come back at a specific time on another day.

Where can I make a phone call?	aht-KOO-duh MAWZH-nuh puh-zvah-NEET'?	Откуда можно позвонить?
Is there a phone booth here?	zdyehs' yehyst' tee-lee-FAWN-uh-yuh BOOT-kuh?	Здесь есть телефонная будка?
Is there a telephone directory?	zdyehys' yehyst' tee-lee-FAWN-ny SPRAH-vuhch-neek?	Здесь есть телефонный справочник?
Operator	ah-peh-RAH-tuhr	Оператор
I'd like to call	YAH khah-CHOO puh-zvah-NEET'	Я хочу позвонить
• this number.	• pah EH-tuh-moo NAW-meer-oo	• по этому номеру

129

the United States.	vsuh-yee-dee-NYA-W-ny-yeh SHTAH-ty ah-LAW	• в Соединённые Штаты.
Hello.	EH-tuh ahn-DRYEH	Алло́.
This is Andrei.	MAWZH-nuh pah-guh-vah-REET' s vah-DEEM-uhm?	Это Андре́й.
May I speak with Vadim?		Мо́жно поговори́ть с Вади́мом?
My number is . . .	moy NAW-meer . . .	Мой но́мер . . .
How do I get the operator?	kahk mnyeh svee-ZAHT'-suh suh-pee-RAH-tuhr-uhm?	Как мне связа́ться с опера́тором?
I was cut off.	mee-NYAH ruhz-yee-dee-NEE-lee	Меня́ разъедини́ли.
To whom am I speaking?	s kyehm yah guh-vah-RYOO?	С ке́м я говорю́?
Speak slowly, please.	guh-vah-REE-tyeh MYEH-dlee-nuh, pah-ZHAHL-stuh	Говори́те ме́дленно, пожа́луйста.
Could you telephone for me?	vy mah-GLEE by puh-zvah-NEET' dlyah mee-NYAH?	Вы могли́ бы позвони́ть для меня́?
I'd like to speak to . . .	yah khah-TYEHL(-uh) by puh-guh-vah-REET' s . . .	Я хоте́л(-а) бы поговори́ть с . . .
Please tell him I called.	skah-ZHY-tyeh yee-MOO, pah-ZHAHL-stuh, shtaw yah zvah-NEEL(-uh)	Скажи́те ему́, пожа́луйста, что я звони́л(-а).

What You May Hear

Алло́!	ah-LAW!	Hello!
Говори́т . . .	guh-vah-REET . . .	This is . . .
Кто́ звони́т?	ktaw zvah-NEET?	Who is calling?
Одну́ мину́точку.	ahd-NOO mee-NOO-tuhch-koo	One moment.
Его́ нет.	yee-VAW nyeht	He's not here.
Вы набра́ли не то́т но́мер.	vy nah-BRAH-lee nee tawt NAW-meer	You dialed the wrong number.

Вы хоти́те ему́ что́-то переда́ть?	vy khah-TEE-tyeh yee-MOO SHTAW-tuh pee-ree-DAHT'?	Would you like to leave a message for him?
Позвони́те, пожа́луйста, попо́зже.	puh-zvah-NEE-tyeh, pah-ZHAHL-stuh, pah-PAW-zheh	Please call back later.
Тебе́ звоня́т.	tee-BYEH zvahn-YAHT	You have a phone call.
По како́му но́меру вы зво́ните?	puh kah-KAW-moo NAW-mee-roo vy ZVAW-nee-tyeh?	What number are you dialing?
Повтори́те, пожа́луйста.	puhf-tah-REET-yeh, pah-ZHAHL-stuh	Please say that again.
Вас не слы́шно.	vahs nee SLYSH-nuh	I can't hear you.
Говори́те погро́мче, пожа́луйста.	guh-vah-REET-yeh pah-GRAWM-cheh, pah-ZHAHL-stuh	Speak louder, please.

POST OFFICE AND MAIL

There is usually a post office in each major hotel. Check with the clerk at the front desk of the hotel for the hours of the post office. Stamps can also be purchased at kiosks on the street.

Mail from the Soviet Union to the United States can take up to a month to arrive.

I'm looking for the main post office.	yah EE-shoo glahv-pahch-TAHMT	Я ищу́ Главпочта́мт.
Where's the nearest mailbox?	gdyeh nah-KHAW-deet-suh blee-ZHAHY-shy pahch-TAW-vy YAH-sheek?	Где нахо́дится ближа́йший почто́вый я́щик?
How much is it for	SKAWL'-kuh STAW-eet aht-PRAH-veet'	Ско́лько сто́ит отпра́вить
• a letter (to the U.S.)?	• pees'-MAW (v sshAH)?	• письмо́ (в США)?
• a postcard?	• aht-KRYT-koo?	• откры́тку?
I would like to buy stamps.	yah khah-CHOO koo-PEET' MAHR-kee	Я хочу́ купи́ть ма́рки.

131

| I would like to send this package to the United States. | yah khah-CHOO pah-SLAHT' EH-too pah-SYL-koo f sshAH | Я хочу́ посла́ть э́ту посы́лку в США. |

TELEGRAMS

Telegraph offices are usually located near a post office and are sometimes in the same building. Some hotels provide telegram services as well. Even though you will be told your telegram will take 24 hours to arrive overseas, it may well take up to a week.

May I send a telegram to New York?	MAWZH-nuh pah-SLAHT' tee-lee-GRAHM-oo v nyoo-YAWRK?	Мо́жно посла́ть телегра́мму в Нью Йо́рк?
How much is it per word?	SKAWL'-kuh STAW-eet zah SLAW-vuh?	Ско́лько сто́ит за сло́во?
Will it arrive tomorrow morning?	pree-DYAWT lee ah-NAH ZAHF-truh OO-truhm?	Придёт ли она́ за́втра у́тром?
Which window is it for telegrams?	kah-KAW-yeh ah-KNAW dlyah tee-lee-GRAHM?	Како́е окно́ для телегра́мм?

THE MEDIA

Some English-language newspapers are available in hotels, but they arrive some three to seven days late. Books in the English language, however, can be bought in bookstores such as Dom Knigi or at foreign currency bookshops for tourists. If you want to try your hand at reading a Russian newspaper, these can be purchased at any kiosk along the street. Also available at kiosks, or at your hotel newsstand, are cultural guides to what is going on in town, such as plays, movies, and musical events. The television schedule is printed in the daily newspaper. There are no programs in English on television or the radio.

Books and Newspapers

I'd like to buy a newspaper.	yah khah-CHOO koo-PEET' gah-ZYEH-too	Я хочу купить газету.
I'd like to buy a magazine.	yah khah-CHOO koo-PEET' zhoor-NAHL	Я хочу купить журнал.
Do you have any books in English?	oo vahs yehst' KNEE-gee nah ahn-GLEES-kuhm yee-zy-KYEH?	У вас есть книги на английском языке?

Radio and Television

Is there a	yehst'	Есть
• music station?	• moo-zy-KAHL'-nuh-yuh prah-GRAH-muh?	• музыкальная программа?
• news station?	• prah-GRAH-muh nuh-vah-STYEHY?	• программа новостей?
• weather station?	• prah-GRAH-muh prah-GNAW-zuh pah-GAW-dy?	• программа прогноза погоды?
What number is it on the dial?	kah-KOY NAW-meer nah tsee-feer-BLAH-tyeh?	Какой номер на циферблате?
What time is the program?	vah SKAWL'-kuh nah-CHAH-luh pee-ree-DAH-chee?	Во сколько начало передачи?
Do you have a television guide?	oo vahs yehst' tee-lee-vee-zee-AW-nuh-yuh prah-GRAH-muh?	У вас есть телевизионная программа?
When is the weather forecast?	vah SKAWL'-kuh prah-GNAWS pah-GAW-dy?	Во сколько прогноз погоды?
What channel is it on?	puh kah-KAW-moo kah-NAHL-oo ee-DYAWT pee-ree-DAH-chuh?	По какому каналу идёт передача?

11/SEEING THE SIGHTS

PLACES OF INTEREST

Before your trip, you should read about the Soviet Union. In addition to guidebooks, your travel agent or the Intourist office offers the information that will help you plan a sight-seeing itinerary. Ask at your hotel for a guide to the city and activities of the week. You may also be able to obtain information about bus tours and places of interest to visit. If you prefer to get a very different view of the city, use public transportation.

DIALOGUE: В МУЗЕЕ (AT THE MUSEUM)

Ни́на:	Зна́ете, я о́чень интересу́юсь ру́сским иску́сством.	ZNAH-yeh-tyuh, yah AW-cheen' een-tee-ree-SOO-yoos' ROOS-keem ees-KOOST-vuhm.
Ива́н:	Я то́же! Како́й ваш люби́мый пери́од?	yah TAW-zhuh! kah-KOY vahsh lyoo-BEE-my pee-REE-uht?
Ни́на:	Я обожа́ю передви́жников! Смотри́те! Вот карти́на жудо́жника-жередви́пника. Кто её написа́л?	yah ahb-ah-ZHAH-yoo pee-ree-DVEEZH-neek-uhf! smah-TREE-tyuh! vawt kahr-TEEN-uh khoo-DAWZH-nee-kuh pee-ree-DVEEZH-nee-kuh. ktaw yee-YAW nuh-pee-SAHL?
Ива́н:	Это карти́на Ре́пина.	EH-tuh kahr-TEEN-uh RYEH-pee-nuh.
Ни́на:	Да, ве́рно. В како́м году́ он её написа́л?	dah, VYEHR-nuh. fkah-KAWM gah-DOO awn yee-YAW nuh-pee-SAHL?
Ива́н:	Одну́ мину́точку. Я посмотрю́ . . . В ты́сяча восемьсо́т во́семьдесят четвёртом году́.	ahd-NOO mee-NOO-yah-twch-koo. puh-smah-TRYOO . . . FTY-see-chuh vuh-seem-SAWT VAW-seem-dee-see-set cheet-VYAWRT-uhm gah-DOO.

. . . .

Nina:	You know, I'm very interested in Russian art.
Ivan:	Me too! What period do you like the best?
Nina:	I love the Wanderers (the *Peredvizhniki*)! Look! There's a picture by one of the Wandering painters! Who painted it?
Ivan:	That's by Repin.
Nina:	Oh, yes. What year did he complete it?
Ivan:	Just a moment. I'll look . . . in 1884.

SIGHT-SEEING

What should one see in town?	shtaw NAH-duh puh-smah-TRYEHT' VGAWR-uhd-dyeh?	Что́ на́до посмотре́ть в го́роде?
How far is it from here?	kahk dah-lee-KAW EH-tuh aht-SYOO-duh?	Ка́к далеко́ э́то отсю́да?
Please tell me about guided tours.	rah-skah-ZHY-tyuh mnyeh ahb eeks-KOORS-ee-ee ZGEED-uhm pee-ree-VAWT-cheek-uhm	Расскажи́те мне́ об экску́рсии с ги́дом-перево́дчиком.
Do you have an English-speaking guide?	oo vahs yehyst' ahn-gluh-yee-ZYCH-ny geet?	У ва́с е́сть англоязы́ч-ный ги́д?
We'd like a guide	my khah-TYEHL-ee by zuh-kah-ZAHT' GEED-uh	Мы́ хоте́ли бы заказа́ть ги́да
• for a day.	• nah ah-DEEN dyehn'	• на оди́н де́нь.
• for half a day.	• nah puh-lah-VEE-noo dnyah	• на полови́ну дня́.
When does the excursion begin?	kahg-DAH nuh-chee-NAH-eet-suh eeks-KOOR-see-yuh?	Когда́ начина́ется экску́рсия?

Is breakfast/ lunch/dinner included?	ZAHF-truhk/ah-BYEHT/ OO-zhuhn fklyoo-CHAH-ee-tsuh?	За́втрак/Обе́д/ Ужин включа́ется?
How much is the excursion, everything included?	SKAWL'-kuh STAW-eet eeks-KOOR-see-yuh sah fsyehm?	Ско́лько сто́ит экску́рсия со всем?
When do we return to the hotel?	kahg-DAH my vuhz-vrah-SHAH-eem-suh vgah-STEE-nee-tsoo?	Когда́ мы возвраща́емся в гости́ницу?
Where do the tours start from?	gdyeh nuh-chee-NAH-eet-suh eeks-KOOR-see-yuh?	Где́ начина́ется экску́рсия?
I'd like to see	yah by kha-TYEHL (-uh) puh-smah-TRYEHT'	Я бы хоте́л(-а) посмотре́ть
• the aquarium.	• ah-KVAH-ree-oom	• аква́риум.
• the art gallery.	• guhl-lee-RYEH-yoo	• галере́ю.
• the botanical gardens.	• buh-tah-NEE-chees-kee saht	• ботани́ческий са́д.
• the castle.	• ZAH-muhk	• за́мок.
• the catacombs.	• kuh-tah-KAWMB-y	• катако́мбы.
• the cathedral.	• sah-BAWR	• собо́р.
• the caves.	• pee-SHEHR-y	• пеще́ры.
• the cemetery.	• KLAHD-bee-sheh	• кла́дбище.
• the central square.	• tsyn-TRAHL'-noo-yoo PLOSH-uht'	• центра́льную пло́щадь.
• the chapel.	• chee-SAWV-nyoo	• часо́вню.
• the church.	• TSEHR-kawf'	• це́рковь.
• the citadel.	• tsy-tah-DYEHL'	• цитаде́ль.
• the convent.	• muh-nahs-TYR'	• монасты́рь.
• the courthouse.	• ZDAH-nyeh soo-DAH	• зда́ние суда́.
• downtown.	• TSEHN-tuhr	• це́нтр.
• the exhibition hall.	• VY-stuhv-uhch-ny-zahl	• вы́ставочный за́л.
• the factories.	• zah-VAWD-y	• заво́ды.
• the folk-art museum.	• moo-ZYEHY nah-RAWD-nuh-vuh ees KOOST-vuh	• музе́й наро́дного иску́сства.

• the fortress.	• KRYEHP-uhst'	• крéпость.
• the fountains.	• fahn-TAHN-y	• фонтáны.
• the grave of . . .	• mah-GEEL-oo . . .	• моги́лу . . .
• the harbor.	• pawrt	• порт.
• historic sites.	• ees-tahr-EE-chees-kee-yeh mees-TAH	• истори́ческие местá.
• the library.	• bee-blee-ah-TYEHK-oo	• библиотéку.
• the market.	• RYN-uhk	• ры́нок.
• the monastery.	• muh-nahs-TYR'	• монасты́рь.
• the mosque.	• mee-CHYEHT'	• мечéть.
• the museums.	• moo-ZYEHY-ee	• музéи.
• the old city.	• STAHR-y GAWR-uht	• стáрый гóрод.
• the opera house.	• AWP-eer-ny tee-AHT-uhr	• óперный теáтр.
• the palace.	• dvahr-YEHTS	• дворéц.
• the park.	• pahrk	• пáрк.
• the planetarium.	• pluh-nee-TAHR-ee	• планетáрий.
• the ruins.	• roo-EEN-y	• руи́ны.
• the shopping district.	• tahr-GAWV-y TSEHN-tuhr	• торгóвый цéнтр.
• the stadium.	• stuh-dee-AWN	• стадиóн.
• the statue of . . .	• PAHM-eet-neek . . .	• пáмятник . . .
• the stock exchange.	• BEERZH-oo	• би́ржу.
• the synagogue.	• see-nah-GAWG-oo	• синагóгу.
• the tower.	• BAHSH-nyoo	• бáшню.
• the town hall.	• RAH-too-shoo	• рáтушу.
• the university.	• oo-nee-veer-see-TYEHT	• университéт.
• the zoo.	• zuh-ah-PAHRK	• зоопáрк.
When does the museum open/close?	kahg-DAH aht-kry-VAH-yeht-suh/zah-kry-VAH-yeht-suh moo-ZYEHY?	Когдá открывáется/ закрывáется музéй?
How much is it . . .	SKAWL'-kuh STAW-eet fkhahd-NOY bee-LYEHT . . .	Скóлько стóит входнóй билéт . . .
• for an adult?	• dlyah VZRAWS-luh-vuh?	• для взрóслого?

137

	for a child?	• dlyah ree-BYAWN-kuh?	• для ребёнка?
•	for a student?	• dlyah stoo-DYEHNT-uh?	• для студе́нта?
•	for seniors?	• dlyah peen-see-ah-NYEHR-uh?	• для пенсионе́ра?

Would you take our picture?	BOOT-tyuh dah-BRY, sfuh-tuh-grah-FEER-oo-yee-tyuh nahs?	Бу́дьте добры́, сфотографи́руйте нас.
One more shot?	yee-SHAW ah-deen SNEEM-uhk, pah-ZHAHL-stuh	Ещё оди́н сни́мок, пожа́луйста.
Smile!	soo-LYP-kuhy!	С улы́бкой!

AT THE MUSEUM

Where can I get an English-speaking guide?	oo vahs yehyst' poo-tee-vah-DEE-teel' puh-ahn-GLEES-kee?	У вас есть путеводи́тель по-англи́йски?
How long does a tour take?	SKAWL'-kuh VRYEH-mee-nee DLEET-suh eeks-KOOR-see-yuh?	Ско́лько вре́мени дли́тся экску́рсия?
Where can one buy postcards and reproductions?	gdyeh MAWZH-nuh koo-PEET' aht-KRYT-kee ee reeh-prah-DOOK-tsy-ee?	Где мо́жно купи́ть откры́тки и репроду́кции?
Is there a restaurant here?	vmoo-ZYEHY-yeh rees-tah-RAHN yehyst'?	В музе́е есть рестора́н?
Where is the bathroom?	gdyeh too-ah-LYEHT?	Где туале́т?
The bathroom is . . .	too-ah-LYEHT . . .	Туале́т . . .
• upstairs.	• nuh-veer-KHOO.	• наверху́.
• downstairs.	• vnee-ZOO.	• внизу́.
Can I take pictures?	MAWZH-nuh fuh-tuh-grah-FEER-uh-vut'?	Мо́жно фотографи́ровать?

I'm interested in	yah een-teer-ee-SOO-yoos'	Я интересу́юсь
• antiques.	• ahn-tee-kvah-ree-AHT-uh-mee	• антиквари-а́тами.

138

• anthropology.	• ahn-truh-pah-LAWG-ee-yehy	• антрополо́гией.
• archaeology.	• ahr-khee-ah-LAWG-ee-yehy	• археоло́гией.
• . . . art.	• . . . ees-KOOST-vuhm	• . . . иску́сством.
Russian	ROOS-keem	ру́сским
Dutch	gah-LAHNTS-keem	голла́ндским
French	frahn-TSOOS-keem	францу́зским
applied	pree-klahd-NYM	прикладны́м
classical	klah-SEE-chees-keem	класси́ческим
fine	eez-uh-brah-ZEE-teel'-nym	изобрази́-тельным
medieval	sreed-nuh-vee-KAWV-ym	средневеко́вым
modern	suh-vree-MYEHN-nym	совреме́нным
• Renaissance art.	• ees-KOOST-vuhm vuhz-RAHZH-dyehy-nyuh	• иску́сством Возрожде́ния.
• socialist realism.	• suhts-ree-ah-LEEZ-muhm	• соцреали́змом.
• surrealism.	• syoo-ree-ah-LEEZ-muhm	• сюрреали́змом.
• impressionism.	• eem-pryehs-see-ah-NEEZ-muhm	• импрессиони́-змом.
• ceramics.	• kee-RAHM-ee-kuhy	• кера́микой.
• furniture.	• preed-MYEHT-uhm-ee BYT-uh	• предме́тами бы́та.
• geography.	• gee-ah-GRAHF-ee-yehy	• геогра́фией.
• geology.	• gee-ah-LAWG-ee-yehy	• геоло́гией.
• handicrafts.	• koos-TAHR-nym-ee eez-DYEHYL-yuh-mee	• куста́рными изде́лиями.
• history.	• ees-TAWR-ee-yehy	• исто́рией.
• natural history.	• yees-YEHYST-veen-ny ees-TAWR-ee-yehy	• есте́ственной исто́рией.
• pottery.	• guhn-CHAHR-nym-ee eez-DYEHYL-yuh-mee	• гонча́рными изде́лиями.

139

- sculpture.
- zoology.

- skool'p-TOOR-oy
- zuh-ah-LAWG-ee-yehy

- скульпту́рой.
- зооло́гией.

MUSEUMS IN MOSCOW

Moscow has about 150 museums and permanent exhibitions. Here is a list of some of them. Their hours of opening change seasonally, so it is advisable to inquire at the service bureau of your hotel if you are not visiting in the course of your Intourist group sightseeing. The opening times we give here are according to the latest information but it is still best to check them. *They may close early on days preceding holidays.*

Museums of Soviet Revolutionary History

Central Lenin Museum, 2 Revolution Square, near Red Square. Open Tues. through Thurs. 11–7.30; Fri. through Sun. 10–6.30. Closed Mon. Free. Includes manuscripts by Lenin and his personal belongings.

Karl Marx and Friedrich Engels Museum, 5 Marx-Engels Street. Open 1–7 Monday, Wednesday, Friday; 11 A.M.–5 P.M., Thursday, Saturday, Sunday; closed Tuesday. The exhibits include letters, early editions, documents and photographs of Marx and Engels and their close associates and friends, together with drawings and paintings.

Lenin's House Museum, in Gorki Leninskiye, 85 kilometers (about 50 miles) from Moscow. Open from 11 to 7, closed on Tuesdays. This is where Lenin spent the last years of his life and where he died on January 21, 1924. Built in 1830, the house stands in a park of 175 acres; it was the home of the Mayor of Moscow before the revolution. Intourist runs group excursions, 4 hours, 28 rubles.

Museum of the Revolution, 21 Gorky Street. Open 10–6, Tues., Sat., Sun.; 12–8 Wed.; 11–7 Fri.; closed Mon., Thurs. Opened in 1926, the 37-room museum houses relics and mementos of the Revolution, starting with the history of the first worker's organizations in the 19th century. Also deals with the 1918–20 Civil War and World War II.

140

Underground Press of the C.C., 55 Lesnaya Street. The premises of a revolutionary printing press deep below a house where the newspaper *Rabochii* (Worker) was printed.

Other History Museums

Museum of the History and Reconstruction of Moscow, 12 Novaya Square. Open 10–6 on Sat., Mon., Thurs.; 2–9 Wed., Fri.; closed Tues. and the last day of each month.

State History Museum, 1–2 Red Square. Open Mon., Thurs., Sat. and Sun., 10–6; Wed. and Fri. 11–7. Closed Tues., and last Mon. of each month. Russian history to the end of the 19th century. Being refurbished 1986–89; may be partly closed. Check.

Art Galleries and Museums

Art Gallery of the U.S.S.R., Krymskaya Naberezhnaya (Crimean Embankment), opposite Gorky Park. The Tretyakov's extension. Newly opened. Opening hours not available at presstime.

Exhibition Hall of the U.S.S.R. Academy of Arts, 21 Kropotkin Street.

Exhibition Halls of the Union of Soviet Artists, are located at 20 Kuznetsky Most, at 25 Gorky Street, at 5 Chernyakhovsky Street, at 46b Gorky Street, at 7/9 Begovaya Street and 17 Zholtovsky Street. For the various exhibitions and opening times, check with Intourist or the galleries themselves.

Manège Central Exhibition Hall, on Marx Prospekt near the Kremlin. Designed as a riding school, it has Russian and foreign exhibitions of art, textiles, furnishing and glass.

Museum of Russian Folk Art, 7 Stanislavsky Street. Open 12–7 daily; Mondays 12–6. Closed Tuesdays and the last day of the month. Antique and modern pottery, ceramics, glassware, metalware, wood, bone, embroideries, lace and popular prints. In the Naryshkin House (17th century), 22 rooms restored.

Museum of Victor Vasnetsov, 13 Pereulok Vasnetsova. The former home, "a typical Russian fairyland house," of the famous 19th-century Russian artist. Open 10–6; closed Sat. and Sun.

141

Pushkin Fine Arts Museum, 12 Volkhonka Street. **New Gallery**, 4 Marshal Shaposhnikov Street. Mostly reproductions and copies. Open 10–8; Sun. 10–6. Closed Mon.

Tretyakov Art Gallery, 10 Lavrushinsky Pereulok, near Novokuznetskaya Metro Station. Open 10–8 (but Ticket Office closes at 7), except Mon.

Economic, Scientific and Technical Museums

The Anthropological Museum, 18 Marx Prospekt, has an excellent collection of fossils of primitive man.

The Darwin Museum, 1 Malaya Pirogovskaya Street, is open 10–5, closed on Sat. and Sun. Devoted to life of Charles Darwin.

Exhibition of Economic Achievements of the U.S.S.R., Prospekt Mira, Metro: VDNKh. Open 9.30 A.M. to 10 P.M., Mon. through Fri.; 9.30 A.M. to 11 P.M. Sat. and Sun. From September 1 to May 1, the pavilions closed for refurbishment.

The Frunze Central Museum of Aviation and Cosmonautics, 4 Krasnoarmeiskaya Street. A museum devoted to the history of Russian aviation. Open 10–6; closed Mon.

Museum of Bread, a new museum on the scene. (Details not available at press-time.) You can see and taste replicas of bread as baked in the times of Peter the Great, and the mini-loaves that Soviet cosmonauts take on their space flights.

The Zoological Museum, 6 Herzen Street. Thousands of exhibits of mammals, birds, amphibians, reptiles and almost a million insects. A collection of more than 100,000 butterflies was recently donated by a citizen of Moscow. Open 10–6; Wed. and Fri. 12–8 P.M.; closed Mon.

Literary, Musical and Theatrical Museums

Alexei Bakhrushin Museum, 31/12 Bakhrushin Street. Open Thurs., Sat., Sun., and Mon. 12–7; Wed. and Fri. 2–9; closed on Tues. and first Mon. of each month. It presents the history of Russian drama, opera and ballet theaters from the 18th century to our own time.

Chekhov Museum, 6 Sadovo-Kudrinskaya Street. Open

142

11–5.30 Tues., Thurs. Sat. and Sun; 2–8.30 Weds. and Fri. Closed Mon.

Dostoyevsky Museum, 2 Dostoyevsky Street, open 11–6 Thurs., Sat., Sun., Mon.; 10–4, Wed. and Fri. 1–9; closed Tues.

Gogol Museum, Suvorov Street, in Gogol's former apartment.

Gorky Museum, 25a Vorovsky Street, and the **Gorky Memorial Museum,** 6/2 Kachalov Street. The Memorial Museum, a fine example of Russian art nouveau architecture, is the house where he lived from 1931 to 1936; the Gorky Museum itself is open Tues. and Fri., 1–8; Wed., Thurs., and Sun., 10–5, and on Sat. 10.30–4 (closed Mon.).

The Leo Tolstoy Museum and the **Tolstoy Home** are, respectively, at 11 Kropotkinskaya Street and at 21 Lev Tolstoy Street. The Museum is open 11–5 Thurs., Sat., and Sun., 10–3; Mon. 2–8; Wed. and Fri.; and is closed on Tues. The Moscow Tolstoy Home can be visited every day 10–4.30, except Mon.

Museum of Literature, 28 Petrovka Street. Open 11–5.30 Tues., Thurs., Sat., and Sun., 2–8 Wed. and Fri. Closed Mon. and last day of the month. A fine collection of material on Russian writers.

Puppet Museum, 3 Sadovaya-Samotechnaya. The Obraztsov Puppet Theater has a collection of old and modern theatrical puppets from over 30 countries.

Pushkin Museum, 12/2 Kropotkinskaya Street. Open on Sat., 1–7.30; Sun., 11–5.30. New branch at *Pushkin's House,* 53 Arbat Street.

Parks and Gardens

Gorky Park, 9 Krymsky Val. Open 10 A.M.–11 P.M. The most popular in Moscow.

Hermitage Garden, 3 Karetny Ryad. Open May 1 to Sept. 1, 10 A.M.–11 P.M. This is a small park in the center of the city, in which there are concerts and variety and puppet performances in the summer. Several cafes and a restaurant.

Izmailovo Park, 17 Narodny Prospekt. Covering almost 3,000 acres, it includes large stretches of pine forest. Once the manor of the Romanovs, a favorite retreat of the Czars. Amusement park, open air theater and several cafes.

Main Botanic Garden of the U.S.S.R. Academy of Sciences, at Ostankino, (trolley buses 36 or 9 go much nearer than the "Botanicheskaya" metro station) covers an area of some 900 acres and has been planted in and among the original beech-oak-spruce forests of the Moscow area.

Sokolniki Park, 62 Rusakovskaya Street. Open 10 A.M.–11 P.M. Named after the falconers *(sokolniki)* who used to live here. Open-air theater, an amusement park, a shooting gallery, restaurants and cafes. There are bicycles and horses to hire, which you may need to explore all 1,530 acres of the park, including part of an ancient forest.

The Zoo is at 1 Bolshaya Gruzinskaya Street. Open 10–5.

Bitsa Forest Park, outside the city, features an arts and crafts market. Weekends only.

MUSEUMS IN LENINGRAD
Leningrad has some of the greatest collections in the world—indeed, many people visit the city simply to see the paintings and other treasures in the Hermitage alone. Whatever your historical or artistic interest, it is likely to discover a great deal to feed on in these fascinating galleries.

Museums of Fine Art and Art History
I.I. Brodsky Museum, 3 Ploshchad Iskusstv. Open daily 11–8 except Thurs. A memorial museum to the artist, well-known for his revolutionary scenes, portraits of Lenin, etc. Rather a matter of taste.

Hermitage Museum, Winter Palace, 36 Dvortsovaya Naberezhnaya, open 10.30–6; closed Mon. Entrance 1.5 roubles. One of the world's great museums. Intourist charges over 4 roubles for tour—better to go alone at your leisure, preferably several times. Last entry 5. Some parts closed for refurbishment.

Permanent Exhibition of Leningrad Artists, 8 Nevsky Prospekt. Open every day 10–9. Various exhibitions of contemporary work.

Peter I's Cottage (Domik Petra), Petrogradskaya Storona, 1 Petrovskaya Naberezhnaya. Open May to November, 12–7, except Tues.

Repin Museum, (Penates), Repino Railroad station, on the Karelian Isthmus, in the resort region of Leningrad. Open from May to September daily, from October to April daily except Tues. This was the estate of the Russian painter Ilya Repin (1844–1930).

State Museum of Russian Art known as the "Russian Museum," 4/2 Inzhenernaya Street. Open daily 10–6.15 except Tues; Thurs. 10–8.15. Last entry 1 hr. before closing.

Historical, Revolutionary and Military Museums

Aurora. After repairs, the Cruiser is back at her mooring on the Neva near Nakhimov Naval College.

Central Naval Museum, Vasilevsky Ostrov, 4 Pushkinskaya Square. Open 10.30–5.45 weekdays, Sun. 11–6, closed Tues. and last Thurs. of each month. Last entry 4.45.

History of Leningrad Museum, 44 Krasnovo Flota Embankment. Open Mon., Thur., Sat. and Sun., 11–6 and Tues. and Fri., 1–9; Closed Wed.

Lenin Museums, 5/1 Khalturin Street. Open 10.30–6.30 weekdays; 11–5 Sun.; closed Wed. Other memorial museums are at Lenin's various homes scattered throughout the city.

Museum of the Great October Revolution, 4 Kuibyshev Street. Open Mon. and Fri. 12–8; Tues., Wed., Sat. and Sun. 11–7. Closed Thurs. Housed in the former mansion of Mathilde Kshessinskaya, the famous ballerina and mistress of Czar Nicholas II.

Museum of the History of Religion and Atheism (in the Kazan Cathedral), 2 Kazanskaya Ploshchad. Open 11–6 daily except Wed. Last entry 4.30.

Ethnographic, Literary and Theatrical Museums

Anthropological and Ethnographical Museum of the U.S.S.R. Academy of Sciences, 3 Universitetskaya Naberezhnaya. Open daily, except Fri. and Sat., 11–6. Last entry 5.

145

Circus Art Museum, 3 Fontanka Naberezhnaya. Open daily 12–5, except Sun. A collection illustrating Soviet and world circus history: posters, programmes, photographs, costumes, models, large library, 6,000 postcards.

Museum of the Ethnography of the Peoples of the U.S.S.R., 1/4 Inzhenernaya Street. Open 10–6 daily, except Mon. and last Fri. of each month. Last entry 5.

Pushkinsky Dom (Pushkin House, Literary Museum of the Academy of Sciences), 4 Naberezhnaya Makarova. Open daily 11–5.30; closed Mon. and Tues. Last entry 5. The Pushkinsky Dom was founded in 1899, the centenary of Pushkin's birth. It has a vast collection of manuscripts and books illustrating the life and works of Pushkin, Lermontov, Gogol, Turgenev, Dostoevsky, Tolstoy, Gorky, Mayakovsky and other writers.

Pushkin Memorial Museum, 12 Moyka. The poet's last residence. English-speaking guide available. Now re-opened after major restoration. You may see this one also called Pushkinsky Dom—but it's not to be confused with the previous entry.

Theater Museum, 6 Ostrovsky Square. Open daily 12–7; closed Tues.

Technical and Scientific Museums

Arctic and Antarctic Museum, 24 Marat Street, open daily 10–6; closed Mon. and Tues. Last entry 5.15.

Komarov Botanical Gardens, 2 Professor Popov Street, is open from May to October daily; the hot-houses are open every day, except Fri., 11–4 in summer and 10.30–3 in winter.

Popov Communications Museum, 4 Podbelsky Street, near the Central Post Office. Open daily 12–6; Mon. 12–3. Closed Tues.

Railway Museum, 50 Sadovaya Street. Open daily, 12–6; Mon. 12–3. Closed Tues.

The Zoo is at 1 Lenin Park, Petrogradskaya Storona. Open from May to August 10–10, from September to November, 10–6, from December to February, 10–4, in March and April, 10–7.

Zoological Museum, 1 Universitetskaya Embankment. Open daily 11–5, except Mon.; Tues. 11–4.

Parks and Gardens

Botanical Gardens, 2 Professor Popov Street, and the **Zoological Gardens** in Lenin Park have already been mentioned under the *Museums* section.

Kirov Park on Yelagin Ostrov (Island). The park was laid out in 1932; more than 18,000 trees have been planted in recent years. There is a summer theater, seating 1600, a variety theater, movie-theater, exhibition halls, boating facilities and a bathing beach.

Lenin Park, Maxim Gorky Prospekt, a crescent-shaped strip of land on Kronwerk Strait, is not very large but a favorite spot for walkers and lovers.

Park Pobedy (Park of Victory), Moskovsky Prospekt. Leningrad has two victory parks, both established in 1945. The second is the Seaside Victory Park **(Primorsky Park Pobedy)** at 7 Rubin Street on Krestovsky Island.

Piskarevskoye Memorial Cemetery, just outside the city. The graves of well over half-a-million Leningraders who died in the siege. The three-hour trip costs 22 roubles including Intourist car seating 3 people. It is part of some city tours.

Summer Garden. 2 Pestel Street, founded by Peter the Great.

IN THE OLD PART OF TOWN

Which are the most historic sites?	kah-KEE-yeh mees-TAH SAHM-y-eh ees-tah-REE-chees-kee-yeh?	Какие места самые исторические?
How many churches are there here?	SKAWL'-kuh tahm tsyrk-VYEHY?	Сколько там церквей?
Is that church old?	EH-tuh STAHR-uh-yuh TSEHR-kuhf'?	Это старая церковь?

147

What religion is it?	kah-KOY ree-lee-gee-AWZ-ny ahp-SHEE-nyeh pree-nahd-lee-ZHYT EH-tuh TSEHRK-uhf'?	Како́й религио́зной общи́не принадлежи́т э́та це́рковь?
Are there any monuments nearby?	yehyst' pah-BLEEZ-uhs-tee kah-KEE-yeh nee-BOOT' PAHM-eet-nee-kee?	Есть побли́зости каки́е-нибу́дь па́мятники?
What does that monument commemorate?	chee-MOO puh-svee-SHAWN EH-tuht PAHM-eet-neek?	Чему́ посвящён э́тот па́мятник?
When was it built?	kahg-DAH EH-tuh BYL-uh pah-STRAW-ee-nuh?	Когда́ э́то бы́ло постро́ено?
How old is that building?	SKAWL'-kuh lyeht EHT-uh-moo strah-YEH-nee-yoo?	Ско́лько лет э́тому строе́нию?
Are there many statues there?	tahm MNAW-guh STAH-too-ee?	Там мно́го ста́туй?
Who does that statue depict?	kah-VAW eez-uh-brah-ZHAH-eet EH-tuh STAH-too-yuh?	Кого́ изобража́ет э́та ста́туя?
Who was that?	ktaw EH-tuh byl?	Кто э́то бы́л?

IN THE BUSINESS DISTRICT

At what time do the stores open?	kahg-DAH rah-BAW-tuh-yoot muh-gah-ZEE-ny?	Когда́ рабо́тают магази́ны?
Which department stores are nearby?	kah-KEE-yeh zdyehys' oo-nee-veer-MAHG-ee?	Каки́е здесь универма́ги?
Are they open on weekends?	ah-NEE rah-BAW-tah-yoot pah vy-khahd-NYM dnyahm?	Они́ рабо́тают по выходны́м дня́м?
Where is a souvenir shop?	gdyeh muh-gah-ZEEN soo-vee-NEER-y?	Где́ магази́н «Сувени́ры»?
Where is a Beriozka store?	gdyeh muh-gah-ZEEN bee-RYAWS-kuh?	Где́ магази́н «Берёзка»?

| Where is the money exchange? | gdyeh bahnk ahb-MYEHN-uh vah-LYOOT-y? | Где банк обмена валюты? |

IN THE COUNTRYSIDE

Attitudes toward life in the Soviet countryside have changed radically since World War II. Before the war, it was the aim of every rural dweller to escape to the nearest big city: few villages had electricity or running water or proper schools, and collective farm workers were at the bottom of the social scale, tied to the land where they were born and unable to move. Things have improved greatly in recent years, although many village houses are still without water mains (women carrying buckets with a yoke are still a commonplace sight). Electricity is now almost universal; and since 1974, farm workers have been issued with internal passports at the age of 16—which means they have the legal right to leave and seek their fortunes elsewhere in the Soviet Union. To keep their workers on the land, *kolkhoz* chairmen now offer inducements in the form of better wages and living accommodations.

The worst problem in the Russian countryside, and one which tourists will readily see for themselves if their visit takes place in spring or fall, is the lack of good roads. For about seven months of the year—while the snow is falling or melting, and during midsummer thunderstorms—the village streets are a sea of mud, which only a tractor can get through. No wonder that many of the eight million Russian families who own a house in the country spend only the summer months in their second residences. Strangely, however, the very backwardness of the rural transport system is an added attraction for many Russians, who would like to escape from the stresses of urban civilization and return to a simpler way of life.

Can you tell me how to get to the country?	vy nee mah-GLEE by mnyeh skah-ZAHT' kahk dah-YEKH-uht' duh dee-RYEHV-nee?	Вы не могли́ бы мне сказа́ть, как дое́хать до дере́вни?
Can I get there by . . .	too-DAH MAWZH-nuh dah-YEKH-uht' . . .	Туда́ мо́жно дое́хать . . .
• bus?	• ahf-TAW-boos-uhm?	• авто́бусом.
• metro?	• mee-TRAW?	• метро́.
• train?	• ee-leek-TREECH-kuhy?	• электри́чкой.
How long does it take?	kahk DAWL-guh too-DAH YEHKH-uht'?	Как до́лго туда́ е́хать?
Is there any place to have lunch there?	tahm yehyst' gdyeh puh-ah-BYEHD-uht'?	Та́м есть где́ пообе́дать?
Should we take some food with us?	NOOZH-nuh lee vzyaht' sah-BOY yee-DOO?	Ну́жно ли взя́ть с собо́й еду́?
Are there restrooms?	tahm yehyst' too-ah-LYEHT-y?	Та́м есть туале́ты?
Where are the most beautiful landscapes?	gdyeh SAH-my-yeh krah-SEE-vy-yeh pee-ZAHZH-y?	Где́ са́мые краси́вые пейза́жи?
I like (the)	mnyeh NRAH-veet-suh	Мне нра́вятся
• mountains.	• GAWR-y	• го́ры.
• lakes.	• ah-ZYAWR-uh	• озёра.
• rivers.	• RYEHK-ee	• ре́ки.
• fields.	• pahl-YAH	• поля́.
• flowers.	• tsfee-TY	• цветы́.
• plants.	• rahs-TYEHY-nyeh	• расте́ния.
• hills.	• kholm-Y	• холмы́.
• woods.	• lees-AH	• леса́.
• birds.	• PTEE-tsy	• пти́цы.
• wild animals.	• DEE-kee-yeh zhy-VAWT-ny-yeh	• ди́кие живо́тные.
• farms.	• FYEHRM-y	• фе́рмы.
• houses.	• dah-MAH	• дома́.

150

• cottages.	• DAH-chee	• да́чи.
• gardens.	• sah-DY	• сады́.
• villages.	• pah-SYAWL-kee	• посёлки.
Look! There's a	smah-TREE-tyuh! vawn tahm	Смотри́те! Вон там
• bridge.	• mawst	• мост.
• church.	• TSEHR-kuhf'	• це́рковь.
• waterfall.	• vu-dah-PAHT	• водопа́д.
• sailboat.	• PAH-roos-nuh-yuh LAWT-kuh	• па́русная ло́дка.
• stream.	• roo-CHAY	• руче́й.
• lake.	• AW-zee-ruh	• о́зеро.
• pond.	• proot	• пруд.
• village.	• pah-SYAWL-uhk	• посёлок.
The view is	veet	Вид
• breathtaking.	• dookh zah-KHVAHT-y-vuh-yeht	• дух захва́тывает.
• magnificent.	• zuh-mee-CHAH-teel'-ny	• замеча́тельный.
This place is . . .	EH-tuh MYEHS-tuh . . .	Э́то ме́сто . . .
• pleasant.	• pree-YAHT-nuh-yuh	• прия́тное.
• very pretty.	• AW-cheen' krah-SEE-vuh-yuh	• о́чень краси́вое.
What is a typical souvenir from here?	kah-KOY soo-vee-NEER tee-PEECH-ny dlyah EH-teekh myehst?	Како́й сувени́р типи́чный для э́тих мест?
Do you tip the . . .	PREEN-yuh-tuh dah-VAHT' chee-yee-VY-yeh . . .	При́нято дава́ть чаевы́е . . .
• driver?	• vah-DEE-teel-yoo?	• води́телю?
• guide?	• GEED-oo?	• ги́ду?

RELIGIOUS SERVICES

The Russian Orthodox Church was Russia's official church under the Tsars. Estimates of its following today vary between 30 and 70 million people; it claims 9,734 operating parishes, and many old churches have been preserved as monuments, or house museums or even offices. The Church, headed by the Patriarch

151

of Moscow, is allowed to print bibles and other religious literature, but only in limited quantities.

The Catholic Church has about 4½ million adherents, many of them in the Baltic state of Lithuania, and in the western Ukraine (formerly part of Poland). Gorbachev's 1989 visit to the Pope and the establishing of relations with the Vatican has strengthened the position of the Catholic community. The Uniate Church of the Ukraine, with about 4 million followers, is Orthodox by ritual but Catholic by association.

Of the Protestant churches the official Baptist is probably the fastest-growing. There are sizeable Lutheran communities in Latvia and Estonia. The Armenians and the Georgians each have their own Christian churches, both of which predate Orthodoxy in Russia; their adherents number 5 million and 4 million respectively. Minority religions are often associated with nationalist sentiment in non-Russian regions.

Much the largest non-Christian group are the Moslems, with a potential congregation of about 55 million. They are organized under four boards, one for the Shi'ite Azeris and three for the much more numerous Sunni Moslems in Central Asia, Kazakhstan, the North Caucasus, and southern Siberia. Although legal worship is limited in the U.S.S.R., there are a number of underground congregations and many more people observe *some* Islamic rites.

Since the war, Jews have suffered most of all from religious persecution. Despite relatively large scale emigration, there are still about 2 million Jews in the Soviet Union. Anti-Semitism, always a potent force in the Slav areas, received semi-official encouragement under both Stalin and Brezhnev, but Gorbachev has encouraged the Jewish religion and culture. There were 113 registered synagogues and one Jewish seminary in the U.S.S.R. in 1988, and a new center for Jewish culture has recently been opened in Moscow.

| a Russian Orthodox church | pruh-vah-SLAHV-nuh-yuh TSEHR-kuhf' | Правосла́вная це́рковь |

a Catholic church	kuh-tah-LEECH-ees-kuh-yuh TSEHR-kuhf'	Католи́ческая це́рковь
a mosque	mee-CHEHYT'	мече́ть
a Protestant church	pruh-tees-TAHN-skuh-yuh TSER-kuhf'	Протеста́нтская це́рковь
a synagogue	see-nah-GAWG-uh	синаго́га
When does the mass (service) begin?	kahg-DAH nuh-chee-NAH-eet-suh SLOOZH-buh?	Когда́ начина́ется слу́жба?
I'm looking for an English-speaking	yah ee-SHOO ahn-gluh-guh-vah-RYAH-sheh-vuh	Я ищу́ анг-логоворя́щего
• minister.	• PAHS-tuhr-ruh	• па́стора.
• priest.	• svee-SHEHN-eek-uh	• свяще́нника.
• rabbi.	• rahv-VEEN-uh	• равви́на.

RELIGIOUS SERVICES IN MOSCOW

Protestant church service and Sunday school is held on alternate Sundays at Spaso House (U.S. Embassy) and the British Embassy, 14 Nab. Morisa Toreza, at 10:30 A.M. The chaplain (according to most recent information) is the Rev. Alphonz Lamprecht (tel. 143-3562, 38 Lomonosovsky Propekt, Apt. 59–60.). The visiting Anglican chaplain (who normally resides in Helsinki) can be contacted at the British Embassy.

Baptist services are held on Sundays at 10, 2, and 6; and on Thursdays at 6 P.M. at 3 Maly Vuzovsky Per. (tel. 297-5167).

Catholic services: St. Louis des Français, 12 Malaya Lubyanka (masses in Latin, sermons in Polish and Russian); Sundays 8.30, 11.30, and 7. Chapel of our Lady of Hope, 7/4 Kutuzovsky Prospekt, Korp. 5, Entr. 3, Fl. 3, Apt. 42. The Chaplain is Father Robert J. Fortin, A.A. (tel. 243-9621). Saturday evening Mass in English and French at 6 P.M. at Our Lady of Hope Chapel. Sunday Masses at the American Embassy Snack Bar, 19/23 Tchaikovsky Street, at 10 A.M. in English and at 12 noon in French. Weekday Masses at Our Lady of Hope Chapel Mon., Tues., Wed. and Fri. at 8.30 A.M., Thurs. at 7 P.M..

Synagogues: 8 Arkhipova Street. Services daily at 10 A.M.

153

and one hour before sundown; also at 8 Bolshoi Spasoglinisch-chevsky.

Russian Orthodox churches open to worship include: Yelokhovsky Cathedral, 15 Spartakovskaya; Uspensky Church, in the Novodevichy Convent, 2 Bolshaya Pirogovskaya Street; Ivan Voin Church, 46 Dimitrov Street; Voskresenskaya Church, on the Brusovsky Per.; The Old Believers' Cathedral, 29 Rogozhsky Per.; and the Moscow Patriarchate at Kropotkin Street, 5 Chisty Per. There are 30–40 in Moscow. Most have services at 8 A.M. and 6 P.M. every weekday and at 7 A.M. and 10 A.M. on Sundays and holidays. Women should always wear a head covering when visiting, especially if service is in progress. Men should remove hats. Do not put hands in pockets; it is considered disrespectful.

In the South of Moscow, exact address unavailable, is the Danilovsky Monastery which was restored for the celebrations of 1,000 years of Kievan Russia's Christianity in 1988. One of its churches, the Church of the Intercession, is already used for worship, and two others, the Church of the Resurrection and the Trinity Cathedral, were to be reconsecrated. Eventually the Patriarch, head of the Orthodox Church, will move his seat here from Zagorsk.

Mosque: 7 Vypolzov Per. The *Hammaz* is recited five times daily and on Fridays at 1 P.M.

RELIGIOUS SERVICES IN LENINGRAD

Orthodox Russian churches open for worship: Saint Nicholas, 13 Ploshchad Kommunarov, open daily 8–7. Sun. and holidays, 9, 11.30, and 7. Trinity Cathedral, Ploshchad Alexandra Nevskogo, open daily 9–6; Sun. 9–7.

Baptist Church, 29a Bolshaya Ozornaya (in the suburbs), open Tues. and Thurs. at 7 P.M., Sun. 10, 2, and 6; **Roman Catholic Church,** 7 Kovensky Pereulok, open daily 7, 10 and 6; Sun. at 1, too.

Synagogue, 2 Lermontovsky Prospekt, open daily 10–12, Sat. 10–2.

Mosque, 7 Maxim Gorky Prospekt, open Fri. 1 P.M.

Check times of services at your hotel or at the Intourist office.

SHOPPING

12/SHOPPING

Tourists in the Soviet Union will want to shop at the Beriozka stores located in all the Intourist hotels. These are foreign currency stores, which are considerably better stocked than the average Soviet store. In the Beriozka stores the staff will usually speak English. Soviet customs laws may be unpredictable but you are always safe at customs with items you have bought in a Beriozka store. Remember to save all your receipts, as you are accountable for all the money you spend in the Soviet Union and you may be asked to present these receipts when you leave the country.

Russia is well known for its amber, lacquer boxes, wooden bowls and spoons, and *matryoshka* dolls, which fit one into the other. These, as well as fur hats, books, records, vodka, and caviar, may all be purchased at the Beriozka stores.

You may also want to investigate one of the big department stores. Shopping here can be a little bit more complicated. When you have chosen the item you would like to purchase, you must ask the salesperson to find out the price. Then you go to the central cash register, where you tell the cashier the price of your purchase, pay for it, and get a receipt. After this you take the receipt back to the salesperson and pick up your purchase. This process entails waiting on line three separate times. You must follow the same procedure in food stores as well.

DIALOGUE: В МАГАЗИ́НЕ "БЕРЁЗКА" (AT THE BERIOZKA STORE)

| Тури́стка: | У ва́с есть наро́дные изде́лия? | oo vahs yehyst' nah-RAW-dny-yeh eez-DYEH-lee-yuh? |
| Продаве́ц: | Да́. У на́с мно́го таки́х веще́й. | dah. oo nahs MNAW-guh tah-KEEKH vee-SHAY. |

Туристка:	Я хотел(-а) бы посмотреть что-нибудь из янтаря.	yah khah-TYEHL(-uh) by puh-smah-TREHT' SHTAW-nee-boot' eez yeen-tahr-YAH.
Продавец:	Вас интересуют серьги, браслеты или ожерелья?	vahs een-tee-ree-SOO-yoot SYEHR'-gee, brah-SLYEH-ty, EE-lee uh-zheye-RYEHL'-yuh?
Туристка:	Серьги, пожалуйста.	SYEHR-gee, pah-ZHAHL-stuh.
Продавец:	Эти красивые.	EH-tee krah-SEE-vy-yeh.
Туристка:	Я возьму их.	yah vahz'-MOO eekh.
Продавец:	Одну минуту.	ahd-NOO mee-NOO-too.
Туристка:	Спасибо.	spah-SEE-buh.

. . . .

Tourist:	Do you have any handicrafts?
Vendor:	Yes, we have many typical items.
Tourist:	May I see some amber?
Vendor:	Are you interested in earrings, bracelets, or necklaces?
Tourist:	Earrings, please.
Vendor:	These are pretty.
Tourist:	I'll take them.
Vendor:	One moment please.
Tourist:	Thank you.

TYPES OF FOLK ART

amber	yeen-TAHR'	янтáрь
basketwork	kahr-ZEE-ny	корзи́ны
blanket	uh-dee-YAH-luh	одея́ло
clay	GLEE-nuh	гли́на
copper	myeht'	мéдь
embroidery	vy-shy-VAH-nee-yeh	вышива́ние
glass	steek-LYAH-nuh-yuh pah-SOO-duh	стекля́нная посу́да
gold	ZAW-luh-tuh	зóлото
icons	ee-KAWN-y	икóны
jade	neef-REET	нефри́т
lacquerware	lahk	лáк
leather	KAW-zhuh	кóжа
malachite	muh-lah-KHEET	малахи́т
marble	MRAH-muhr	мрáмор
musical instruments	moo-zy-KAHL'-ny-yeh een-stroo-MYEHN-ty	музыка́льные инструме́нты
onyx	AW-neeks	óникс
pottery	guhn-CHAHR-ny-yeh eez-DYEHL-ee-yuh	гонча́рные изде́лия
shawl	shal'	шáль
silver	see-ree-BRAW	серебрó
toy	ee-GROOSH-kuh	игру́шка
weaving	TKAH-cheest-vuh	тка́чество
wood carvings	DYEH-ree-vuh	де́рево
wooden dolls	mah-TRYAWSH-kee	матрёшки
wool	shehrst'	шéрсть

GENERAL SHOPPING LIST

I need to buy	mnyeh NOOZH-nuh koo-PEET'	Мнé ну́жно купи́ть
• books.	• KNEE-gee	• кни́ги.
• a roll of film.	• PLYAWN-koo	• плёнку.
• some food.	• yee-DOO	• еду́.
• candy.	• kahn-FYEH-ty	• конфéты.
• shoes.	• TOO-flee	• ту́фли.
• clothes.	• ah-DYEHZH-doo	• одéжду.

157

• medicine.	• lee-KAHR-stvuh	• лека́рство.
• jewelry.	• druh-gah-TSYEH-nuh-stee	• драгоце́нности.
• cigarettes.	• see-gah-RYEH-ty	• сигаре́ты.
• gifts.	• pah-DAHR-kee	• пода́рки.
• souvenirs.	• soo-vee-NEE-ry	• сувени́ры.
• postcards.	• aht-KRYT-kee	• откры́тки.

TYPES OF STORES

shop	muh-gah-ZEEN	магази́н
bookstore	KNEEZH-ny muh-gah-ZEEN	кни́жный магази́н
grocery store	guh-strah-NAWM	гастроно́м
bakery	BOO-luhch-nuh-yuh	бу́лочная
candy store	kahn-DEE-tehr-skuh-yuh	конди́терская
shoe store	ah-BOOV-noy muh-gah-ZEEN	обувно́й магази́н
clothing store	muh-gah-ZEEN ah-DYEHZH-dy	магази́н оде́жды
jewelry store	yoo-vee-LEER-ny muh-gah-ZEEN	ювели́рный магази́н
local market	RY-nuhk	ры́нок
butcher shop	mees-NOY muh-gah-ZEEN	мясно́й магази́н
department store	oo-nee-veer-MAHK	универма́г
flower store	tsvee-TAWCH-ny muh-gah-ZEEN	цвето́чный магази́н
liquor store	VEE-ny muh-gah-ZEEN	ви́нный магази́н
hardware store	skaw-bee-NUHY muh-gah-ZEEN	скобяно́й магази́н
record store	muh-gah-ZEEN plah-STEEN-uhk	магази́н пласти́нок
tobacco store	tah-BAHCH-ny mu-gah-ZEEN	таба́чный магази́н
newsstand	kee-AWSK	кио́ск
supermarket	oo-nee-veer-SAHM	универса́м

AT THE CLOTHING STORE

I want to buy

yah khah-CHOO koo-PEET'

Я хочу́ купи́ть

- a blouse.
- a sweater.
- a dress.
- a skirt.
- stockings/panty hose.
- an evening gown.
- a tie.
- a shirt.
- a belt.
- a hat.
- a robe.
- an overcoat.
- handkerchiefs.

My size is
- small.
- medium.
- large.
- 34.

- 36.

- 38.

Do you have it in

- black?
- dark blue?
- light blue?
- brown?
- gray?
- white?
- red?
- green?
- yellow?

- BLOOS-koo
- SVEE-tuhr
- PLAH-t'yeh
- YOOP-koo
- kahl-GAWT-kee

- veeh-CHYEHR-neh-yeh PLAH-t'yeh
- GAHL-stook
- roo-BAHSH-koo
- ree-MYEHYN'
- SHAHP-koo
- khah-LAHT
- pahl'-TAW
- plaht-KEE

moy rahz-MYEHR
- MAH-leen'-kee
- SRYEHD-nee
- bahl'-SHOY
- TREE-tseet' chee-TY-ree
- TREE-tseet' shehst'

- TREE-tseet' VAW-seem'

oo vahs yehyst' TAWCH-nuh tah-KOY zheh
- CHAWR-ny?
- SEE-nee?
- guh-loo-BOY?
- kah-REECH-nuh-vy?
- SYEH-ry?
- BYEH-ly?
- KRAH-sny?
- zee-LYAW-ny?
- ZHAWL-ty?

- блу́зку.
- сви́тер.
- пла́тье.
- ю́бку.
- колго́тки.

- вече́рнее пла́тье.
- га́лстук.
- руба́шку.
- реме́нь.
- ша́пку.
- хала́т.
- пальто́.
- платки́.

Мой разме́р
- ма́ленький.
- сре́дний.
- большо́й.
- три́дцать четы́ре.
- три́дцать шесть.
- три́дцать во́семь.

У вас есть то́чно тако́й же
- чёрный?
- си́ний?
- голубо́й?
- кори́чневый?
- се́рый?
- бе́лый?
- кра́сный?
- зелёный?
- жёлтый?

159

• orange?	• ah-RAHN-zhuh-vy?	• ора́нжевый?
• purple?	• fee-ah-LYEHT-uh-vy?	• фиоле́товый?
I prefer something in	yah preet-puh-CHYAWL (-CHLAH) by SHTAW-nee-boot' ees	Я предпоуёл (предпочпа́ [f.]) бы что́-нибудь из
• cotton.	• KHLAWP-kuh	• хло́пка.
• silk.	• SHAWL-kuh	• шёлка.
• corduroy.	• veel'-VYEH-tuh	• вельве́та.
• lace.	• KROO-zhuhf	• кру́жев.
• linen.	• l'nah	• льна́.
• leather.	• KAW-zhy	• ко́жи.
• nylon.	• zhnyen-LAW-nuh	• нейло́на.
• satin.	• aht-LAHS-uh	• атла́са.
• suede.	• ZAHM-shy	• за́мши.
• synthetic.	• seen-TYEH-tee-kee	• синте́тики.
• taffeta.	• tahf-TY	• тафты́.
• velvet.	• BAHR-khuh-tuh	• ба́рхата.
• wool.	• SHYEHR-stee	• шёрсти.
I'd like to try it on.	yah khah-CHOO yeh-VAW pah-MYEH-reet'	Я хочу́ его́ поме́рить.
It does not fit me.	EH-tuh mnyeh nee pahd-KHAW-deet	Это мне́ не подхо́дит.
It fits well.	mnyeh EH-tuh ee-DYAWT	Мне́ э́то идёт.
I'll take it.	yah yee-VAW bee-ROO	Я его́ беру́.

Shoes

I'd like a pair of	yah khah-CHOO PAH-roo	Я хочу́ па́ру
• boots.	• sah-PAWK	• сапо́г.
• shoes.	• TOO-feel'	• ту́фель.
• sandals.	• bah-sah-NAWZH-uhk	• босоно́жек.
• slippers.	• TAH-puh-cheek	• та́почек.
• sneakers.	• krah-SAW-vuhk	• кроссо́вок.
They fit me well.	paht-KHAW-deet FSAH-my rahs	Подхо́дят в са́мый раз.

They don't fit.	ah-NEE mnyeh nee ee-DOOT	Они мне не идут.
They're too	ah-NEE SLEESH-kuhm	Они слишком
• big.	• vee-lee-KEE	• велики.
• small.	• mah-LY	• малы.
• wide.	• shy-rah-KEE	• широки.
• narrow.	• oos-KEE	• узки.
I don't know my size.	yah nee ZNAH-yoo svuh-yee-VAW rahz-MYEHR-uh	Я не знаю своего размера.
I wear size . . .	yah nah-SHOO . . . rahz-MYEHR	Я ношу . . . размер.
Where do I pay?	koo-DAH mnyeh plah-TEET'?	Куда мне платить?
Wait on line over there.	pah-dahzh-DEE-tyeh v'AW-chee-ree-dee VAWN tahm	Подождите в очереди вон там.
Are you the last person on line?	vy pah-SLYEHD-ny?	Вы последний?

Sizes

We recommend trying on all clothing before buying because sizes vary and do not always correlate exactly with U.S. sizes. Also, it is not customary in the Soviet Union to return clothing already purchased. Sizes in the Soviet Union are the same as those in Europe.

WOMEN'S CLOTHING AND SHOE SIZES

Suits/Dresses
| U.S. | 6,8 | 8,10 | 10,12 | 12,14 | 14,16 |
| USSR | 44 | 46,48 | 48,50 | 50,52 | 52,54 |

Blouses/Sweaters
| U.S. | small | medium | large |
| USSR | 44,46 | 48,50 | 52,54 |

Shoes
| U.S. | 5 | 6 | 7 | 8 | 9 |
| USSR | 38 | 39 | 41 | 42 | 43 |

161

MEN'S CLOTHING AND SHOE SIZES

Suits/Coats

U.S.	36	38	40	42	44
USSR	46	48	50	52	54

Dress Shirts

U.S.	14	14½	15	15½	16	16½	17
USSR	36	37	38	40	41	42	43

Sleeve Lengths

короткий	(kah-ROHT-kee)	= short
средний	(SREHD-nee)	= medium
длинный	(DLEEN-ee)	= long

Shoes

U.S.	7	8	9	10	11	12
USSR	41	42	43	44	46	47

AT THE JEWELRY STORE

I'd like to see some — yah khah-TYEHL(-uh) by puh-smah-TREHT' — Я хоте́л(-а) бы посмотре́ть

- rings. — KAWL'-tsuh — кольца.
- necklaces. — uh-zhy-RYEHL'-yuh — ожере́лья.
- chains. — tsy-PAWCH-kee — цепо́чки.
- bracelets. — brah-SLYEHT-y — брасле́ты.
- brooches. — BRAWSH-kee — бро́шки.
- earrings. — SYEHR'-gee — се́рьги.
- watches. — chee-SY — часы́.

Do you have this in — oo vahs yehyst' EH-tuh ees — У ва́с е́сть э́то из

- gold? — ZAW-luh-tuh? — зо́лота?
- white gold? — BYEH-luh-vuh ZAW-luh-tuh? — бе́лого зо́лота?
- silver? — see-ree-BRAH? — серебра́?
- stainless steel? — nee-rzhah-VYEH-yoo-shee STAH-lee. — нержаве́ющей ста́ли?
- platinum? — PLAH-tee-ny? — пла́тины?

162

I would like it with	yah khah-TYEHL(-uh) by EH-tuh s	Я хоте́л(-а) бы . . . с
• jade.	• nee-FREET-uhm	• нефри́том.
• onyx.	• AW-neeks-uhm	• о́никсом.
• a pearl.	• ZHYEHM-choog-uhm	• же́мчугом.
• a diamond.	• breel-YAHNT-uhm	• бриллиа́нтом.
• an emerald.	• eez-oom-ROOD-uhm	• изумру́дом.
• an aquamarine.	• ahk-vuh-mah-REEN-uhm	• аквамари́ном.
• an amethyst.	• ah-mee-TEEST-uhm	• амети́стом.
• turquoise.	• bee-RYOO-zoy	• бирю́зой.

AT THE CAMERA SHOP

The Soviets develop film differently from the rest of the Western world so it's a good idea to hold on to your film until you are back in the United States. If you do get your film developed in the Soviet Union you will not be able to have prints made from your negatives in the United States.

You can buy Kodak film in the Beriozka stores but it is quite expensive, so we recommend bringing as many rolls as you think you'll need and not relying on finding it in the Soviet Union. Take a supply of hi-speed film (Kodak ASA 1000 color print is recommended) for interiors of churches, where flash may be forbidden (it damages icons, frescoes, etc.), and for those gloomy winter days on end-of-season tours. A wide-angle and/or zoom lens is another must. Also, avoid running your camera and film through the airport X-ray machines. Have your camera bag examined by hand and use a lead-lined film bag, available at most camera stores in the United States.

You can photograph or film most things, but use your common sense: don't photograph anything that is clearly a "sensitive" installation—airports, factories, military installations or personnel, prisons, railway junctions or stations, telephone exchanges, etc. If in doubt, ask your guide. Photography and video-filming is *un*restricted in most tourist locations, but it is wiser *not* to take pictures from airplanes or trains, etc. If you intend to take close-ups of people, *ask them,* even if only by gestures . . . this isn't security, just politeness.

I would like a roll of film.	yah khah-TYEHL(-uh) by PLYAWN-koo	Я хотéл(-а) бы плёнку.
Do you have	oo vahs yehyst'	У вас есть
• film for prints?	• nee-gah-TEEV-nuh-yuh PLYAWN-kuh?	• негативная плёнка?
• film for slides?	• PLYAWN-kuh dlyah dee-uh-puh-zee-TEE-vuhf?	• плёнка для диапозитивов?
• color film?	• tsveet-NAH-yuh PLYAWN-kuh?	• цветная плёнка?
• black-and-white film?	• cheer-nah-BYEH-luh-yuh PLYAWN-kuh?	• черно-белая плёнка?

ELECTRICAL APPLIANCES

Make sure you check the voltage when buying or bringing in electrical appliances, since 220 volts AC is the rule all over the Soviet Union. You will need a transformer to use U.S. equipment, as well as auxiliary adapter plugs.

What is the voltage?	kah-KAW-yeh zdyehys' nuh-pree-ZHEH-nee-yeh?	Какое здесь напряжéние?
I need batteries for this.	mnyeh noozh-NY buh-tah-RYEH-kee dlyah EH-tuh-vuh	Мне нужны батарéйки для этого.
I'd like	yah khah-TYEL(-uh) by	Я хотéл(-а) бы
• a bulb.	• LAHM-puhch-koo	• лáмпочку.
• a clock.	• chee-SY	• часы́.
• a radio.	• RAH-dee-aw	• рáдио.
• a hair dryer.	• fehn	• фéн.
• an iron.	• oo-TYOOK	• утю́г.
• a lamp.	• LAHM-poo	• лáмпу.

• a record player.	• prah-EE-gree-vuh-teel'	• проигрыватель.
• a shaver.	• BREET-voo	• бритву.
• a tape recorder.	• muh-gnee-tah-FAWN	• магнитофон.
• a black-and-white TV.	• cheer-nah-BYEH-ly tee-lee-VEE-zuhr	• черно-белый телевизор.
• a color TV.	• tsveet-NOY tee-lee-VEE-zuhr	• цветной телевизор.
• a transformer.	• truhns-fawr-MAH-huhr	• трансформатор

AT THE MUSIC STORE

Do you have	oo vahs yehyst'	У вас есть
• records?	• plah-STEEN-kee?	• пластинки?
• cassettes?	• kah-SEH-ty?	• кассеты?
Where is the	gdyeh nah-KHAW-deet-suh	Где находится
• classical music?	• klah-SEE-chees-kuh-yuh MOO-zy-kuh?	• классическая музыка?
• folk music?	• nah-RAWD-nuh-yuh MOO-zy-kuh?	• народная музыка?
• popular music?	• puh-poo-LYAHR-nuh-yuh MOO-zy-kuh?	• популярная музыка?
• Russian music?	• ROOS-kuh-yuh MOO-zy-kuh?	• русская музыка?
• rock 'n' roll?	• rawk MOO-zy-kuh?	• рок-музыка?
Do you sell	vy pruh-dah-YAW-tyeh	Вы продаёте
• balalaikas?	• buh-lah-LAHY-kee?	• балалайки?
• accordions?	• gahr-MAWSH-kee?	• гармошки?
• other musical instruments?	• droo-GEE-yeh moo-zy-KAHL'-ny-yeh een-stroo-MYEHN-ty?	• другие музыкальные инструменты?

AT THE BOOKSTORE

Where is there a bookstore?	gdyeh zdyehys' KNEE-zhny muh-gah-ZEEN?	Где здесь книжный магазин?

165

Is there a bookstore that carries English books?	yehyst' KNEE-zhny muh-gah-ZEEN kah-TAW-ree pruh-dah-YAWT KNEE-gee nah ahn-GLEE-skum yee-zy-KYEH?	Есть кни́жный магази́н, кото́рый продаёт кни́ги на англи́йском языке́?
Do you have	Oo vahs yehyst'	У ва́с есть
• novels?	• rah-MAH-ny?	• рома́ны?
• books?	• KNEE-gee?	• кни́ги?
• magazines?	• zhoor-NAH-ly?	• журна́лы?
• a map of the city?	• KAHR-tuh GAW-ruh-duh?	• ка́рта го́рода?
Do you have the book . . . ?	oo vahs yehyst' KNEE-guh . . . ?	У ва́с есть кни́га . . . ?
Do you have this guidebook in English?	oo vahs yehyst' EH-tuht poo-tee-vah-DEE-tyehl' nah ahn-GLEE-skuhm yee-zy-KYEH?	У вас есть э́тот путеводи́тель на англи́йском языке́?
Do you have a Russian-English dictionary?	oo vahs yehyst' ROO-skuh-uhn-GLEE-ske-e slah-VAHR'?	У ва́с есть ру́сско-англи́йский слова́рь?

AT THE PAPER GOODS STORE

a ballpoint pen	ahf-tah-ROOCH-kuh	авторучка
envelopes	kahn-VYEHR-ty	конве́рты
a notebook	tee-TRAHT'	тетра́дь
posters	plah-KAH-ty	плака́ты
ribbon	LYEHN-tuh	ле́нта
stamps	MAHR-kee	ма́рки
stationery	pahch-TAW-vuh-yuh boo-MAH-guh	почто́вая бума́га
string	vee-RYAWF-kuh	верёвка
wrapping paper	ah-BYAWR-tuhch-nuh-y-uh boo-MAH-guh	обёрточная бума́га

166

AT THE DRUGSTORE

toiletries	too-ah-LYEHT-ny-yeh pree-nahd-LYEHZH-nuh-stee	туалétные принадлéжности
a brush	SHAWT-kuh	щётка
a comb	rahs-SHAWS-kuh	расчёска
deodorant	dee-aw-dah-RAHNT	деодорáнт
hair spray	lahk	лáк
a mirror	ZYEHR-kuh-luh	зéркало
moisturizing lotion	kryehm dlyah lee-TSAH	крéм для лицá
mouthwash	zoob-NOY ee-leek-SEER	зубнóй эликсѝр
nail clippers	NAWZH-nee-tsee dlyah nahk-TYEHY	нóжницы для ногтéй
nail polish	lahk dlyah nahk-TYEHY	лáк для ногтéй
nail polish remover	ZHEET-kuhst' dlyah snee-TYAH LAH-kuh	жѝдкость для снятия лáка
perfume	doo-KHEE	духѝ
shampoo	shahm-POON'	шампýнь
shaving cream	kryehm dlyah breet'-YAH	крéм для бритья́
soap	MY-luh	мы́ло
tissues	boo-MAHZH-nee sahl-FYEHT-kee	бумáжные салфéтки
toilet paper	too-ah-LYEHT-nuh-yuh boo-MAH-guh	туалéтная бумáга
a toothbrush	zoob-NAH-yuh SHAWT-kuh	зубнáя щётка
toothpaste	zoob-NAH-yuh PAHS-tuh	зубнáя пáста
tweezers	peen-TSEHT	пинцéт

AT THE GROCERY STORE

I would like	yah khah-CHOO	Я хочý
• juice.	• sawk	• сóк.
• milk.	• muh-lah-KAW	• молокó.

167

• oatmeal.	• ahf-SYAHN-koo	• овся́нку.
• cookies.	• pee-CHEHN-yeh	• пече́нье.
• tomato sauce.	• tah-MAHT-noo-yoo PAH-stoo	• тома́тную па́сту.
• a dozen eggs.	• DYOO-zhy-noo yee-EETS	• дю́жину яи́ц.
• candy.	• kahn-FYEH-ty	• конфе́ты.
• cheese.	• syr	• сы́р.
• mineral water.	• mee-nee-RAHL'-noo-yoo VAW-doo	• минера́льную во́ду.
• cigarettes.	• see-gah-RYEH-ty	• сигаре́ты.
• matches.	• SPEECH-kee	• спи́чки.

WEIGHTS AND MEASURES

Metric Weight	U.S.
1 gram (g)	0.035 ounce
28.35 grams	1 ounce
100 grams	3.5 ounces
454 grams	1 pound
1 kilogram (kilo)	2.2 pounds

Liquids	U.S.
1 liter (l)	4.226 cups
1 liter	2.113 pints
1 liter	1.056 quarts
3.785 liters	1 gallon

Dry Measures	U.S.
1 liter	0.908 quart
1 decaliter	1.135 pecks
1 hectoliter	2.837 bushels

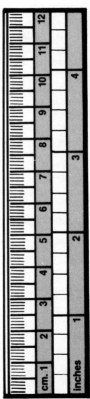

One inch = 2.54 centimeters
One centimeter = .39 inch

	inches	feet	yards
1 mm	0.039	0.003	0.001
1 cm	0.39	0.03	0.01
1 dm	3.94	0.32	0.10
1 m	39.40	3.28	1.09

.39 (# of centimeters) = (# of inches)
2.54 (# of inches) = (# of centimeters)

	mm	cm	m
1 in.	25.4	2.54	0.025
1 ft.	304.8	30.48	0.304
1 yd.	914.4	91.44	0.914

13/LEISURE AND ENTERTAINMENT

In the Soviet Union, people spend their leisure time in a variety of ways. You will see people sitting in parks or cafés reading a magazine or newspaper, talking, or playing chess. There are also many other entertainment activities to consider—movies, theater, operas, and concerts. In Moscow you can pick up a copy of the weekly **Досуг в Москве**, *Leisure in Moscow*, to find out about the latest exhibitions, plays, films, and sports events. Many Russians enjoy the famous Russian **баня** (BAH-nyuh), steambath, and beat one another with birch branches to improve circulation. At the famous Sandunovskaya baths in Moscow, one has a chance to try the Russian custom of eating, drinking, socializing, and bathing all rolled into one. The variety of climates and temperatures in the Soviet Union allow for cross-country skiing or troika rides in the winter as well as sunbathing and swimming at one of the many Caspian or Black Sea resorts in the summer. Soccer and hockey are very popular, as is, of course, the circus. Numerous athletic clubs and stadiums offer an array of opportunities for spectators of sports competitions and for those wishing to get a little exercise themselves.

DIALOGUE: ПЛАВАНИЕ (SWIMMING)

Иван:	Как жáрко!	kahk ZHAHR-kuh!
Джéйн:	Да. Пойдём купáться?	dah. pah-ee-DYAWM koo-PAHT'-suh?
Иван:	Хорóшая идéя! Кудá пойдём—в бассéйн или на мóре?	khah-RAWSH-uh-yuh ee-DYEHY-uh! koo-DAH pah-ee-DYAWM—vbah-SYEHYN EE-lee nah MAWR-yeh?
Джéйн:	Я обожáю мóре. А онó не холóдное?	yah ah-bah-ZHAH-yoo MAWR-yeh. a ah-NAW nee khah-LAWD-nuh-yeh?

170

Ива́н:	Совсе́м нет! Чёрное мо́ре о́чень тёплое.	sahv-SYEHM nyeht! CHAWR-nuh-yuh MAWR-yeh AW-cheen' TYAWP-luh-yuh.
Джейн:	Ла́дно. Встре́тимся на пля́же че́рез пять мину́т.	LAHD-nuh. FSTRYEHYT-eem-suh nah PLAYAHZH-uh CHEHR-ees pyaht' mee-NOOT.
Ива́н:	Дава́й. И не забу́дь крем про́тив зага́ра! Со́лнце о́чень я́ркое.	dah-VAHY. ee nee zah-BOOT' KRYEHM PRAWT-eef zah-GAHR-uh! SAWN-tsuh AWH-cheen' YAHR-kuh-yuh.

. . . .

Ivan:	It's so hot out!
Jane:	Yes. Why don't we go swimming?
Ivan:	Good idea! Shall we go to the pool or the beach?
Jane:	I love the sea. But isn't the water cold here?
Ivan:	Not at all! The Black Sea is very warm.
Jane:	Good. Then I'll see you on the beach in five minutes.
Ivan:	Right. And don't forget the suntan lotion! The sun is very strong.

AT THE BEACH

Where are the best beaches?	gdyeh LOOCH-shee-yeh PLYAHZH-y?	Где́ лу́чшие пля́жи?
How do we get there?	kahk too-DAH pah-PAHST'?	Как туда́ попа́сть?

171

Do we have to pay for admission to the beach?	NAH-duh lee plah-TEET' zah fkhawt nah plyahsh?	Надо ли платить за вход на пляж?
Is there a lifeguard?	tahm yehyst' spah-SAHT-eel'?	Там есть спасатель?
Is it dangerous for children?	tahm ah-PAHS-nuh dlyah dee-TYEHY?	Там опасно для детей?
Are there dangerous currents?	tahm SEEL'nuh-yeh tee-CHEHY-nee-yuh?	Там сильное течение?
When is	fkah-KEE-yeh chee-SY by-VAH-eet	В какие часы бывает
• high tide?	• SEEL'ny pree-LEEF?	• сильный прилив?
• low tide?	• SEEL'ny aht-LEEF?	• сильный отлив?
We would like	my khah-TYEHY-lee by	Мы хотели бы
• some chaise lounges.	• shehz-LAWNG-ee	• шезлонги.
• some beach towels.	• puh-lah-TYEHN-tsuh	• полотенца.
• an umbrella.	• zawnt	• зонт.
• to rent a rowboat.	• vzyaht' na prah-KAHT LAWT-koo	• взять на-прокат лодку.
• to rent a pedal boat.	• vzyaht' na prah-KAHT VAWD-ny vee-luh-see-PYEHT	• взять на-прокат водный велосипед.
• to rent a Ping-Pong table.	• vzyaht' nah prah-KAHT nah-STAWL'-ny TYEHN-ees	• взять на-прокат настольный теннис.
• to rent a volleyball.	• vzyaht' nah prah-KAHT vuh-lee-BAWL'-ny myahch	• взять на-прокат волейбольный мяч.
• suntan lotion.	• kryehm PRAW-teef zah-GAHR-uh	• крем против загара.
Is the pool	bah-SYEHYN	Бассейн
• indoors?	• snah-ROOZH-y?	• снаружи?
• outdoors?	• vnoo-TREE?	• внутри?

172

• heated?	• ah-TAH-plee-vah-eet-suh?	• отапливается?
When does the pool open?	kahg-DAH aht-kry-VAH-eet-suh bahs-SYEHYN?	Когда открывается бассейн?
When does the pool close?	kahg-DAH zah-kry-VAH-eet-suh bahs-SYEHYN?	Когда закрывается бассейн?

CAMPING

Camping in the Soviet Union is more popular among adventurous tourists and those who like to rough it. Campsites, кéмпинг (KYEHM-peenk), also provide low-budget accommodations for young people. You can learn more about them from your Intourist travel agent.

I'm looking for a campsite near Moscow.	yah ee-SHCHOO KYEHMP-eenk fpuhd-mahs-KAWV-yeh	Я ищу кéмпинг в Подмоскóвье.
Can we camp here?	zdyehys MAWZH-nuh puh-loo-CHEET' MYEHS-tuh FKYEHMP-een-gyeh?	Здесь мóжно получить мéсто в кéмпинге?
Is there room for a trailer?	zdyehys pah-MYEHYST-eet-suh moy pree-TSEHP?	Здесь помéстится мой прицéп?
What does it cost for one night?	SKAWL'-kuh STAW-eet ZAH-nuhch?	Скóлько стóит зá ночь?
How's the drinking water?	kahk pee-tyee-VAH-yuh vah-DAH?	Кáк питьевáя водá?
You can drink the water.	VAW-doo peet' MAWZH-nuh	Вóду пить мóжно.
Use bottled water.	PEHY-tyeh TAWL'-kuh VAW-doo eez boo-TYL-kee	Пéйте тóлко вóду из бутылки.
Is there . . . nearby?	yehyst' . . . pah-BLEEZ-uhs-tee?	Есть . . . поблизости?

173

• electricity	• ee-leek-TREE-cheest-vuh	• электри́чество
• butane gas	• boo-TAHN-uhv-y gahs	• бута́новый га́з
• a place to take shower	• MYEHST-uh gdyeh MAWZH-nuh pree-nyaht' doosh	• ме́сто, где мо́жно приня́ть ду́ш
• a grocery store	• pruh-dook-TAW-vy muh-gah-ZEEN	• продукто́вый магази́н

MOVIES

Check a local newspaper like **Досу́г в Москве́** (dah-SOOK v mahsk-VYEH) to see what's playing at the movies. American and European movie titles are sometimes changed, so you may not always recognize what is showing. The names of the actors will help identify some well-known movies. Many English-language films are dubbed into Russian, but occasionally Russian subtitles are added instead. On the other hand, you may find it a valuable experience to see some locally produced films even if you don't understand everything you hear. Moviegoing is sometimes a weekend activity for the entire family, and movie theaters can be crowded. It is not uncommon to purchase numbered tickets in advance for a specific seat as one does in a theater. For a really different experience, try a showing at one of the new, privately run video halls, which feature more out of the ordinary movies on a monitor or small screen.

Let's go to the movies.	pah-yee-DYAWM fkee-NAW	Пойдём в кино́.
What's playing?	shtaw ee-DYAWT?	Что́ идёт?
Is it in Russian or English?	EH-tuh puh-ahn-GLEES-kee EE-lee pah-ROOS-kee?	Это по-англи́йски и́ли по-ру́сски?
Is the movie subtitled?	feel'm ssoop-TEE-truh-mee?	Фи́льм с субти́трами?
Is it dubbed?	awn doob-LEER-uh-vuhn-y?	Он дубли́-рованный?
What kind of film is it?	shtaw EH-tuh zah feel'm?	Что́ э́то за фи́льм?

It's	EH-tuh	Это
• a comedy.	• kah-MYEHY-dee-yuh	• коме́дия.
• a drama.	• mee-lah-DRAH-muh	• мелодра́ма.
• an adventure movie.	• buh-ee-VEEK	• боеви́к.
When does the show start?	kahg-DAH nuh-chee-NAH-yeht-suh see-YAHNS?	Когда́ начина́ется сеа́нс?
How much are the tickets?	SKAWL'-kuh STAW-yuht bee-LYEHT-y?	Ско́лько сто́ят биле́ты?
What theater is showing the new film	fkah-KAWM tee-AH-tryeh ee-DYAWT NAWV-y feel'm	В како́м теа́тре идёт но́вый фи́льм
• directed by . . .	• pah-STAHV-lyehn-y . . .	• поста́влен-ный . . .
• with . . .	• soo-CHAHS-tyehm . . .	• с уча́стием . . .

THEATER, CONCERTS, AND BALLET

In the Soviet Union, buying tickets for performing arts events is often very difficult at a theater box office. You can find out what tickets are available and order them through the service bureau in an Intourist hotel.

Moscow and Leningrad boast many world-class theaters, the most famous of which are the Bolshoi in Moscow and the Kirov in Leningrad, both of which offer ballet and opera. Sometimes the Bolshoi company performs on the stage of the Kremlin Palace of Congresses, which, while lacking the atmosphere of the old theater, has the advantage of allowing more viewers to enjoy the performance. The famous Tchaikovsky Concert Hall in Mayakovsky Square presents the finest musical talents of the Soviet Union and the world. For those interested in the theater, Moscow and Leningrad have very active repertory companies playing in the more conventional well-known theaters as well as in the experimental "theater studios." For children of all ages there are numerous puppet theaters, circuses, and theaters spe-

175

cializing in programs for young people. Performances of folk singing and dancing are easily available and tickets are sold by Intourist.

What's playing at the theater?	shtaw ee-DYAWT ftee-AH-tryeh?	Что́ идёт в теа́тре?
I'd like to go to	yah kha-TYEHL(-uh) by pah-ee-TEE	Я хоте́л(-а) бы пойти́
• a play.	• nuh PYEHS-oo	• на пье́су.
• an opera.	• VAW-peer-oo	• в о́перу.
• an operetta.	• vaw-peer-EHT-oo	• в опере́тту.
• a ballet.	• nuh bah-LYEHT	• на бале́т.
• a musical.	• nah moo-zee-KAHL'-noo-yoo PYEHS-oo	• на музыка́льную пье́су.
• a concert.	• nuh kahn-TSEHRT	• на конце́рт.
• a folk concert.	• nuh fahl'k-LAWR	• на фолькло́р.
• the circus.	• ftsyrk	• в цирк.
What kind of play is it?	shtaw EH-tuh zah PYEHS-uh?	Что э́то за пье́са?
Who wrote it?	ktaw yee-YAW nuh-pee-SAHL?	Кто её написа́л?
Are there tickets for today?	bee-LYEHT-y nah see-VAWD-nyuh yehys't?	Биле́ты на сего́дня есть?
How much are tickets?	SKAWL'-kuh STAW-eet bee-LYEHT?	Ско́лько сто́ит биле́т?
Do we need to reserve tickets?	nahm NAH-duh zuh-kah-ZAHT' bee-LYEHT-y?	Нам на́до заказа́ть биле́ты?
Please give me	DAHY-tyeh pah-ZHAHL-stuh	Да́йте, пожа́луйста,
• one ticket.	• ah-DEEN bee-LYEHT	• оди́н биле́т.
• two tickets.	• dvah bee-LYEHT-uh	• два биле́та.
• five tickets.	• pyaht' bee-LYEHT-uh	• пять биле́тов.
I'd like a seat . . .	yah by khah-TYEHL(-uh) MYEHS-tuh . . .	Я бы хоте́л(-а) ме́сто . . .

176

• in the orchestra.	• fpahr-TEHR-yeh	• в партере.
• in the balcony.	• nuh bahl-KAWN-yeh	• на балконе.
• in the mezzanine.	• VLAWZH-yeh	• в ложе.
I'd like . . .	yah by khah-TYEHL (-uh) . . .	Я бы хотел(-а) . .
• seats up front.	• pah-BLEEZH-uh KSTSYEHN-yeh	• поближе к сцене.
• seats in the back.	• pah-DAHL'-shuh aht STSYEHN-y	• подальше от сцены.
• seats on the side.	• ZBAWK-oo	• сбоку.
• good seats.	• khah-RAWSH-ee-yeh mees-TAH	• хорошие места.
• inexpensive tickets.	• nee-duh-rah-GEE-yeh bee-LYEHT-y	• недорогие билеты.
• tickets for the matinee.	• bee-LYEHT-y nah dneev-NAW-yeh preed-stah-VLEHY-nyeh	• билеты на дневное представление.
• tickets for the evening.	• bee-LYEHT-y nah vee-CHEHR-nuh-yeh preed-stah-VLEHY-nyeh	• билеты на вечернее представление.
• a program	• ahd-NOO prah-GRAHM-oo	• одну программу.
Who's . . .	ktaw . . .	Кто . . .
• playing?	• ee-GRAH-yeht?	• играет?
• singing?	• pah-YAWT?	• поёт?
• dancing?	• tahn-TSOO-yeht?	• танцует?
• directing?	• ree-zhy-SYAWR?	• режиссёр?
• speaking?	• guh-vah-REET?	• говорит?
• announcing?	• kuhn-fee-rahn-SYEH?	• конферансье?

CLUBS, DISCOS, AND CABARETS

In the Soviet Union, many restaurants, especially in Intourist hotels, are also nightclubs where you can have dinner and see a floorshow, **варьете** (vuh-ryeh-TEH), which can include everything from folk dancing to magicians. People in the Soviet Union

177

love to dance, and the orchestras in restaurants will play music for all ages and tastes. For younger people, discos, bars, and video clubs offer Western music and a grittier nightlife. Discos are often organized, like high school dances, at a Komsomol Youth Palace or a similar venue and alcohol is not officially allowed on the premises. All nightlife is at a premium, however, and sometimes gaining entry to an average spot can be as difficult as walking into the hottest New York nightclub. Most clubs, restaurants, and discos close by 11:00 P.M.

Why don't we go dancing tonight?	puh-chee-MOO by nee pah-yee-TEE tahn-tseh-VAHT' see-VAWD-nyuh VYEHY-cheer-uhm?	Почему́ бы не пойти́ танцева́ть сего́дня ве́чером?
Can you suggest a good nightclub?	vy nee MAWZH-eh-tyeh puh-ree-kuh-meen-dah-VAHT' kha-RAWSH-y nahch-NOY kloop?	Вы не мо́жете пореко-мендова́ть хоро́ший ночно́й клуб?
Do they serve dinner?	tahm MAWZH-nuh pah-OO-zhyn-uht'?	Та́м мо́жно поу́жинать?
What kind of show do they have?	kah-KOY-yeh tahm vuh-ree-ee-TEH?	Како́е та́м варьете́?
Is there an entrance fee?	tahm yehyst' fkhahd-NOY bee-LYEHT?	Та́м е́сть входно́й биле́т?
What kind of dress is required?	kah-KEE-yeh TRYEHB-uh-vuh-nyuh kah-DYEHZH-dyeh?	Каки́е тре́бования к оде́жде?
Good evening.	DAWB-ry VYEHYCH-eer	До́брый ве́чер.
We would like a table near the stage.	my kha-TYEHYL-ee by STAWL-eek BLEE-zheh KTSYEHN-yeh	Мы хоте́ли бы сто́лик бли́же к сце́не.
Do you have any special drinks?	oo vahs yehyst' kah-KEE-yeh nee-BOOT' FEER-mee-ny-yeh nah-PEET-kee?	У ва́с есть каки́е-нибу́дь фи́рменные напи́тки?

178

What kind of nonalcoholic drinks do you serve?	kah-KEE-yeh oo vahs beez-uhl-kah-GAWL'-ny-yeh nah-PEET-kee?	Каки́е у вас безалко-го́льные напи́тки?
Could we see the menu?	MAWZH-nuh puh-smah-TREHYT' meen-YOO?	Мо́жно посмотре́ть меню́?
At what time is the show?	fkah-TAWH-ry chahs nuh-chee-NAH-eet-suh SHAWH-oo?	В кото́ром чау начина́ется шо́у?
How many shows are there?	SKAWHL'-kuh aht-dee-LYEHN-ee?	Ско́лько отделе́ний?

SPECTATOR SPORTS

Soccer and hockey are probably what first come to mind when one thinks of sports in the Soviet Union. But the options are much broader and more exciting. World-class Soviet athletes can be seen in figure skating competitions, track and field, gymnastics, and many events at stadiums all over the country.

I would like to see a soccer match.	yah by khah-TYEHL (-uh) pah-ee-TEE nah food-BOL'-ny mahch	Я бы хоте́л(-а) пойти́ на футбо́льный ма́тч.
Who is playing?	ktaw ee-GRAH-eet?	Кто́ игра́ет?
Which is the best team?	kah-KAH-yuh LOOCH-uh-yuh kah-MAHND-uh?	Кака́я лу́чшая кома́нда?
Is the stadium far from here?	stuh-dee-YAWN duh-lee-KAW aht-SYOOD-uh?	Стадио́н далеко́ отсю́да?
How much are the tickets?	SKAWL'-kuh STAW-eet bee-LYEHT?	Ско́лько сто́ит биле́т?
Are there better seats?	nyeht oo vahs LOOCH-eekh myehst?	Не́т у ва́с лу́чших мест?
What is the score?	kah-KOY shchawt?	Како́й счёт?
Who is winning?	ktaw vy-EE-gree-vuh-yeht?	Кто выи́грывает?

ENTERTAINMENT IN MOSCOW

Opera and Ballet

You can get tickets at the Intourist office beside the Intourist Hotel at the bottom of Gorky Street or at your hotel's service bureau. They will charge you in foreign currency and often at a *very* high price, but it may be your only way of getting in on a popular night. Evening performances 7.30, sometimes earlier, matinees 12 noon, but check.

The Bolshoi Opera and Ballet Theater, Sverdlov Square. Tickets from 1 rouble to 5 roubles. Its ballet company is justly world famous; there are many Russian and foreign operas in its repertory, and its orchestra is also outstanding. The Bolshoi also presents regular performances on the stage of the Kremlin Palace of Congresses.

Stanislavsky and Nemirovich-Danchenko Musical Theater, 17 Pushkinskaya Street. For classical and modern operas, ballets and operettas.

The Operetta, 6 Pushkinskaya Street. 2,000 seats. Classical and modern works. Obtain tickets for all performances through your hotel service bureau.

Moscow Chamber Opera Theater. Experimental theater; worth a visit.

Drama

Even if you do not speak Russian, you might want to explore the dramatic theaters. Evenings at 7; matinees at 12 noon; puppets at 7.30 P.M., but always check ahead. The puppet theater is excellent.

Central Soviet Army Theater, 2 Commune Square, has two auditoria.

Lenin Komsomol Theater, 6 Chekhov Street. The student and youth theater, presenting new plays by young authors.

The Maly Theater has *two* houses. The major is at 1/6 Sverdlov Square, its associated studio theater at 60 Bolshaya Ordynka Street.

Mayakovsky Theater, 19 Herzen Street.

Moscow Art Theater (MKhAT), 3 Proyezd Khudozhestvennogo Teatra. An affiliated smaller house, the MKhAT Filial, is at 3 Moskina Street. New building on Tverskoi Boulevard. The old building was refurbished in 1985.

Moscow Drama Theater, (also known as the Malaya Bronnaya) on Malaya Bronnaya Street.

The Moscow Music Hall performs at summer theaters in the parks, in the Variety Theatre, the Exhibition of Economic Achievements, etc.

Moscow Theater of Miniatures, 3 Karetny Ryad, offers popular programs of "witty melodrama, merry tragedy, dramatized songs and dances"; its motto is brevity.

Obraztsov Puppet Theater, 3 Sadovo-Samotechnaya. Puppetry is a particularly popular art form in the U.S.S.R. and this is a world-famous troupe. Though primarily a children's theater it also puts on excellent satirical shows for adults which the visitor can enjoy even without Russian language ability. It also boasts a "puppet cuckoo clock" which, at noon or midnight, is one of Moscow's tourist attractions.

Poezia Hall, 12 Gorky Street. For poetry recitals and experimental drama.

Pushkin Drama Theater, 23 Tverskoi Boulevard.

Romany Theater, 32 Leningradsky Prospekt, in the Hotel Sovetskaya.

Satire Theater, 18 Bolshaya Sadovaya Street, specializes in satirical comedies such as Mayakovsky's *The Bathhouse, The Bedbug* and *Mystery Bouffe.*

Sovremennik Theater, Christiye Prudy. One of the youngest of Moscow's theaters; experimental, with a company of young actors and good designers.

Taganka Drama and Comedy Theater, 75 Chkalov Street. The best known of Moscow's avant-gardist and experimental companies. Almost impossible to get seats for productions like *Master and Margarita,* so popular are they.

Vakhtangov Theater, 26 Arbat.

Variety Theater, 20/2 Bersenevskaya Embankment, also known as the **Estrada**, the center of Moscow's music hall life.

Yermolova Theater, 5 Gorky Street.

LEISURE

Concerts

The musical life of Moscow is particularly rich; there are a number of symphony orchestras and song and dance ensembles, and the soloists are often world famous—from Igor Oistrakh to Sviatoslav Richter.

Variety and symphony concerts are given in the **Hall of Columns** (Kolonnyi Zal) of the House of Trade Unions, 1 Pushkinskaya Street. Chamber music is performed in the **October Hall** of the House of Trade Unions, and the **Hall of the Gnesin Music Institute** 30–36 Vorovsky Street, while symphony concerts and solo recitals, oratorios and concert performances of operas are given in the **Grand Hall of the Conservatory**, 13 Herzen Street, the **Rakhmaninov Hall**, also in Herzen Street, and the **Tchaikovsky Concert Hall**, 20 Mayakovsky Square.

Organ recitals are held in the Small Hall of the Conservatory and there are poetry readings in the **Lenin Library Hall**, 5 Kalinin Prospekt, and in the concert hall of the Rossia Hotel. There are scores of excellent halls where concerts are frequently given. A recently opened one is the **Glinka Concert Hall**, in the Glinka Musical Museum at 4 Fadeyev Street.

Pop Music

A whole new scene has opened up under Mr. Gorbachev. Lots of rock performances are now officially advertised; discos are proliferating; and a country-and-western club was about to open in 1989. Some of these are in restaurants and cafés.

The Circus

Often a hit with foreign tourists. The old **Moscow Circus** is at 13 Tsvetnoi Boulevard. **New Circus** at 7 Vernadsky Prospekt. In summer there are tent circuses in the Gorky Park and at the Exhibition of Economic Achievements.

There is a **circus on ice** which claims to rival the great ice shows of the West and has one extraordinary feature, *Bruins Play Hockey,* a troupe of bears playing on skates. The **Moscow Ice Ballet** usually performs in the Palace of Sport of the Lenin Stadium. For times and places of performance check with Intourist.

ENTERTAINMENT IN LENINGRAD

Opera, Ballet and Drama

Academic Maly Theater of Opera and Ballet, 1 Ploshchad Iskusstv (Arts Square).

Comedy Theater, 56 Nevsky Prospekt.

Gorky (Bolshoi) Drama Theater, 65 Fontanka Naberezhnaya. Founded in 1919 by the writer himself.

Great Puppet Theater, 10 Nekrasov Street.

Kirov Academic Opera and Ballet Theater (often known as the Marinsky Theater), 2 Teatralnaya Square.

Komsomol (Youth) Theater, 46 Zagorodny Prospekt.

Musical Comedy Theater, 13 Rakov Street. The only theater that continued to perform throughout the siege of Leningrad. Mainly operettas.

Pushkin Theater, 2 Ostrovsky Square. Classical and modern drama.

Theater of the Music and Drama Institute, 35 Mokhovaya Street, also presents musical productions.

Concerts

Leningrad has a very intensive musical life; the concert halls include:

Glinka Kapella (Choral Hall), 20 Moyka Naberezhnaya. Built in 1880 by L.N. Benois; the choir was founded by Peter the Great in 1713. Glinka, Rimsky-Korsakov and many other famous musicians have appeared here.

Leningrad Philharmonia Concert Hall, 2 Brodsky Street. A second, smaller hall of the Leningrad Philharmonia is at 30 Nevsky Prospekt.

October Concert Palace, 6 Ligovsky Prospekt, three minutes from the Ploshchad Vosstaniya Metro station.

Circus

The **Leningrad Circus** is at 3 Fontanka Naberezhnaya. Designed in 1876 it is one of the oldest circuses in the country. Its programs feature many Soviet and foreign artists.

14/GENERAL TERMS AND EXPRESSIONS

DAYS, MONTHS, DATES, AND SEASONS

Days of the Week	dnee nee-DYEH-lee	Дни неде́ли
What day is it?	kah-KOY see-VAWD-nyuh dyehyn'?	Како́й сего́дня день?
Today is	see-VAWD-nyuh	Сего́дня
• Monday.	• puh-nee-DYEHL'-neek	• понеде́льник.
• Tuesday.	• FTAWR-neek	• вто́рник.
• Wednesday.	• sree-DAH	• среда́.
• Thursday.	• cheet-VYEHRK	• четве́рг.
• Friday.	• PYAT-neet-suh	• пя́тница.
• Saturday.	• soo-BAW-tuh	• суббо́та.
• Sunday.	• vuhs-kree-SYEH-nyuh	• воскресе́нье.

Months of the Year	MYEHS-eets-y GAWD-uh	Ме́сяцы
January	yeen-VAHR'	янва́рь
February	fee-VRAHL'	февра́ль
March	mahrt	ма́рт
April	ah-PREHL'	апре́ль
May	mahy	май
June	ee-YOON'	ию́нь
July	ee-YOOL'	ию́ль
August	AHF-goost	а́вгуст
September	seen-TYAHBR'	сентя́брь
October	ahk-TYAHBR'	октя́брь
November	nah-YAHBR'	ноя́брь
December	dee-KAHBR'	декабрь

The Date	DAHT-uh	Да́та
What is today's date?	kah-KAW-yuh see-VAWD-nyuh chees-LAW?	Како́е сего́дня число́?

184

| Today is April 1. | see-VAWD-nyuh PYEHR-vuh-yuh ah-PRYEHL-yuh | Сего́дня пе́рвое апре́ля. |
| Today is March 15, 1990. | see-VAWD-nyuh peet-NAHT-tsuh-tuh-yuh MAHRT-uh, TY-see-chuh dee-veet-SAWT dee-vee-NAWST-uh-vuh GAWD-uh | Сего́дня пятна́дцатое ма́рта, ты́сяча девятьсо́т девяно́стого го́да. |

Seasons	vree-mee-NAH GAW-duh	Времена́ го́да
winter	zee-MAH	зима́
spring	vees-NAH	весна́
summer	LYEHT-uh	ле́то
fall	AWS-een'	о́сень
in winter	zee-MOY	зимо́й
in spring	vees-NOY	весно́й
in summer	LYEHT-uhm	ле́том
in fall	AWS-een-yoo	о́сенью

Age	VAWZ-ruhst	Во́зраст
How old are you?	SKAWL'-kuh vahm LYEHT?	Ско́лько ва́м ле́т?
I'm 36.	mnyeh TREET-tsuht' shehst' lyeht	Мне три́дцать ше́сть лет.
How old is she?/he?	SKAWL'kuh yehy/yee-MOO lyeht?	Ско́лько ей/ему́ лет?
She's/He's 20.	yehy/yee-MOO DVAHT-tsuht' lyeht	Ей/Ему́ два́дцать лет.
I'm younger than he is.	yah mah-LAWZH-uh yee-VAW	Я моло́же его́.
I was born in 1941.	yah rah-DEEL-suh f TY-suh-chuh dee-veet-SAWT SAWR-uhk PYEHR-vuhm gah-DOO	Я роди́лся в ты́сяча девятьсо́т со́рок пе́рвом году́.

185

| His birthday is December 2. | yee-VAW dyehyn' rahzh-DYEHYN-yuh ftah-RAW-vuh dee-kah-BR'. | Его день рождения второго декабря. |

TIME EXPRESSIONS

now	sehy-CHAS	сейча́с
earlier	RAHN'-shuh	ра́ньше
later	PAW-zhuh	по́зже
before . . .	daw . . . (genitive)	до . . . (род.)
after . . ./afterward	PAWS-lee . . . (genitive)	по́сле . . . (род.)
soon	SKAWR-uh	ско́ро
once	ahd-NAHZH-dy	одна́жды
in the morning	OO-truhm	у́тром
at noon	FPAWL-deen'	в по́лдень
in the afternoon	dnyawm	днём
in the evening	VYEH-cheer-uhm	ве́чером
at night	NAWCH-yoo	но́чью
at midnight	FPAWL-nuch	в по́лночь
tomorrow	ZAHF-truh	за́втра
yesterday	fchee-RAH	вчера́
the day after tomorrow	puhs-lee-ZAHF-truh	послеза́втра
the day before yesterday	puhz-ah-fchee-RAH	позавчера́
this week	nah EHT-uhy nee-DYEHL-yeh	на э́той неде́ле
next week	nah SLYEHD-oo-yoo-shchey nee-DYEHL-yeh	на сле́дующей неде́ле
last week	nah PRAWSH-luhy nee-DYEHL-yee	на про́шлой неде́ле
every day	KAHZH-dy dyehyn'	ка́ждый день
in 3 days	CHEHR-ees tree dnyah	че́рез три дня
2 days ago	dvah dnyah tah-MOO nah-ZAHT	два́ дня́ тому́ наза́д
on Saturdays	puh soo-BAWT-uhm	по суббо́там

186

GENERAL TERMS

on weekends	puh vy-khahd-NYM dnyahm	по выходны́м дня́м
on weekdays	pah BOOD-neem	по бу́дням
a working day	rah-BAWCH-ee dyehyn'	рабо́чий де́нь
a day off	vy-khahd-NOY dyehyn'	выходно́й де́нь
in January	vyeen-vahr-YEH	в январе́
last January	vyeen-vahr-YEH PRAWSH-luh-vuh GAW-duh	в январе́ про́шлого го́да.
next January	FSLYEHD-oo-yoo-shchee yeen-VAHR'	в сле́дующий янва́рь
each month	KAHZH-dy MYEHS-eets	ка́ждый ме́сяц
since August	SAHV-goost-uh	с а́вгуста
this month	VEHT-uhm MYEHS-eets-eh	в э́том ме́сяце
next month	FSLYEHD-oo-yoo-shchehm MYEHS-eets-uh	в сле́дующем ме́сяце
last month	FPRAWSH-luhm MYEHS-eets-uh	в про́шлом ме́сяце
this year	VEHT-uhm gah-DOO	в э́том году́
next year	FSLYEHD-oo-yoo-shcheem gah-DOO	в сле́дующем году́
last year	FPRAWSH-luhm gah-DOO	в про́шлом году́
every year	KAHZH-dy goht	ка́ждый год
In what year . . . ?	fkah-KAWM-gah-DOO . . . ?	В како́м году́ . . . ?
In 1985 . . .	FTY-suh-chuh dee-veet-SAWT VAWS-eem-dee-seet PYAHT-uhm gah-DOO . . .	В ты́сяча девятьсо́т во́семьдесят пя́том году́ . . .
In the nineteenth century . . .	vdee-veet-NAHT-tsuht-uhm VYEHK-yeh . . .	В девятна́дцатом ве́ке . . .
In the forties . . .	fsuh-ruhk-ah-VY-yeh GAWD-y . . .	В сороковы́е го́ды . . .

187

HOLIDAYS

The following are public holidays in the Soviet Union. Though no official holiday falls in the month of August, it is the favorite month for Soviets to take their annual vacation. Some holidays in the Soviet Union, such as New Year's Day, are already familiar to you. However, there are many holidays that are specific to the Soviet Union. Most of these are related to the history and political culture of the country, such as the Anniversary of the Great October Socialist Revolution. Keep holidays in mind when you are planning your trip, because most public offices, banks, and museums are closed on these dates. Visiting the Soviet Union on a holiday, though, is a wonderful opportunity to see how the people celebrate.

January 1 New Year's Day	NAWV-y gawt	Но́вый го́д
February 23 Soviet Army Day	dyehyn' sah-VYEHT-skuhy AHRM-ee-ee	Де́нь сове́тской а́рмии
March 8 International Women's Day	myehzh-doo-nah-RAWD-ny dyehyn ZHEHN-sheen	Междунаро́дный де́нь же́нщин
May 1–2 International Worker's Solidarity Day	myehzh-doo-nah-RAWD-ny dyehyn' suh-lee-DAHR-nuhs-tee troo-DYAH-sheekh-syuh (PYEHR-vuh-yeh MAH-yuh)	Междунаро́дный день солида́рности трудя́щихся (Пе́рвое ма́я)
May 9 Victory Day	dyehyn' pah-BYEHD-y (nahd fah-SHYZ-muhm)	Де́нь побе́ды (над фаши́змом)
October 7 Constitution Day	dyehyn' kuhn-stee-TOO-tsy-ee	Де́нь конститу́ции
November 7–8 Anniversary of the Great October Socialist Revolution	guh-dahf-SHCHEEN-uh vee-LEEK-uhy ahk-TYAHBR-skuhy suhts-ee-uhl-eest-EECH-ee-skuhy ree-vah-LYOO-tsy-ee	Годовщи́на вели́кой октя́брьской социалисти́ческой револю́ции

188

Christmas	rahzh-deest-VAW	Рождество́
Easter	PAHS-khuh	Па́сха
Merry Christmas!	sruhzh-deest-VAWM!	С Рождество́м!
Happy New Year!	SNAWV-ym GAWD-uhm!	С Но́вым го́дом!
Happy Easter!	SPAHS-khuhy!	С Па́схой!
Happy holidays!	SPRAHZ-neek-uhm!	С пра́здником!
Happy birthday!	zdnyawm rahzh-DYEHYN-yuh!	С днём рожде́ния!

SEASONAL EVENTS

These include the May Day celebrations, the anniversary of V.E. Day (May 9) and the military parades of the Great October Revolution (commemorated on November 7 each year). The parades are followed by mass pageants and sports displays in Moscow's Red Square and other city centers.

The Russian Winter Festival lasts 12 days from December 25 to January 5. Carnivals take place in the immense Luzhniki Stadium in Moscow and elsewhere there are circuses and special theatrical performances. The Russian New Year is usually celebrated in restaurants and cafés. The Festival is also celebrated in Leningrad, Suzdal, Novgorod and Irkutsk where events are laid on for foreign visitors.

There are the Festival of Moscow Stars (May 5–13), the Kiev Spring Festival (May 18–30), the Leningrad White Nights (June 21–29), various art festivals and the Riga Song Festival (August 1–9). The Moscow International Film Festival is held every odd-numbered year in July, with entries from all over the world.

Sporting highlights include national and international ice-hockey and soccer (football) matches, skating and skiing championships, athletic meets, boxing competitions and many other events.

The November 7 celebrations are particularly brilliant in Moscow, with the whole city decked out in bunting, gaily-colored streamers and flags. The Soviet leaders take the salute on top of the Lenin Mausoleum while the long colorful parade rolls past

189

to the strains of a large brass band. (The exact position of the leaders is supposed to be an indication of their actual standing in the hierarchy of the Party.) Then follows a spectacular gymnastic display after which folklore groups from all over the country perform. The march-past of workers, many carrying their children on their shoulders, can last three or four hours. In the evening, the buildings are illuminated, fireworks light up the sky, and there is dancing and entertainment in the central squares and streets (which are closed to traffic). In Leningrad, the Soviet Baltic Fleet sails up the Neva and drops anchor opposite the Winter Palace. Illuminated at night, the warships draw great crowds to the embankments.

In Moscow, Leningrad, Kiev and other towns the theatrical season usually starts in October.

WEATHER AND CLIMATE

Weather varies greatly in different parts of the Soviet Union. During the summer, Central Asian temperatures rise well over 100 degrees Fahrenheit, while Siberian winters are well-known for their long and deep freezes. Nevertheless, the country's climate is not only one of extremes, and mild and pleasant weather can be found at almost any time of the year in some part of the country. It is a good idea to check with your travel agent for information about weather conditions in the area where you will be traveling. Some experts consider August and September the best months. This is the high season, so you must reserve well ahead to avoid disappointment. In the central part of the Soviet Union, June and July are fairly hot and on the Black Sea coast it is even hotter. But on the Black Sea May is a particularly attractive month and you can bathe from the beginning of that month through October. If you choose June or July, pick the Baltic countries and Leningrad, which will be just pleasantly warm. Central Asia is best visited in March–April or September–October as you will find the climate in summer almost tropical yet dry and dusty.

190

Winter in Moscow can be fierce in January and early February but the rest of the season is tolerable. There is, of course, plenty of snow and in the dry cold the city looks very attractive under its white cover. Some people find the cold most exhilarating, and Russian interiors are always well-heated.

Here are the average temperature ranges of the five main tourist centers (lowest monthly *average* and highest *average*):

Leningrad: 18.5°F. to 63.5°F. (−7.7°C. to 17.5°C.).
Moscow: 12.6°F. to 65.3°F. (−10.8°C to 18.5°C.).
Odessa: 25.7°F. to 71.6°F. (−3.7°C. to 22.1°C.).
Sochi: 44.4°F. to 73.4°F. (6.2°C. to 23.0°C.).
Yalta: 38.3°F. to 75.2°F. (3.7°C. to 24.2°C.).

What's the weather today?	kah-KAH-yuh see-VAWD-nyuh pah-GAWD-uh?	Кака́я сего́дня пого́да?
It's raining./snowing.	snyehk/dawzht' ee-DYAWT	Снег/Дождь идёт.
It's	see-CHAHS	Сейча́с
• cold.	• KHAW-luhd-nuh	• хо́лодно.
• cool.	• prah-KHLAHD-nuh	• прохла́дно.
• cloudy.	• PAHS-moor-nuh	• па́смурно.
• foggy.	• too-MAHN-nuh	• тума́нно.
• warm.	• tee-PLAW	• тепло́.
• hot.	• ZHAHR-kuh	• жа́рко.
• nice.	• pree-YAHT-nuh	• прия́тно.
• sunny.	• SAWL-neech-nuh	• со́лнечно.
• windy.	• VYEH-treen-nuh	• ве́трено.
What's the forecast for tomorrow?	kah-KOY prahg-NAWS nah ZAHF-truh?	Како́й прогно́з на за́втра?
It's going to rain.	BOOD-eet dawsht'	Бу́дет дождь.
What is the average temperature at this time of year?	kah-KAH-yuh SRYEHD-nuh-yuh teem-pee-rah-TOO-ruh VEH-tuh VRYEHM-yuh GAWD-uh?	Кака́я сре́дняя температу́ра в э́то вре́мя го́да?

191

TEMPERATURE CONVERSIONS

In the Soviet Union, temperature is measured in degrees Celsius, or centigrade. To convert degrees Celsius into degrees Fahrenheit, use this formula:

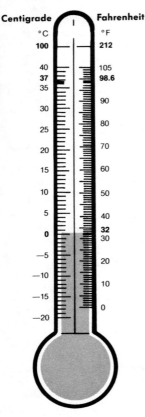

Centigrade **Fahrenheit**

To Convert Centigrade to Fahrenheit

$(\frac{9}{5})C° + 32 = F°$

1. Divide by 5.
2. Multiply by 9.
3. Add 32.

To Convert Fahrenheit to Centigrade

$(F° - 32)\frac{5}{9} = C°$

1. Subtract 32.
2. Divide by 9.
3. Multiply by 5.

GENERAL TERMS

CONTINENTS

Africa	AH-free-kuh	А́фрика
Asia	AH-zee-yuh	А́зия
Australia	ahf-STRAHL-ee-yuh	Австра́лия
Europe	yee-VRAW-puh	Евро́па
North America	SYEH-veern-nuh-yuh ah-MYEH-ree-kuh	Се́верная Аме́рика
South America	YOOZH-nuh-yuh ah-MYEH-ree-kuh	Ю́жная Аме́рика
Antarctica	ahn-tahrk-TEE-duh	Антаркти́да

COUNTRIES AND NATIONALITIES

Where do you come from?	aht-KOO-duh vy?	Отку́да вы?
I come from Finland.	yah ees feen-LYAHN-dee-ee	Я из Финля́ндии.
I am	yah	Я
• from the Soviet Union.	• ees sah-VYEHT-skuh-vuh sah-YOOZ-uh	• из Сове́тского Сою́за.
• from France.	• ees FRAHN-tsy-ee	• из Фра́нции.
• from England.	• eez AHN-glee-ee	• из Áнглии.
• from the United States./U.S.A.	• ees sah-yeed-een-NYAWN-ykh SHTAHT-uhf Ah-MYEH-ree-kee/seh-shuh-AH	• из Соединённых Шта́тов Аме́рики./ США.
• from China.	• ees kee-TAH-yuh	• из Кита́я.
I'm going	yah YEH-doo	Я е́ду
• to the Soviet Union.	• fsah-VYEHT-skee SAH-yoos	• в Сове́тский Сою́з.
• to Europe.	• vee-VRAW-poo	• в Евро́пу.
• to the United States./U.S.A.	• fsah-yeed-een-NY-AWN-y-yeh SHTAHT-y ah-MYEH-me-kee/ sshAH	• в Соединённые Шта́ты Аме́рики./ США.
• to Japan.	• vyee-PAWN-ee-yoo	• Япо́нию.
Algeria	ahl-ZHYR	Алжи́р

Algerian	ahl-ZHYR-eets(-kuh)	алжи́р-ец(-ка)
Argentina	ahr-geen-TEEN-uh	Аргенти́на
Argentinian	ahr-geen-TEEN-eets (-kuh)	аргенти́н-ец(-ка)
Austria	AHF-stree-yuh-EE	А́встрия
Austrian	ahf-STREE-yeets(-kuh)	австри́-ец(-и́йка)
Belgium	BYEHL'-gee-yuh-EE	Бе́льгия
Belgian	beel'-GEE-yeets(-kuh)	бельги́-ец(-и́йка)
Brazil	brah-ZEE-lyuh	Брази́лия
Brazilian	brah-ZEEL-eets/brah-zeel-YAHN-kuh	брази́л-ец(-я́нка)
Canada	kah-NAH-duh	Кана́да
Canadian	kah-NAHD-eets/kah-NAHT-kuh	кана́д-ец(-ка)
China	kee-TAHY	Кита́й
Chinese	kee-TAH-eets/kee-tah-YAHN-kuh	кита́-ец(-я́нка)
Denmark	DAH-nee-yuh	Да́ния
Danish	dah-CHAHN-een (-kuh)	датча́н-ин(-ка)
England	AHN-glee-yuh	А́нглия
English	ahn-glee-CHAHN-een (-kuh)	англича́н-ин(-ка)
Finland	feen-LYAHN-dee-yuh	Финля́ндия
Finnish	feen/FEEN-kuh	фи́нн(-ка)
France	FRAHN-tsy-yuh	Фра́нция
French	frahn-TSOOS/frahn-TSOOZH-ehn-kuh	францу́з/францу́женка
Germany	geer-MAHN-ee-yuh	Герма́ния
Greece	GRYEH-tsy-yuh	Гре́ция
Greek	gryehk/gree-CHAHN-kuh	грек(-ча́нка)
India	EEN-dee-yuh	Инди́я
Indian	een-DEE-eets-een-DYAHN-kuh	инди́-ец(-а́нка)
Ireland	eer-LYAHN-dyee-yuh	Ирла́ндия
Irish	eer-LYAHND-deets/eer-LYAHNT-kuh	ирла́нд-ец(-ка)
Israel	eez-RAH-eel'	Изра́иль
Israeli	eez-rah-eel'-TYAHN-een(-kuh)	израильтя́н-ин(-ка)

194

Italy	ee-TAH-lee-yuh	**Ита́лия**
Italian	ee-tah-LYAHN-eets (-kuh)	**италья́н-ец(-ка)**
Japan	yee-PAWN-ee-yuh	**Япо́ния**
Japanese	yee-PAWN-eets(-kuh)	**япо́н-ец(-ка)**
Korea	kah-RYEH-yuh	**Коре́я**
Korean	kah-RYEH-eets(-YAHN -kuh)	**коре́-ец(-я́нка)**
Luxembourg	lyook-seem-BOORG	**Люксембу́рг**
Luxembourger	lyook-seem-BOORZH-eets(-kuh)	**люксембу́р-жец(-ка)**
Mexico	MYEHK-see-kuh	**Ме́ксика**
Mexican	meek-see-KAHN-eets (-kuh)	**мексика́н-ец(-ка)**
Morocco	mah-RAWK-kuh	**Маро́кко**
Moroccan	mah-rawk AHN-eets/muh-rah-KAH-N-kuh	**марокка́н-ец (-а́нка)**
Netherlands	nee-deer-LAHN-dy	**Нидерла́нды**
Dutch	gah-LAHNHD-eets (-kuh)	**голла́нд-ец(-ка)**
New Zealand	NAW-vuh-yuh zee-LAHN-dee-yuh	**Но́вая Зела́ндия**
New Zealander	nuh-vuh-zee-LAHN-deets(-kuh)	**новозела́нд-ец (-ка)**
Norway	nawr-VYEH-gee-ee	**Норве́гия**
Norwegian	nawr-VYEHZH-eets (-kuh)	**норве́ж-ец(-ка)**
Portugal	puhr-too-GAHL-yee-uh	**Португа́лия**
Portuguese	puhr-too-GAHL-eets (-kuh)	**португа́л-ец(-ка)**
Russia	rah-SEE-yuh	**Росси́я**
Russian	ROOS-kee/ROOS-kuh -yuh	**ру́сск-ий(-ая)**
Scotland	shaht-LAHN-dee-yuh	**Шотла́ндия**
Scottish	shaht-LAHN-deets (-tkuh)	**шотла́нд-ец(-ка)**
Soviet Union	sah-VYEHTS-kee sah-YOOS	**Сове́тский Сою́з**

Soviet	sah-VYEHTS-kee (-kuh -yuh)	сове́тск-ий(-ая)
Spain	ees-PAHN-ee-yuh	Испа́ния
Spanish	ees-PAHN-eets(-kuh)	испа́н-ец(-ка)
Sweden	SHVEH-tsy-yuh	Шве́ция
Swedish	shveht(-kuh)	швед(-ка)
Switzerland	shvay-TSAHR-ee-yuh	Швейца́рия
Swiss	shvay-TSAHR-eets (-kuh)	швейца́р-ец(-ка)
Thailand	tuh-ee-LAHNT	Таила́нд
Thai	tuh-ee-lahn-deets (-kuh)	таила́нд-ец(-ка)
Turkey	TOOR-tsy-yuh	Ту́рция
Turkish	TOOR-uhk/toor-CHA-HN-kuh	ту́р-ок(-ча́нка)
United States	sah-yeed-ee-NYAWN-y-yeh SHTAHT-y ah -MYEH-ree-kee	Соединённые Шта́ты Аме́рики
American	ah-MYEH-ree-KAHN-eets(-kuh)	америка́н-ец(-ка)

LANGUAGES

Note the difference between the name of the language and the adverbial expression signifying an act performed in a specific language.

Arabic	ah-RAHP-skee	ара́бский
in Arabic	puh-ah-RAHP-skee	по-ара́бски
Chinese	kee-TAHY-skee	кита́йский
in Chinese	puh-kee-TAHY-skee	по-кита́йски
English	ahn-GLEE-skee	англи́йский
in English	puh-ahn-GLEE-skee	по-англи́йски
French	frahn-TSOO-skee	францу́зский
in French	puh-frahn-TSOO-skee	по-францу́зски
German	nee-MYEHT-skee	неме́цкий
in German	puh-nee-MYEHT-skee	по-неме́цки
Japanese	yee-PAWN-skee	япо́нский
in Japanese	puh-yee-PAWN-skee	по-япо́нски
Portuguese	puhr-too-GAHL'-skee	португа́льский

196

in Portuguese	puh-pahr-too-GAHL'-skee	по-португа́льски
Russian	ROOS-kee	ру́сский
in Russian	pah-ROOS-kee	по-ру́сски
Spanish	ees-PAHN-skee	испа́нский
in Spanish	puh-ees-PAHN-skee	по-испа́нски
Ukrainian	oo-krah-EEN-skee	украи́нский
in Ukrainian	puh-oo-kroh-EEN-skee	по-украи́нскц
I speak Russian.	yah guh-vah-RYOO pah-ROOS-kee	Я говорю́ по-ру́сски.
I like Russian.	yah lyoo-BLYOO ROOS-kee yee-ZYK	Я люблю́ ру́сский язы́к.

PROFESSIONS AND OCCUPATIONS

accountant	boo-GAHL-teer	бухга́лтер
architect	ahr-khee-TYEHK-tuhr	архите́ктор
artist	khoo-DAWZH-neek	худо́жник
baker	PYEH-kuhr'	пе́карь
blacksmith	kooz-NYEHTS	кузне́ц
butcher	mees-NEEK	мясни́к
cardiologist	kuhr-dee-AWL-uhk	кардио́лог
carpenter	PLAWT-neek	пло́тник
chef	shehf PAW-vuhr	шеф-по́вар
clerk	klyehrk	клерк
cook	PAW-vuhr	по́вар
dentist	zoob-NOY vrahch	зубно́й врач
doctor	vrahch	врач
electrician	ee-LYEHK-treek	эле́ктрик
engineer	een-zhy-NYEHR	инжене́р
housepainter	mah-LYAHR	маля́р
lawyer	yoo-REEST	юри́ст
locksmith	SLEHS-uhr'	сле́сарь
maid	oo-BAWR-shchee-tsuh	убо́рщица
neurologist	nee-VRAW-luhk	невро́лог
nurse	meet-sees-TRAH	медсестра́
ophthalmologist	ahf-tahl'-MAWL-uhk	офтальмо́лог
optometrist	AWP-teek	о́птик
plumber	vuh-duh-prah-VAWT-cheek	водопрово́дчик
salesperson	pruh-dah-VYEHTS/pruh-dahf-SHCHEE-tsuh	продаве́ц/продавщи́ца

197

sculptor	SKOOL'P-tuhr	ску́льптор
shoemaker	sah-PAWZH-neek	сапо́жник
shopkeeper	LAH-vuhch-neek	ла́вочник
waiter	ah-fee-tsy-AHNT	официа́нт
waitress	ah-fee-tsy-AHNT-kuh	официа́нтка
writer	pee-SAH-teel'	писа́тель

COLORS

red	KRAH-snee	кра́сный
yellow	ZHAWL-ty	жёлтый
green	zee-LYAW-ny	зелёный
blue	SEE-nee	си́ний
white	BYEH-ly	бе́лый
brown	kah-REECH-nuh-vy	кори́чневый
orange	ah-RAHNZH-uh-vy	ора́нжевый
purple	fee-ah-LYEHT-uh-vy	фиоле́товый
black	CHAWR-ny	чёрный
gold	zuh-lah-TOY	золото́й
silver	see-RYEH-bree-ny	сере́бряный

EMERGENCY EXPRESSIONS

Fire!	pah-ZHAR!	Пожа́р!
Hurry!	spee-SHY-tyeh!	Спеши́те!
Call the fire department!	VY-zuh-vee-tyeh pah-ZHAHR-nykh!	Вы́зовите пожа́рных!
Help!	nah PAW-mushch!	На по́мощь!
I'm sick.	yah BAWL-een/bahl'-NAH	Я бо́лен./больна́.
Call a doctor.	VY-zuh-vee-tyeh vrah-CHAH	Вы́зовите врача́.
I'm lost.	yah zuh-bloo-DEEL-suh(-uhs')	Я заблуди́лся (-ась).
Can you help me, please?	puh-mah-GEE-tyeh mnyeh pah-ZHAHL-stuh!	Помоги́те мне, пожа́луйста!
Stop, thief!	vawr!	Вор!
Stop him!/her!	ah-stahn-ah-VEE-tyeh yee-VAW!/yee-YAW!	Останови́те его́!/её!

Someone/They stole	oo mee-NYAH oo-KRAHL-ee	У меня́ укра́ли
• my camera!	• fuh-tuh-ah-pah-RA-HT!	• фотоаппара́т!
• my car!	• mah-SHY-noo!	• маши́ну!
• my handbag!	• SOOM-koo!	• су́мку!
• my money!	• DYEHN'-gee!	• де́ньги!
• my passport!	• PAHS-puhrt!	• па́спорт!
• my suitcase!	• chee-mah-DAHN!	• чемода́н!
• my watch!	• chee-SY!	• часы́!
He's the thief.	vawt awn-vawr	Вот он—вор.
Leave me alone!	aht-STAHN-tyeh aht mee-NYAH!	Отста́ньте от меня́!
I'm going to call the police.	yah VY-zuh-voo mee-LEE-tsy-yoo	Я вы́зову мили́цию.
Where's the police station?	gdyeh aht-dee-LYEH-nyeh mee-LEE-tsee-ee?	Где отделе́ние мили́ции?
I want a lawyer.	mnyeh NOOZH-ehn ahd-vah-KAHT	Мне ну́жен адвока́т.
I want an interpreter.	mnyeh NOOZH-ehn pee-ree-VAWT-cheek	Мне ну́жен перево́дчик.
Is there someone here who speaks English?	ktaw-nee-BOOT' ees vahs guh-vah-REET puh-ahn-GLEE-skee?	Кто-нибу́дь из вас говори́м по-англи́йски?
I want to go to the American consulate./ embassy.	yah khah-CHOO pah-ee-TEE vah-mee-ree-KAHN-skuh-yuh KAWN-sool'st-vuh/ pah-SAWL'ST-vuh	Я хочу́ пойти́ в Америка́нское ко́нсульство./ посо́льство.

ABBREVIATIONS

в.	ве́к	century
ГАИ	Госуда́рственная автомоби́льная инспе́кция	State Automobile Inspectorate (civilian highway police)
г.	го́д/го́род/гора́	year/city/mountain

199

г-жа	госпожа́	Ms./Mrs./Miss
г-н	господи́н	Mr.
гр.	граждани́н/гражда́нка	citizen
ГУМ	Госуда́рственный универса́льный магази́н	state department store
д.	до́м	house
до н.э.	до на́шей э́ры	B.C.
и др.	и други́е	et alia
и пр.	и про́чее	et cetera
и т.д.	и та́к да́лее	and so on
и т.п.	и тому́ подо́бное	et cetera
им.	и́мени	named after
к.	копе́йка	kopeck
кв.	кварти́ра	apartment
м.	мину́та	minute
н.э.	на́шей э́ры	A.D.
о.	о́стров	island
обл.	о́бласть	oblast (province)
о-во	о́бщество	society
пл.	пло́щадь	square
п.о.	почто́вое отделе́ние	post office
р.	ру́бль	ruble
р-н	райо́н	region
с.г.	сего́ го́да	of this year
ст.	ста́нция	station
стр.	страни́ца	page
СССР	Сою́з Сове́тских Социалисти́ческих Респу́блик	USSR
США	Соединённые Шта́ты Аме́рики	U.S.A.
ТАСС	Телегра́фное Аге́нство Сове́тского Сою́за	TASS, Telegraph Agency of the Soviet Union
т., тов.	това́рищ	comrade
т.е.	то е́сть	that is, i.e.
т.к.	та́к ка́к	since
ул.	у́лица	street
ч.	ча́с	hour

GRAMMAR IN BRIEF

With this book, you can find and use essential phrases without formal study of Russian grammar. However, by learning some of the basic patterns of the language, you will also be able to construct your own sentences. No book can predict or contain every sentence a traveler may need to use or understand, so any time you invest in learning grammatical patterns will substantially increase your ability to communicate.

NOUNS

Russian is an inflected language, which means that words change their endings to show different grammatical meanings. There are six such basic categories, or cases, of nouns in Russian: the nominative, the genitive, the dative, the accusative, the instrumental, and the prepositional. Depending on its meaning or grammatical function in a sentence, the noun carries a different ending to showing what the case is. Nouns in Russian are either masculine, feminine, or neuter, and this is also reflected in the case ending.

The Nominative Case and Determining Gender

The nominative is used for the subject of a sentence and is the form listed in the dictionary. When a noun in the nominative case ends in a consonant it is generally masculine, such as дóм (house) or стóл (table); words ending in a, я, or ь are feminine, such as кнúга (book) or машúна (car), and words ending in o and e are neuter, such as сóлнце (sun) or окнó (window). Some exceptions worth noting are мужчúна (man), дя́дя (uncle), and дéдушка (grandfather), which are masculine nouns with feminine-like endings, whose modifying adjectives are nonetheless masculine; and nouns ending in мя are neuter, such as врéмя (time).

Other Cases

The other five cases have a variety of functions, depending on the meaning the speaker seeks to convey; use of the other cases is also introduced by certain prepositions. *The prepositional or locative case* is generally employed in expressions of place. For example, in the sentence "The book is on the table," the word *table* is in the prepositional case—**стол** (stawl) becomes **столе́** (stah-LYEH). It is also used after the preposition о (about) as in "to talk about someone." *The accusative case* is used for the direct object in a sentence. In the sentence "Ivan sees the dog," the word *dog* is in the accusative case—**соба́ка** (sah-BAH-kuh) becomes **соба́ку** (sah-BAH-koo). In the affirmative, the direct object requires the accusative case, while in the negative it takes the genitive case. The accusative is also used in time expressions, and to show motion toward an object. The role of *the genitive case* is to quantify things or concepts; the genitive is used in counting, measuring, and generally for nouns that would come after the English word *of*. The word *books*, when quantified by the number five, would be in the genitive—**кни́га** (KNEE-guh) becomes **пять кни́г** (pyaht' kneek). *The dative case* is used to show the indirect object in a sentence as well as in impersonal constructions. An example of this is "I gave the book to the teacher," where the word *teacher* would be in the dative—**преподава́тель** (pree-puh-dah-VAH-tyeel') becomes **преподава́телю** (pree-puh-dah-VAH-tyee-lyoo). *The instrumental case* is generally used to show the agent by which or instrument with which something is done, as the word *pencil* is used in the phrase "I wrote the letter with a pencil" ("I wrote the letter in pencil"). The word pencil, **каранда́ш** (kuh-rahn-DAHSH) becomes **карандашо́м** (kuh-rahn-dahsh-AWM).

ADJECTIVES

All adjectives agree in number, gender, and case with the nouns they modify. Adjectives describe nouns, show possession (possessive adjectives), or are used to point to something (demonstrative adjectives). Examples here are shown in the nominative case. Summary tables of noun, pronoun, and adjective declensions can be found at the end of this chapter.

Possessive Adjectives

Singular*		Plural	
мой, моя, моё		мои	my
твой, твоя, твоё		твои	your
его		его	his
её		её	her
наш, наша, наше		наши	our
ваш, ваша, ваше		ваши	your
их		их	their

*Where there are three different forms listed in the singular, the order is masculine, feminine, neuter.

Demonstrative Adjectives

Singular		Plural	
этот, эта, это	this	эти	these
тот, та, то	that	те	those

ADVERBS

In English, -*ly* is added to an adjective to form an adverb. Russian adverbs usually end in -**o**.

Adjective

(Masc.)	(Fem.)	(Neut.)	
красивый	красивая	красивое	pretty
молодой	молодая	молодое	young
лёгкий	лёгкая	лёгкое	light

Adverb

красиво		prettily
молодо		young
легко		lightly

Note that in adverbial expressions used to show something done in a certain language, you add the prefix **по-** and the suffix -**ски**

203

to the basic adjective—**Я говорю́ по-ру́сски**. This should not be confused with the masculine adjectival ending **-ский**.

COMPARISONS WITH ADJECTIVES AND ADVERBS

In Russian you form the comparative in two ways. The first and simplest way is to place the word **бо́лее** (BOH-lyeh-yeh), "more," or **ме́нее** (MYEHN-yeh-yeh), "less," before the adjective or adverb compared. These words do not agree with the nouns or adjectives compared.

бо́лее у́мный, чем (more intelligent than)
ме́нее у́мный, чем (less intelligent than)

The first noun in the comparison is always in the nominative case and the second noun is preceded by the word **чём** (chehm), than, and is also in the nominative case:

Э́тот до́м бо́лее краси́вый, чём то́т до́м. (This house is prettier than that house.)

To form the superlative, place the adjective **са́мый** (most) before the adjective (**са́мый** is always in agreement with the number, gender, and case of the adjective or noun).

PRONOUNS

The pronoun takes the place of a noun in a sentence, and assumes its gender, number, and case. This table shows the declensions of Russian pronouns:

Case	I	You	He/It	She
Nom.	я́	ты́	о́н/оно́	она́
Acc.	меня́	тебя́	его́	её
Gen.	меня́	тебя́	его́	её
Prep.	обо мне́	о тебе́	о нём	о не́й
Dat.	мне́	тебе́	ему́	е́й
Instr.	мно́й	тобо́й	и́м	е́й

Case	We	You	They	Who	What
Nom.	мы́	вы́	они́	кто́	что́
Acc.	на́с	ва́с	и́х	кого́	что́
Gen.	на́с	ва́с	и́х	кого́	чего́
Prep.	о на́с	о ва́с	о ни́х	о ко́м	о чём
Dat.	на́м	ва́м	и́м	кому́	чему́
Instr.	на́ми	ва́ми	и́ми	ке́м	чём

Relative Pronouns

Relative pronouns must always be expressed in Russian. The main relative pronoun is **кото́рый** (kah-TAW-ry), and it corresponds to English who, which, and that. **Кото́рый** agrees in gender and number with the antecedent but declines based on its function (subject, object, etc.) in the dependent clause. It is used for both persons and things.

Кни́га, кото́рая лежи́т на столе́, . . . (The book, which is lying on the table, . . .)
Кни́га, кото́рую я чита́ю . . . (The book that I read . . .)
Же́нщина, кото́рая уста́ла, . . . (The woman, who is tired, . . .)

Interrogative Pronouns

Interrogative pronouns are used for asking questions.

что́	what	отку́да	where (from)
кто́	who	че́й	whose
ка́к	how	како́й	which
когда́	when	почему́	why
где́	where (at)	заче́м	what for
куда́	where (to)	ско́лько	how much

PREPOSITIONS

Some of the most common prepositions in Russian, and their cases are

205

в (prepositional)	in, at	**Я в шко́ле.** I'm at school.
в (accusative)	to	**Я иду́ в шко́лу.** I'm going to school.
в (accusative)	at (time)	**В два часа́ . . .** At two o'clock . . .
на (prepositional)	on	**Ру́чка на столе́.** The pen is on the table.
на (accusative)	to	**Я е́ду на вокза́л.** I'm going to the station.
у (genitive)	at (a person's house)	**Джон у Ви́ки.** John is at Vika's house.
	in the expression *to have*	**У меня́ маши́на.** I have a car.
к, ко (dative)	to (a person)	**Пошли́ к Ива́ну!** Let's go to Ivan's! **Она́ идёт ко мне́.** She's coming to me.
из (genitive)	from, of	**Я из Аме́рики.** I'm from America. **Я из сре́дней семьи́.** I'm from an average family.
от (genitive)	from	**Кни́га от Ива́на.** The book is from Ivan.
с (genitive)	from	**Она́ пришла́ с вокза́ла.** She arrived from the station.

с (instrumental)	with	**Чай с лимо́ном, пожа́луйста.** Tea with lemon, please.
без (genitive)	without	**Я чита́ю без очко́в.** I read without glasses.
до (genitive)	up to, until	**Я рабо́таю до конца́ дня.** I work until the end of the day.
о, об, о́бо (prepositional)	about	**Он говори́т о любви́.** He's speaking about love.
по (dative)	along,	**Ты идёшь по у́лице.** You walk along the street.
по́сле (genitive)	after	**По́сле рабо́ты . . .** After work . . .
для (genitive)	for	**Это для вас.** This is for you.

VERBS

There are two basic stems for regular Russian verbs, **-a** stems and **-и** stems. The present tense is shown for **-a** verbs by the endings **-у** or **-ю, -ешь, -ет, -ем, -ете, ут**, or **ют**. The present tense is shown for **-и** verbs by the endings **-у** or **-ю, -ишь, -ит, -им, -ите, -ат**, or **-ят**. The infinitive is shown by the ending **-ть**.

	-ать **рабо́тать** (to work)	**-ить** **говори́ть** (to speak)
Present Tense		
I	**я рабо́таю**	**говорю́**
you	**ты рабо́таешь**	**говори́шь**

207

he, she, it	он/она́/оно́ рабо́тает	говори́т
we	мы рабо́таем	говори́м
you	вы рабо́таете	говори́те
they	они́ рабо́тают	говоря́т

Past Tense

The past tense is indicated by the ending -л. For feminine nouns the verb ends with -ла, for neuter nouns with -ло, and for plural nouns with -ли.

я рабо́тал/а	говори́л/а
ты рабо́тал/а	говори́л/а
он/она́/оно́ рабо́тал/а/о	говори́л/а/о
мы рабо́тали	говори́ли
вы рабо́тали	говори́ли
они́ рабо́тали	говори́ли

IRREGULAR VERBS

Some commonly used verbs that do not follow the patterns above, and have slightly irregular forms, are

	хоте́ть (to want) Present Tense	хоте́ть (to want) Past Tense
I	я хочу́	хоте́л/а
you	ты хо́чешь	хоте́л/а
he, she, it	он/она́/оно́ хо́чет	хоте́л/а/о
we	мы хоти́м	хоте́ли
you	вы хоти́те	хоте́ли
they	они́ хотя́т	хоте́ли

	быть (to be)* Present Tense	быть (to be)* Past Tense
I	я бу́ду	был/была́
you	ты бу́дешь	был/была́
he, she, it	он/она́/оно́ бу́дет	был/была́/бы́ло
we	мы бу́дем	бы́ли

you	вы бу́дете	бы́ли
they	они́ бу́дут	бы́ли

*Russian does not use the verb *to be* in the present tense: it is merely implied. So to say "I am a doctor," one would say literally "I doctor." The verb *to be* is used in the past and future. The present-tense conjugation of the verb is used in forming the future tense (see *Aspect,* below).

	идти́ (to walk) Present Tense	идти́ (to walk) Past Tense
I	я иду́	шёл/шла
you	ты идёшь	шёл/шла
he, she, it	он/она́/оно́ идёт	шёл/шла/шло
we	мы идём	шли
you	вы идёте	шли
they	они́ иду́т	шли

	дать (to give) Present Tense	дать (to give) Past Tense
I	я дам	дал/дала́
you	ты дашь	дал/дала́
he, she, it	он/она́/оно́ даст	дал/дала́/дало́
we	мы дади́м	да́ли
you	вы дади́те	да́ли
they	они́ даду́т	да́ли

	есть (to eat) Present Tense	есть (to eat) Past Tense
I	я ем	ел/е́ла
you	ты ешь	ел/е́ла
he, she, it	он/она́/оно́ ест	ел/е́ла/е́ло
we	мы еди́м	е́ли
you	вы еди́те	е́ли
they	они́ едя́т	е́ли

Perfective and Imperfective Russian Verbs

In using Russian verbs one always chooses between two types of meanings. The *perfective* form of the verb describes a completed action, or action completed at once or on one occasion. The *imperfective* does not specify this type of action. The imperfective refers to a wider range of meanings including process, progress (incomplete action), or action performed repetitively.

This distinction in meaning is made by the speaker choosing between paired verbs, either imperfective or perfective. (Verbs are listed in imperfective/perfective pairs in the dictionary at the end of the book.)

Here are some examples of the differences between use of the imperfective and perfective meanings:

Process

Вчера́ я чита́л кни́гу.
(imperfective, emphasis on process)

Yesterday I was reading a book.

Ты прочита́л кни́гу?
(perfective, emphasis on result)

Did you finish reading the book?

Да, я уже́ её прочита́л.
(perfective, emphasis on result)

Yes, I've already finished reading it.

Repetition

Когда́ я учи́лся в университе́те, я чита́л ка́ждый день, писа́л, и мно́го рабо́тал.
(imperfective, emphasis on repeated action)

When I studied at the university, I read every day, wrote, and worked a lot.

Весно́й я ко́нчил университе́т, и тепе́рь я рабо́таю в больни́це.
(perfective, emphasis on the result)

In the spring I graduated, and now I work at a hospital.

Tense and Aspect

Since the perfective refers to completed action, perfective verbs do not appear in the present tense. Only imperfective verbs are used to describe actions that take place in the present. When you want to use an imperfective verb in the future, you use a conjugated form of the verb **быть** (to be), and the infinitive of the imperfective verb. For example, **Я бу́ду чита́ть кни́гу.** (I will read/be reading the book.) Here are some more examples of the perfective and imperfective verbs for you to compare:

Past Tense	Present Tense	Future Tense
Она́ написа́ла письмо́. She wrote the letter. (once, completely)	**Она́ пи́шет письмо.** She is writing the letter.	**Она́ бу́дем писа́мь письмо́.** She will write/She will be writing the letter.
Она́ писа́ла письмо́. She was writing/She used to write a letter.		**Она́ напи́шет письмо́.** She will write the letter. (once, completely)

Note that when two or more perfective verbs are used in a sentence, they usually describe consecutive action; when two or more imperfective verbs are used, the meaning is of simultaneous action.

NOUN ENDINGS

Masculine and neuter nouns decline identically in Russian. To decline nouns properly, take the last letter off the noun, and add the ending shown. If no ending is shown, the noun does not change. In some instances there is a choice of endings, depending on whether the final consonant is hard or soft: hard consonants add endings beginning in **a**, **э**, **o**, or **y**; soft consonants add endings beginning in **я**, **e**, **ё**, or **ю**.*

*The accusative case in Russian distinguishes between nouns denoting animate objects and inanimate objects: inanimate masculine and neuter nouns and pronouns use the same endings as in the genitive case, while the inanimate ones have the same endings as the nominative. Feminine singular nouns do not fall into this category and have their own ending, у/ю.

211

Singular

Case	(Factory)	Masculine and Neuter (Window)	(Boy)
Nom.	заво́д	окно́	ма́льчик
Acc.	заво́д	окно́	ма́льчика -а
Gen.	заво́да	окна́ -а	ма́льчика -а
Prep.	заво́де	окне́ -е	ма́льчке -е
Dat.	заво́ду	окну́ -у	ма́льчику -у
Instr.	заво́дом	окно́м -ом	ма́льчнком -ом

Singular

Case	Feminine (Newspaper)	Feminine Ending in ь (Door)
Nom.	газе́та -а	две́рь
Acc.	газе́ту -у	две́рь
Gen.	газе́ты -ы	две́ри -и
Prep.	газе́те -е	две́ри -и
Dat.	газе́те -е	две́ри -и
Instr.	газе́той -ой	две́рью -ью

Plural

Case	Feminine (Newspaper)	Feminine Endings in ь (Door)	Endings
Nom.	газе́ты	две́ри	-ы, -и, -а
Acc.	газе́ты	две́ри	as Nom. or Gen.
Gen.	газе́т	двере́й	O, -ов, -ей
Prep.	газе́тах	две́рях	-ах, -ях
Dat.	газе́там	две́рям	-ам, -ям
Instr.	газе́тами	деверя́ми	-ами, -ями

PRONOUN DECLENSIONS

Case	I	You	He/It	She
Nom.	я	ты	óн/онó	онá
Acc.	меня	тебя	егó	её
Gen.	меня	тебя	егó	её
Prep.	óбо мнé	о тебé	о нём	о нéй
Dat.	мнé	тебé	емý	éй
Instr.	мнóй	тобóй	и́м	éй

Case	We	You	They	Who	What
Nom.	мы́	вы́	они́	ктó	чтó
Acc.	нáс	вáс	и́х	когó	чтó
Gen.	нáс	вáс	и́х	когó	чегó
Prep.	о нáс	о вáс	о ни́х	о кóм	о чём
Dat.	нáм	вáм	и́м	комý	чемý
Instr.	нáми	вáми	и́ми	кéм	чéм

DEMONSTRATIVE AND POSSESSIVE PRONOUNS

Masculine and Neuter

Case	This	Ours	My	That
Nom.	э́тот э́то	нáш нáше	мóй моё	тóт тó
Acc.	э́тот э́то	нáш нáше	мóй моё	тóт тó
Gen.	э́того	нáшего	моегó	тогó
Prep.	э́том	нáшем	моём	тóм
Dat.	э́тому	нáшему	моемý	томý
Instr.	э́тим	нáшим	мои́м	тéм

Feminine

Case	This	Ours	My	That
Nom.	э́та	нáша	моя́	тá
Acc.	э́ту	нáшу	мою́	тý
Gen.	э́той	нáшей	моéй	тóй
Prep.	э́той	нáшей	моéй	тóй
Dat.	э́той	нáшей	моéй	тóй
Instr.	э́той	нáшей	моéй	тóй

GRAMMAR

213

Plural

Case	This	Ours	My	That
Nom.	э́ти	на́ши	мои́	то́т
Acc.	э́ти	на́ши	мои́	то́т
Gen.	э́тих	на́ших	мои́х	того́
Prep.	э́тих	на́ших	мои́х	то́м
Dat.	э́тим	на́шим	мои́м	те́м
Instr.	э́тими	на́шими	мои́ми	те́ми

ADJECTIVE DECLENSIONS

Case	но́вый (New) Masculine and Neuter		Feminine	Plural
Nom.	но́вый	но́вое	но́вая	но́вые
Acc.	но́вый	но́вое	но́вую	но́вые
Gen.	но́вого		но́вой	но́вых
Prep.	но́вом		но́вой	но́вых
Dat.	но́вому		но́вой	но́вым
Instr.	но́вым		но́вой	но́выми

GRAMMAR

214

ENGLISH-RUSSIAN DICTIONARY

abbr. abbreviated as
adj. adjective
adv. adverb
conj. conjunction
f. feminine noun
imp. imperfective verb
m. masculine noun

n. neuter noun
perf. perfective verb
pl. plural
pron. pronoun
sing. singular
v. verb

Note: Nouns in the dictionary are listed in the nominative case, and adjectives in the nominative masculine form. Please note, however, that usage of the imperfective and perfective verb forms appear only in the Russian/English portion of the dictionary. Verbs are given in the infinitive, with the imperfective form first and perfective last. To learn more about conjugating verbs or declining nouns and adjectives, see **Grammar in Brief**.

A

accept принима́ть/ приня́ть *(pree-nee-MAHT'/ pree-NYAHT')*

accident ава́рия (f.) *(ah-VAH-ree-yuh)*

address а́дрес (m.) *(AH-drees)*

after по́сле *(PAWS-lee)*

afternoon, in the днём *(dnyawm)*

age во́зраст (m.) *(VAWZ-ruhst)*

ago тому́ наза́д (adv.) *(tah-MOO nah-ZAHT)*

aisle прохо́д (m.) *(prah-KHAWT)*

almost почти́ *(pahch-TEE)*

amber янта́рь (m.) *(yeen-TAHR')*

American америка́нец (m.) /америка́нка (f.) *(ah-mee-ree-KAHN-eets/ah-mee-ree-KAHN-kuh)*; америка́нский (adj.) *(amee-ree-KAHN-skee)*

ankle щи́колотка (f.) *(SHEE-kuh-luht-kuh)*

apartment кварти́ра (f.) *(kvahr-TEE-ruh)*

apple я́блоко (n.) *(YAH-bluh-kuh)*

apricot абрико́с (m.) *(ah-bree-KAWS)*

April апре́ль (m.) *(ah-PRYEHL')*

Argentinian аргенти́нец (m.)/аргенти́нка (f.) *(ahr-geen-TEEN-eets/ahr-geen-TEEN-kuh)*

arm рука́ (f.) *(roo-KAH)*

armchair кре́сло (n.) *(KRYEH-sluh)*

artist худо́жник (m.) *(khoo-DAWZH-neek)*

ashtray пе́пельница (f.) *(PYEH-peel'-nee-tsuh)*

aspirin аспири́н (m.) *(ahs-pee-REEN)*

August а́вгуст (m.) *(AHV-goost)*

aunt тётя (f.) *(TYAW-tyuh)*

Austrian австри́ец (m.)/
австри́йка (f.) *(ahf-STREE-
yeets/ahf-STREE-kuh)*

B

back (body part) спина́
(f.) *(spee-NAH)*

  (direction) наза́д *(nah-
ZAHT)*

  (location) сза́ди *(ZAH-dee)*

bad плохо́й *(plah-KHOY)*

badly пло́хо *(PLAW-khuh)*

baggage cart теле́жка
(f.) *(tee-LYEHSH-kuh)*

baked запечённое *(zuh-pee-
CHAW-nuh-yuh)*

balcony балко́н (m.) *(bahl-
KAWN)*

ball мяч (m.) *(myahch)*

ballet бале́т (m.) *(bah-LYEHT)*

bank ба́нк (m.) *(bahnk)*

bar ба́р (m.) *(bahr)*

barber парикма́хер
(m.) *(puh-reek-MAH-khuhr)*

barbershop
парикма́херская (f.) *(puh-
reek-MAH-kheer-skuh-yuh)*

bathing suit купа́льник
(m.) *(koo-PAHL'-neek)*

bathroom ва́нная (f.) *(VAHN-
nuh-yuh)*

battery (automobile)
аккумуля́тор (m.) *(ah-koo-
moo-LYAH-tuhr)*

beach пляж (m.) *(plyahsh)*

beard борода́ (f.) *(buh-rah-
DAH)*

beautiful краси́вый *(krah-
SEE-vy)*

beauty salon
парикма́херская (f.) *(puh-
reek-MAHKH-eer-skuh-yuh)*

beer пи́во (n.) *(PEE-vuh)*

bed крова́ть (f.) *(krah-VAHT')*

bedroom спа́льня
(f.) *(SPAHL'-nyuh)*

before до *(daw)*

belt реме́нь (m.) *(ree-
MYEHN')*

beverages напи́тки
(pl.) *(nah-PEET-kee)*

bill счёт (m.) *(shawt)*

bird пти́ца (f.) *(PTEE-tsuh)*

bite уку́с (m.) *(oo-KOOS)*

  to bite куса́ть *(koo-SAHT')*

black чёрный *(CHAWR-ny)*

blanket одея́ло (n.) *(ah-dee-
YAH-luh)*

block (city) кварта́л
(m.) *(kvahr-TAHL)*

blond белоку́рый *(byeh-lah-
KOO-ry)*

blood кровь (f.) *(krawf')*

blouse блу́зка (f.) *(BLOOS-
kuh)*

blue (dark) си́ний *(SEE-nee)*

  (light) голубо́й *(guh-loo-
BOY)*

boiled варёное *(vah-RYAW-
nuh-yuh)*

bone ко́сть (f.) *(kawst')*

book кни́га (f.) *(KNEE-guh)*

  guidebook
путеводи́тель (m.) *(poo-
tee-vah-DEE-teel')*

bookstore кни́жный
магази́н (m.) *(KNEEZH-ny
muh-gah-ZEEN)*

border грани́ца (f.) *(grah-
NEE-tsuh)*

bottle буты́лка (f.) *(boo-TYL-kuh)*

bracelet брасле́т (m.) *(brahs-LYEHT)*

braised тушёное *(too-SHAW-nuh-yuh)*

brakes (automobile) тормоза́ (pl.) *(tuhr-mah-ZAH)*

Brazilian брази́лец (m.)/ бразилья́нка (f.) *(brah-ZEEL-eets/brah-zeel-YAHN-kuh)*

bread хле́б (m.) *(khlyehp)*

break лома́ть/слома́ть *(lah-MAHT'/slah-MAHT')*

breakfast за́втрак (m.) *(ZAHF-truhk)*

bridge мост (m.) *(mawst)*

bring (by conveyance) привози́ть/ привезти́ *(pree-vah-ZEET'/pree-vees-TEE)*

   (on foot) приводи́ть/ привести́ *(pree-vah-DEET'/pree-vees-TEE)*

broiled обжа́реное *(ahb-ZHAHR-ee-nuh-yuh)*

brooch бро́шка (f.) *(BRAW-shkuh)*

brown кори́чневый *(kah-REECH-nee-vy)*

bruise (injury) синя́к (m.) *(see-NYAHK)*

bulb (electric) ла́мпочка (f.) *(LAHM-puhch-kuh)*

burn (injury) ожо́г (m.) *(ah-ZHAWK)*

   to burn же́чь/ поджё́чь *(zhaych/pahd-ZHAYCH')*

bus авто́бус (m.) *(ahf-TAW-boos)*

bus station автовокза́л (m.) *(ahf-tuh-vahg-ZAHL)*

business дела́ (n. pl.) *(dee-LAH)*

   businessman бизнесме́н (m.) *(beez-nees-MYEHN)*

   business trip командиро́вка (f.) *(kuh-muhn-dee-RAWF-kuh)*

but но *(naw)*

butter ма́сло (n.) *(MAH-sluh)*

button пу́говица (f.) *(POO-guh-vee-tsuh)*

buy покупа́ть/купи́ть *(puh-koo-PAHT'/koo-PEET')*

C

cafe кафе́ (n.) *(kah-FEH)*

call (name) звать/ позва́ть *(zvaht'/pah-ZHAHT')*

   (summon) вызыва́ть/ вы́звать *(vy-zy-VAHT'/VY-zvuht')*

   (telephone) звони́ть/ позвони́ть *(zvah-NEET'/puh-zvah-NEET')*

   to be called называ́ться *(nuh-zy-VAH-tsuh)*

Canadian кана́дец (m.)/ кана́дка (f.) *(kah-NAH-deets/kah-NAHT-kuh)*; кана́дский (adj.) *(kah-NAHT-skee)*

candy конфе́ты (pl.) *(kahn-FYEHT-y)*

car маши́на (f.) *(mah-SHY-nuh)*

carburetor карбюра́тор (m.) *(kahr-byoo-RAH-tuhr)*

carefully осторо́жно (adv.) *(ahs-tah-RAWZH-nuh)*

carry-on luggage ручна́я кладь (f.) *(rooch-NAH-yuh klaht')*

cathedral собо́р (m.) *(sah-BAWR)*

Catholic католи́ческий *(kuh-tah-LEE-chees-kee)*

ceiling потоло́к (m.) *(puh-tah-LAWK)*

center це́нтр (m.) *(TSEHN-tuhr)*

chain (jewelry) цепо́чка (f.) *(tsy-PAWCH-kuh)*

chair стул (m.) *(stool)*

change ме́лочь (f.) *(MYEH-luhch)*

> **to change (bills to coins)** разме́нивать/разменя́ть *(rahz-meen-YAHT'/rahz-MYEH-nee-vuht')*

> **to change (from one currency to another)** меня́ть/поменя́ть *(meen-YAHT'/pah-meen-YAHT')*

cheap дёшево *(DYAW-shuh-vuh)*

check чек (m.) *(chyek)*

> **traveler's check** доро́жный чек *(dah-RAWZH-ny chyek)*

cheese сыр (m.) *(syr)*

chest (body part) грудь (f.) *(groot)*

child ребёнок (m.); де́ти (pl.) *(ree-BYAWN-uhk; DYEHY-tee)*

chill озно́б (m.) *(ah-ZNAWP)*

China Кита́й (m.) *(kee-TAHY)*

Chinese кита́ец/китая́нка (noun) *(kee-TAH-eets/kee-tah-YAHN-kuh)*

Christmas Рождество́ (n.) *(ruhzh-deest-VAW)*

church це́рковь (f.) *(TSEHR-kuhf')*

cigarette сигаре́та (f.) *(see-gah-RYEH-tuh)*

circus цирк (m.) *(tsyrk)*

city го́род (m.) *(GAWR-uht)*

class класс (m.) *(klahs)*

clean убира́ть/убра́ть (v.) *(oo-bee-RAHT'/oo-BRAHT')*

clock часы́ (pl.) *(chee-SY)*

close (near, not far) бли́зко; недалеко́ *(BLEES-kuh; nee-duh-lee-KAW)*

> **closed** закры́т (-a, -o, -ы) *(zah-KRYT-uh, -uh, -y)*

> **to close** закрыва́ть/закры́ть *(zuh-kry-VAHT'/zah-KRYT')*

clothes оде́жда (f.) *(ah-DYEHZH-duh)*

cloud о́блако (n.) *(AW-bluh-kuh)*

> **cloudy** па́смурно *(PAHS-moor-nuh)*

coffee ко́фе (n.) *(KAW-feh)*

coins ме́лочь (f.) *(MYEH-luhch)*

cold (illness) простуда (f.) *(prah-STOO-duh)*
> **(temperature)** холо́дный *(khah-LAWD-ny)*

colleague колле́га (m) *(kah-LYEHG-uh)*

comb расчёска (f.) *(rahs-CHAWS-kuh)*

comedy коме́дия (f.) *(kah-MYEHY-dee-yuh)*

complain жа́ловаться/ пожа́ловаться (v.) *(ZHAHL-uh-vuh-tsuh/pah-ZHAHL-uh-vuy-tsuh)*

convent монасты́рь (m.) *(muh-nahs-TYR')*

cost сто́ить (v.) *(STAW-eet')*

cotton (fabric) хло́пок (m.) *(KHLAWP-uhk)*

   (medical) ва́та (f.) *(VAH-tuh)*

couch дива́н (m.) *(dee-VAHN)*

cough ка́шель (m.) *(KAH-shyl')*

   to cough ка́шлять/ пока́шлять *(KAH-shleet/pah-KAH-shleet')*

country (nation) страна́ (f.) *(strah-NAH)*

country house да́ча (f.) *(DAH-chuh)*

countryside дере́вня (f.) *(dee-RYEHV-nyuh)*

cream сли́вки (pl.) *(SLEEF-kee)*

credit card креди́тная ка́рточка (f.) *(kree-DEET-nuh-yuh KAHR-tuhch-kuh)*

cucumber огуре́ц (m.) *(ah-goo-RYEHTS)*

cup ча́шка (f.) *(CHAHSH-kuh)*

currency валю́та (f.) *(vah-LYOO-tuh)*

customer клие́нт (m.)/ клие́нтка (f.) *(klee-YEHNT/ klee-YEHNT-kuh)*

cut (hair) подстрига́ть/ подстри́чь (v.) *(puhd-stree-GAHT'/puhd-STREECH)*

D

dance та́нец (m.) *(TAH-neets)*

   to dance танцева́ть/ потанцева́ть *(tuhn-tsy-VAHT'/puh-tuhn-tsy-VAHT')*

dangerous опа́сно *(ah-PAHS-nuh)*

dark тёмный *(TYAWM-ny)*

date (calendar) да́та (f.) *(DAH-tuh)*

   (day) число́ (n.) *(chees-LAW)*

daughter до́чь (f.) *(dawch)*

day де́нь (m.) *(dyehn')*

December дека́брь (m.) *(dee-KAH-buhr')*

declaration (customs) деклара́ция (f.) *(dee-klah-RAH-tsy-yuh)*

dentist зубно́й вра́ч (m.) *(zoob-NOY vrahch)*

denture проте́з (m.) *(prah-TYEHS)*

deodorant деодора́нт (m.) *(dee-uh-dah-RAHNT)*

department store универма́г (m.) *(oo-nee-veer-MAHK)*

desk сто́л (m.) *(stawl)*

dictionary слова́рь (m.) *(slah-VAHR')*

different по-друго́му *(puh-droo-GAW-moo)*

difficult тру́дно *(TROOD-nuh)*

dining car ваго́н-рестора́н (m.) *(vah-GAWN rees-tah-RAHN)*

dining room столо́вая (f.) *(stah-LAW-vuh-yuh)*

dinner у́жин (m.) *(OO-zhyn)*

219

ENGLISH/RUSSIAN

direct прямо́й (adj.) (pree-MOY)
  directly пря́мо (PRYAH-muh)
dish (food) блю́до (n.) (BLYOO-duh)
  (plate) таре́лка (f.) (tah-RYEHL-kuh)
disturb меша́ть/помеша́ть (mee-SHAHT'/puh-mee-SHAHT')
dizziness головокруже́ние (n.) (guh-luh-vuh-kroo-ZHEH-nee-yuh)
doctor врач (m.) (vrahch)
double bed двухспа́льная крова́ть (f.) (dvookh-SPAHL'-nuh-yuh krah-VAHT')
double room двухме́стный но́мер (m.) (dvookh-MYEHS-ny NAW-meer)
down вниз (adv.) (vnees)
downstairs внизу́ (adv.) (vnee-ZOO)
dozen дю́жина (f.) (DYOO-zhy-nuh)
drama дра́ма (f.) (DRAH-muh)
dress пла́тье (n.) (PLAH-tyuh)
  to dress одева́ться/оде́ться (ah-dee-VAH-tsuh/ah-DYAY-tsuh)
drink напи́ток (m.) (nah-PEE-tuhk)
  to drink пить/попи́ть (peet'/pah-PEET')
drive (a car) води́ть маши́ну (vah-DEET' mah-SHY-noo)

driver шофёр (m.) (shah-FYAWR)
  driver's license води́тельские права́ (pl.) (vah-DEET-eel'-skee-yuh prah-VAH)
dry сухо́й (soo-KHAWY)
dry cleaning химчи́стка (f.) (kheem-CHEEST-kuh)
Dutch голла́ндец (m.)/голла́ндка (f.) (gah-LAHN-deets/gah-LANHT-kuh); голла́ндский (adj.) (gah-LAHNT-skee)
  in Dutch по-голла́ндски (adv.) (puh-gah-LAHNT-skee)
duty (customs) по́шлина (f.) (PAWSH-lee-nuh)
  duty-free беспо́шлинный (bees-PAWSH-ly-ny)

E

ear у́хо (n.) (OO-khuh)
early ра́нний (adj.) (RAH-nee); ра́но (adv.) (RAH-nuh)
east восто́к (m.) (vah-STAWK)
Easter Па́сха (f.) (PAHS-khuh)
eat есть/пое́сть (yayst'/pah-YAYST')
egg яйцо́ (n.) (yee-TSAW)
eight во́семь (VAW-seem')
eighteen восемна́дцать (VAW-seem-nuht-suht')
eighth восьмо́й/восьма́я/восьмо́е (vahs'-MOY/vahs'-MAH-yuh/vahs'-MAW-yeh)
eighty во́семьдесят (VAW-seem'-dee-seet)

220

electric электри́ческий *(ee-leek-TREE-chees-kee)*

elevator лифт *(m.)* *(leeft)*

eleven оди́ннадцать *(ah-DEEN-uht-suht')*

England Англия *(f.)* *(AHN-glee-yuh)*

English англича́нин *(m.)*/ англича́нка *(f.)* *(ahn-glee-CHAHN-een/ahn-glee-CHAHN-kuh)*; англи́йский *(adj.)* *(ahn-GLEE-skee)*

   in English по-англи́йски *(adv.)* *(puh-ahn-GLEE-skee)*

enough доста́точно *(adv.)* *(dah-STAH-tuhch-nuh)*

   to be enough хвата́ть/ хвати́ть *(khvah-TAHT'/ khvah-TEET')*

entrance вход *(m.)* *(fkhawt)*

evening, in the ве́чером *(VYEH-chee-ruhm)*

exchange (money) меня́ть /поменя́ть *(v.)* *(meen-YAHT'/ puh-meen-YAHT')*

   exchange office ба́нк обме́на валю́ты *(m.)* *(bahnk ahb-MYEH-nuh vah-LYOO-ty)*

excursion экску́рсия *(f.)* *(eeks-KOOR-see-yuh)*

excuse извиня́ть/ извини́ть *(v.)* *(ee-zvee-NYAHT'/ee-zvee-NEET')*

exit вы́ход *(m.)* *(VY-khuht)*

expensive до́рого *(DAW-ruh-guh)*

extract удаля́ть/удали́ть *(v.)* *(oo-dah-LYAHT'/oo-dah-LEET')*

eye глаз *(m.)* *(glahs)*

eyebrow бро́вь *(f.)* *(brawf')*

eyelash ресни́ца *(f.)* *(rees-NEE-tsuh)*

F

face лицо́ *(n.)* *(lee-TSAW)*

facial ма́ска для лица́ *(f.)* *(MAH-skuh dlyah lee-TSAH)*

factory заво́д *(m.)* *(zah-VAWT)*

fall (season) о́сень *(f.)* *(AW-seen')*

family семья́ *(f.)* *(see-MYAH)*

fan вентиля́тор *(m.)* *(veen-tee-LYAH-tuhr)*

far далеко́ *(duh-lee-KAW)*

fare (fee) проездна́я пла́та *(f.)* *(prah-yeez-NAH-yuh PLAH-tuh)*

fat жир *(m.)* *(zhyr)*

favorite люби́мый *(adj.)* *(lyoo-BEE-my)*

February февра́ль *(m.)* *(fee-VRAHL')*

feel чу́вствовать себя́/почу́вствовать себя́ *(v.)* *(CHOOST-vuh-vuht' see-BYAH/pah-CHOOST-vuh-vuht' see-BYAH)*

fever жар *(m.)* *(zhahr)*

fifteen пятна́дцать *(peet-NAHT-suht')*

fifth пя́тый *(PYAH-ty)*

fifty пятьдеся́т *(pee-dee-SYAHT)*

fill заполня́ть/запо́лнить *(v.)* *(zuh-pahl-NYAHT'/zah-PAWL-neet')*

   fill a tooth запломби́ровать *(zuh-plahm-BEER-uh-vuht')*

221

filling (tooth) пломба (f.) *(PLAWM-buh)*

film (camera) плёнка (f.) *(PLYAWN-kuh)*
(movie) кино (n.) *(kee-NAW)*

finally наконец *(nuh-kah-NYEHTS)*

finger палец (m.) *(PAH-leets)*

finish заканчивать/закончить (v.) *(zah-KAHN-chee-vuht'/zah-KAWN-cheet')*

first первый *(PYEHR-vy)*
first aid первая помощь (f.) *(PYEHR-vuh-yuh PAW-muhsh)*

fish рыба (f.) *(RY-buh)*

fit (clothing) подходить *(paht-khah-DEET')*

five пять *(pyaht')*

fix чинить/починить *(chee-NEET'/puh-chee-NEET')*

flashlight фонарь (m.) *(fah-NAHR')*

flight рейс (m.) *(ryehys)*

floor пол (m.) *(pawl)*

flour мука (f.) *(moo-KAH)*

flower цветок (m.) *(tsvyeht-OHK)*

foggy туманно *(too-MAH-nuh)*

food еда (f.) *(yee-DAH)*

foot нога (f.) *(nah-GAH)*
on foot пешком (adv.) *(peesh-KAWM)*

for для (gen.) *(dlyah)*

forbidden нельзя *(neel'-ZYAH)*

foreign иностранный *(ee-nah-STRAH-ny)*

fork вилка (f.) *(VEEL-kuh)*

form анкета (f.) *(ahn-KYEH-tuh)*

forty сорок *(SAW-ruhk)*

four четыре *(chee-TY-ree)*

fourteen четырнадцать *(chee-TYR-nuht-suht)*

fourth четвёртый *(cheet-VYAWR-ty)*

fowl птица (f.) *(PTEE-tsuh)*

free (independent, unoccupied) свободно *(svah-BAWD-nuh)*
(of charge) бесплатно *(bees-PLAHT-nuh)*

French
French person француз (m.)/француженка (f.) *(frahn-TSOOS/frahn-TSOO-zhyn-kuh);* французский (adj.) *(frahn-TSOO-skee)*
in French по-французски (adv.) *(puh-frahn-TSOOS-kee)*

Friday пятница (f.) *(PYAHT-nee-tsuh)*

friend друг (m.)/подруга (f.) *(drook/pah-DROO-guh)*

from из; от; с *(ees; awt; suh)*

front (position) впереди *(fpee-ree-DEE)*

fruit фрукт (m.) *(frookt)*

G

garage гараж (m.) *(gah-RAHSH)*

garden сад (m.) *(saht)*

gas (fuel) бензи́н (m.) *(been-ZEEN)*

gas station бензозапра́вочная ста́нция (f.) *(been-zuh-zah-PRAH-vuhch-nuh-yuh STAHN-tsy-yuh)*

gauze ма́рля (f.) *(MAHR-lyuh)*

gears (automobile) переключе́ние (n.) *(pee-ree-klyoo-CHEH-nye)*

German не́мец (m.)/не́мка (f.) *(NYEH-meets/NYEHM-kuh)*; неме́цкий (adj.) *(nee-MYEHT-skee)*

in German по-неме́цки (adv.) *(puh-nee-MYEHT-skee)*

get (obtain) получа́ть/получи́ть *(puh-loo-CHAHT'/puh-loo-CHEET')*

to get off/out выходи́ть /вы́йти *(vy-khah-DEET'/VY-tee)*

to get on сади́ться/ сесть *(sah-DEET-suh/syehst')*

to get to проходи́ть/ пройти́ *(pruh-khah-DEET'/pruh-ee-TEE)*

gift пода́рок (m.) *(pah-DAHR-uhk)*

girl де́вушка (f.) *(DYEH-voosh-kuh)*

glass (drinking) стака́н (m.) *(stah-KAHN)*

(material) стекло́ (n.) *(stee-KLAW)*

glasses (eye) очки́ (pl.) *(ahch-KEE)*

to go* (on foot →) идти́/ пойти́ *(ee-TEE'/puh-ee-TEE')*

(on foot ↔) ходи́ть/ походи́ть *(khah-DEET'/puh-khah-DEET')*

(by vehicle →) е́хать/ пое́хать *(YEH-khuht'/pah-YEH-khuht')*

(by vehicle ↔) е́здить/ пое́здить *(YEHZ-deet'/pah-YEHZ-deet')*

gold зо́лото (n.) *(ZAW-luh-tuh)*

good добро́ (n.) *(dah-BRAW)*; до́брый (adj.) *(DAW-bry)*

good-bye! до свида́ния! *(duh svee-DAH-nee-yuh!)*

grandfather де́душка (m.) *(DYEH-doosh-kuh)*

grandmother ба́бушка (f.) *(BAH-boosh-kuh)*

gray се́рый *(SYEH-ry)*

green зелёный *(zee-LYAW-ny)*

guest гость (m.) *(gawst')*

guest card (hotel) визи́тная ка́рточка (f.) *(vee-ZEET-nuh-yuh KAHR-tuhch-kuh)*

gum (chewing) жва́чка (f.) *(ZHVAHCH-kuh)*

---

*The verb *to go* in Russian is different depending on whether you go on foot or by a vehicle. Different verbs are used to show that the subject is moving in one direction (→), or going back and forth as when making a round trip (↔).

H

hair во́лосы (pl.) *(VAW-luh-sy)*

hairbrush щётка (f.) *(SHAWT-kuh)*

haircut стри́жка (f.) *(STREESH-kuh)*

hair spray лак (m.) *(lahk)*

half полови́на (f.) *(puh-lah-VEE-nuh)*

hand рука́ (f.) *(roo-KAH)*

handbag су́мка (f.) *(SOOM-kuh)*

handkerchief плато́к (m.) *(plah-TAWK)*

hanger ве́шалка (f.) *(VYEH-shuhl-kuh)*

happy счастли́вый *(SHAST-lee-vy)*

Happy New Year! С Но́вым го́дом! *(S'NAW-vym GAWD-uhm!)*

hat ша́пка (f.) *(SHAHP-kuh)*

he он *(awn)*

head голова́ (f.) *(guh-lah-VAH)*

> **headache** головна́я боль (f.) *(gah-lahv-NAH-yuh bowl')*

headlights фа́ры (pl.) *(FAH-ry)*

health здоро́вье (n.) *(zdah-RAWV-yeh)*

hear слы́шать *(SLYSH-uht')*

heart се́рдце (n.) *(SYEHR-tsuh)*

heat отопле́ние (n.) *(ah-tah-PLYEH-nyeh)*

hello! здра́вствуйте! *(ZDRAH-stvooy-tyeh!)*

(telephone) алло́! *(ah-LAW!)*

help помога́ть/помо́чь (v.) *(puh-mah-GAHT'/pah-MAWCH')*

Help! На по́мощь! *(nah PAW-muhsh!)*

her её/ей *(yee-YAW/yehy)*

here (location) вот *(vawt)*; тут *(toot)*; здесь *(zdyehys')*
> **(motion)** сюда́ *(syoo-DAH)*

hers её *(yee-YAW)*

high высо́кий *(vy-SAW-kee)*

highway шоссе́ (n.) *(shah-SEH)*

him его́/ему́ *(yee-VAW/yee-MOO)*

hip бедро́ (n.) *(bee-DRAW)*

his его́ *(yee-VAW)*
> **his/her/one's own** свой *(svoy)*

hospital больни́ца (f.) *(bahl'-NEE-tsuh)*

hospitality гостеприи́мство (n.) *(guhs-tee-PREE-eems-tvuh)*

hot горя́чий *(gah-RYAH-chee)*

hotel гости́ница (f.) *(gah-STEE-nee-tsuh)*

hour час (m.) *(chahs)*

house дом (m.) *(dawm)*

how как *(kahk)*

how much ско́лько *(SKAWL'-kuh)*

hundred сто *(staw)*
> **a hundred and . . .** сто . . . *(staw . . .)*

hurry спеши́ть (v.) *(spee-SHYT')*

husband муж (m.) *(moosh)*

I

I я *(yah)*

ice лёд (m.) *(lyawt)*

ignition (automobile) зажига́ние (n.) *(zuh-zhy-GAH-nyuh)*

ill больно́й *(bahl'-NOY)*

illness боле́знь (f.) *(bah-LYEHZN')*

imagine представля́ть/ предста́вить *(preet-stah-VLYAHT'/preet-STAH-veet')*

in, into в *(v)*

included, to be включа́ться (imp.) *(fklyoo-CHAHT-suh)*

information спра́вки (f.pl.) *(SPRAHF-kee)*

injection уко́л (m.) *(oo-KAWL)*

insect насеко́мое (m.) *(nuh-see-KAW-muh-yeh)*

insurance страхо́вка (f.) *(strah-KHAWF-kuh)*

interesting интере́сно *(een-tee-RYEHS-nuh)*

international междунаро́дный *(meezh-doo-nah-RAWD-ny)*

interpreter перево́дчик (m.) *(pee-ree-VAWT-cheek)*

introduce (oneself) представля́ть(-ся)/ предста́вить(-ся) *(preet-stah-VLYAHT-suh/preet-STAH-veet-suh)*

invite приглаша́ть/ пригласи́ть *(pree-glah-SHAHT'/pree-glah-SEET')*

iodine йод (m.) *(yawt)*

iron (flat-) утю́г (m.) *(oo-TYOOK)*

(metal) желе́зо (n.) *(zhy-LYEH-zuh)*

to iron гла́дить/ погла́дить *(GLAH-deet'/pah-GLAH-deet')*

J

jack (automobile) домкра́т (m.) *(dahm-KRAHT)*

jam варе́нье (n.) *(vah-RYEH-nyuh)*

January янва́рь (m.) *(yeen-VAHR')*

jaw че́люсть (f.) *(CHEH-lyoost')*

jewelry драгоце́нности (pl.) *(druh-gah-TSEH-nuhs-tee)*

jewelry store ювели́рный магази́н (m.) *(yoo-vee-LEER-ny muh-gah-ZEEN)*

Jewish евре́йский *(yee-VREHY-skee)*

journey пое́здка (f.) *(pah-YEHST-kuh)*

juice сок (m.) *(sawk)*

July ию́ль (m.) *(ee-YOOL')*

June ию́нь (m.) *(ee-YOON')*

K

key ключ (m.) *(klyooch)*

kilogram килогра́мм (m.) *(kee-lah-GRAHM)*

kilometer киломе́тр (m.) *(kee-lah-MYEH-tuhr)*

kitchen ку́хня (f.) *(KOOKH-nyuh)*

knife нож (m.) *(nawsh)*

know знать *(znaht')*

225

lace крýжево (n.) (KROO-zhy-vuh)

ladies' room жéнский туалéт (m.) (ZHEHN-skee too-ah-LYEHT)

lamb барáнина (f.) (bah-RAH-nee-nuh)

lamp лáмпа (f.) (LAHM-puh)

language язы́к (m.) (yee-ZYK)

large большóй (bahl'-SHOY)

last (final) послéдний (adj.) (pah-SLYEHD-nee)
   (preceding) прóшлый (PRAWSH-ly)

late пóздний (adj.) (PAWZ-nee); пóздно (adv.) (PAWZ-nuh)

laundry прáчечная (f.) (PRAH-cheech-nuh-yuh)

lawyer адвокáт (m.) (ahd-vah-KAHT)

laxative слабúтельное (n.) (slah-BEE-teel'-nuh-yuh)

leather кóжа (f.) (KAW-zhuh)

leave (by conveyance) уезжáть/уéхать (oo-yee-ZHAHT'/oo-YEH-khuht')
   (by foot) уходúть/уйтú (oo-khah-DEET'/oo-ee-TEE)

left (direction) налéво (nah-LYEH-vuh)
   (location) слéва (SLYEH-vuh)

leg ногá (f.) (nah-GAH)

lemon лимóн (m.) (lee-MAWN)

lens лúнза (f.) (LEEN-zuh)

library библиотéка (f.) (bee-blee-ah-TYEHK-uh)

lie (down) ложúться/лечь (lah-ZHY-tsuh/lyehych)

life жизнь (f.) (zhyzn')
   lifeguard спасáтель (m.) (spah-SAH-teel')

light свет (m.) (svyeht)
   to light зажигáть/зажéчь (zuh-zhy-GAHT'/zah-ZHAYCH)

lighter (cigarette) зажигáлка (f.) (zah-zhy-GAHL-kuh)

like нрáвиться (NRAH-veet-suh)

line лúния (f.) (LEE-nee-yuh)

linen лён (m.) (lyawn)

lip губá (f.) (goo-BAH)

liter литр (m.) (LEE-tuhr)

little мáло (adv.) (MAH-luh); мáленький (adj.) (MAH-leen'-kee)

live жить (zhyt')

liver пéчень (f.) (PYEH-cheen')

living room гостúная (f.) (gah-STEE-nuh-yuh)

lobby вестибю́ль (m.) (vees-tee-BYOOL')

located, be находúться (nuh-khah-DEET-suh)

lock замóк (m.) (zah-MAWK)

long длúнный (adj.) (DLEE-ny)
   long time дóлго (DAWL-guh)

look смотрéть/посмотрéть (smah-TREHYT'/puh-smah-TREHYT')

lose теря́ть/потеря́ть (tee-RYAHT'/puh-tee-RYAHT')

lost-baggage office ро́зыск багажа́ (RAWZ-ysk buh-gah-ZHAH)

lot, much мно́го (adv.) (MNAW-guh)

lotion (face) крем для лица́ (m.) (kryehm dlyah lee-TSAH)

love люби́ть (v.) (lyoo-BEET')

luggage бага́ж (m.) (bah-GAHSH)

  luggage tag би́рка (f.) (BEER-kuh)

lunch обе́д (m.) (ah-BYEHT)

M

magazine журна́л (m.) (zhoor-NAHL)

maid го́рничная (f.) (GAWR-neech-nuh-yuh)

mailbox почто́вый я́щик (m.) (pahch-TAW-vy YAH-sheek)

make де́лать/сде́лать (DYEH-luht'/ZDYEH-luht)

man мужчи́на (m.) (moo-SHY-nuh)

manager администра́тор (m.) (ahd-mee-nee-STRAH-tuhr)

manicure маникю́р (m.) (muh-nee-KYOOR)

map ка́рта (f.) (KAHR-tuh)

March март (m.) (mahrt)

market ры́нок (m.) (RY-nuhk)

mass слу́жба (f.) (SLOOZH-buh)

matches спи́чки (pl.) (SPEECH-kee)

May май (m.) (mahy)

me меня́/мне/мной (mee-NYAH/mnyeh/mnoy)

meal пита́ние (n.) (pee-TAH-nyeh)

meat мя́со (n.) (MYAH-suh)

medicine лека́рство (n.) (lee-KAHRST-vuh)

meet (encounter) встреча́ться/встре́титься (fstree-CHAHT-suh/FSTRYEH-teet-suh)

  (for the first time) знако́миться/познако́миться (znah-KAW-meet-suh/puh-znah-KA-W-meet-suh)

memory па́мять (f.) (PAH-myet')

mend што́пать/зашто́пать (SHTAW-puht'/zah-SHTAW-puht')

menu меню́ (n.) (mee-NYOO)

Merry Christmas! С рождество́м! (s'ruzh-deest-VAWM!)

meter (length) метр (m.) (MYEH-tuhr)

  (taxi) счётчик (m.) (SHAWT-cheek)

middle (location) середи́на (f.) (see-ree-DEE-nuh)

midnight по́лночь (f.) (PAWL-nuhch)

milk молоко́ (n.) (muh-lah-KAW)

million миллио́н (m.) (mee-LYAWN)

mine мой (moy)

227

mineral water
минера́льная вода́ (f.) (mee-nee-RAHL'-nuh-yuh vah-DAH)

minister па́стор (m.) (PAHS-tuhr)

minute мину́та (f.) (mee-NOO-tuh)

mirror зе́ркало (n.) (ZYEHR-kuh-luh)

miss (fail to . . .)
пропуска́ть/
пропусти́ть (pruh-poos-KAHT'/pruh-poos-TEET')

(someone) скучать (skoo-CHAHT')

mistake оши́бка (f.) (ah-SHYP-kuh)

to be mistaken
ошиба́ться/
ошиби́ться (ah-shy-BAHT-suh/ah-shy-BEET-suh)

monastery монасты́рь (m.) (muh-nahs-TYR')

Monday понеде́льник (m.) (puh-nee-DYEHL'-neek)

money де́ньги (pl.) (DYEHN'-gee)

month ме́сяц (m.) (MYEH-seets)

monument па́мятник (m.) (PAH-meet-neek)

more ещё (ee-SHAW)

morning у́тром (adv.) (OO-truhm)

most са́мый (adj.) (SAH-my)

mother мать (f.) (maht')

mountain гора́ (f.) (gah-RAH)

mouth рот (m.) (rawt)

mouthwash зубно́й эликси́р (m.) (zoob-NOY ee-leek-SEER)

movies кино́ (n.) (kee-NAW)

museum музе́й (m.) (moo-ZYEHY)

mustache усы́ (pl.) (oo-SY)

mustard горчи́ца (f.) (gahr-CHEE-tsuh)

N

nail (finger-, toe-) но́готь (m.) (NAW-guht')

name и́мя (n.) (EE-myuh)

last name фами́лия (f.) (fah-MEE-lyuh)

napkin салфе́тка (f.) (sahl-FYEHT-kuh)

narrow у́зкий (OOS-kee)

nationality
национа́льность (f.) (nuh-tsy-ah-NAHL'-nuhst')

nausea тошнота́ (f.) (tuhsh-nah-TAH)

near (close to) о́коло (adv.) (AW-kuh-luh)

nearest ближа́йший (blee-ZHAHY-shee)

neck ше́я (f.) (SHEH-yuh)

necklace ожере́лье (n.) (ah-zhy-RYEH-lyuh)

need ну́жно/нужна́/ну́жен (adv.) (NOOZH-nuh/noozh-NAH/NOOZH-uhn)

new но́вый (NAW-vy)

newspaper газе́та (f.) (gah-ZYEH-tuh)

newsstand кио́ск (m.) (kee-AWSK)

New Year Но́вый Год (m.) (NAW-vy gawt)

next пото́м (adv.) (pah-TAWM); сле́дующий (adj.) (SLYEH-doo-yoo-shee)

nice прия́тно (adv.) *(pree-YAHT-nuh);* прия́тный (adj.) *(pree-YAHT-ny)*

night ночь (f.) *(nawch')*

nightclub ночно́й клуб (m.) *(nahch-NOY kloop)*

nine де́вять (DYEH-veet')

nineteen девятна́дцать *(dee-veet-NAH-tsuht')*

ninety девяно́сто *(dee-vee-NAWS-tuh)*

ninth девя́тый *(dee-VYAH-ty)*

no нет *(nyeht)*

noisy шу́мный *(SHOOM-ny)*

none нет *(nyeht)*

noon по́лдень (m.) *(PAWL-dyeen)*

north се́вер (m.) *(SYEH-veer)*

nose нос (m.) *(naws)*

November ноя́брь (m.) *(nah-YAH-buhr')*

now сейча́с *(syehy-CHAHS)*

number но́мер (m.) *(NAW-meer)*

nurse медсестра́ (f.) *(meed-see-STRAH)*

O

occupied за́нято (ZAHN-yee-tuh)

ocean океа́н (m.) *(ah-kee-AHN)*

October октя́брь (m.) *(ahk-TYAH-buhr')*

of course коне́чно *(kah-NYEHSH-nuh)*

offer предложе́ние (n.) *(preed-lah-ZHEH-nyeh)*
  to offer предлага́ть/предложи́ть *(preed-lah-GAHT'/preed-lah-ZHYT')*

office конто́ра (f.) *(kahn-TAW-ruh)*

oil ма́сло (n.) *(MAH-sluh)*

once оди́н раз *(ah-DEEN rahs)*

one оди́н *(ah-DEEN)*

only то́лько *(TAWL'-kuh)*

open открыва́ть/откры́ть (v.) *(aht-kry-VAHT'/aht-KRYT')*
  opened откры́т (-а, -о, -ы) *(aht-KRYT-uh, -uh, -y)*

opera о́пера (f.) *(AW-pee-ruh)*

operator (telephone) телефони́стка (f.) *(tee-lee-fah-NEEST-kuh)*

orange (color) ора́нжевый *(ah-RAHN-zhy-vy)*
  (fruit) апельси́н (m.) *(ah-peel'-SEEN)*

orchestra орке́стр (m.) *(ahr-KYEHS-tuhr)*

order зака́зывать/заказа́ть (v.) *(zuh-KAH-zy-vaht'/zuh-kah-ZAHT')*

ours наш *(nahsh)*

outlet розе́тка (f.) *(rah-ZYEHT-kuh)*

outside на у́лице *(nah OO-lee-tseh)*

overcoat пальто́ (n.) *(pahl'-TAW)*

P

package посы́лка (f.) *(pah-SYL-kuh)*

pain боль (f.) *(bawl')*

pair па́ра (f.) *(PAH-ruh)*

palace дворе́ц (m.) *(dvah-RYEHTS)*

pants брю́ки (pl.) *(BRYOO-kee)*

229

paper бума́га (f.) *(boo-MAH-guh)*

park парк (m.) *(pahrk)*
  to park (a car) ста́вить маши́ну *(STAH-veet' mah-SHY-noo)*

part часть (f.) *(chahst')*
  to part hair сде́лать пробо́р *(ZDYEH-luht' prah-BAWR)*

passport па́спорт (m.) *(PAHS-puhrt)*

pay плати́ть/ заплати́ть *(plah-TEET'/zuh-plah-TEET')*

pen ру́чка (f.) *(ROOCH-kuh)*

pencil каранда́ш (m.) *(kuh-rahn-DAHSH)*

pepper пе́рец (m.) *(PYEHR-eets)*

perfume духи́ (pl.) *(doo-KHEE)*

permanent (wave) пермане́нт (m.) *(peer-mah-NYEHNT)*

pharmacy апте́ка (f.) *(ahp-TYEH-kuh)*

photograph фотогра́фия (f.) *(fuh-tah-GRAH-fee-yuh)*
  to photograph фотографи́ровать *(fuh-tuh-grah-FEER-uh-vuht')*

picture (art) карти́на (f.) *(kahr-TEE-nuh)*
  motion picture кино́ (n.) *(kee-NAW)*

pill табле́тка (f.) *(tah-BLYEHT-kuh)*

pillow поду́шка (f.) *(pah-DOOSH-kuh)*

pineapple анана́с (m.) *(ah-nah-NAHS)*

place (seat) ме́сто (n.) *(MYEHS-tuh)*

plane (air-) самолёт (m.) *(suh-mah-LYAWT)*

plate таре́лка (f.) *(tah-RYEHL-kuh)*

platform перро́н (m.) *(pee-RAWN)*

play пье́са (f.) *(PYEH-suh)*
  to play игра́ть/ поигра́ть *(ee-GRAHT'/puh-ee-GRAHT')*

pleasant прия́тно *(pree-YAHT-nuh)*

please пожа́луйста *(pah-ZHAHL-stuh)*

pliers плоскогу́бцы (pl.) *(pluhs-kah-GOOP-tsy)*

poison отра́ва (f.) *(ah-TRAH-vuh)*

porter носи́льщик (m.) *(nah-SEEL'-sheek)*

portion по́рция (f.) *(PAWR-tsy-uh)*

postcard откры́тка (f.) *(aht-KRYT-kuh)*

post office почта́мт (m.) *(pahch-TAHMT)*

prefer предпочита́ть *(preed-pah-chee-TAHT')*

prepare гото́вить/ пригото́вить *(gah-TAW-veet'/pree-gah-TAW-veet')*

prescription реце́пт (m.) *(ree-TSEHPT)*

pretty краси́во *(krah-SEE-vuh)*

priest свяще́нник (m.) *(svee-SHEN-eek)*

230

profession профéссия (f.)
(prah-FYEH-see-yuh)

Protestant
протестáнтский (pruh-tees-
TAHN-tskee)

purple фиолéтовый (fee-ah-
LYEHT-uh-vy)

push (sign) от себя́ (aht see-
BYAH)

Q

question вопрóс (m.) (vah-
PRAWS)

to ask a question
задавáть/задáть
вопрóс (zuh-dah-VAHT'/
zah-DAHT' vah-PRAWS)

R

rabbi раввин (m.) (rah-VEEN)

radiator радиáтор (m.) (ruh-
dee-AH-tuhr)

radio рáдио (n.) (RAH-dee-
uh)

razor бритва (f.) (BREET-vuh)

ready готóвый (gah-TAW-vy)

real настоя́щий (nuh-stah-
YAH-shee)

reception (hotel) приёмная
(f.) (pree-YAWM-nuh-yuh)

recommend
рекомендовáть/
порекомендовáть (ree-kah-
meen-dah-VAHT'/puh-ree-kah-
meen-dah-VAHT')

record (phonograph)
пластинка (f.) (plah-STEEN-
kuh)

red крáсный (KRAHS-ny)

rent брать/взять на-
прокáт (v.) (braht'/vzyaht'
nah-prah-KAHT)

repeat повторя́ть/
повторить (v.) (puhf-tuh-
RYAHT'/puhf-tah-REET')

reservation закáз (m.) (zah-
KAHS)

reserve закáзывать/
заказáть (zuh-KAH-zy-vaht'/
zuh-kah-ZAHT')

restaurant ресторáн
(m.) (rees-tah-RAHN)

reverse обрáтно (adv.) (ah-
BRAHT-nuh)

rib ребрó (n.) (ree-BRAW)

right (correct)
прáвильный (PRAH-veel'-ny)

(direction) напрáво (nah-
PRAH-vuh)

(location) спрáва (SPRAH-
vuh)

all right лáдно (LAHD-nuh)

right now сейчáс (syay-
CHAHS)

ring (on finger) кольцó
(n.) (kahl'-TSAW)

river рекá (f.) (ree-KAH)

road дорóга (f.) (dah-RAW-
guh)

robe халáт (m.) (khah-LAHT)

rug ковёр (m.) (kah-VYAWR)

Russian рýсский (m.)/
рýсская (f.) (noun) (ROOS-
kee/ROOS-kuh-yuh)

in Russian по-
рýсски (pah-ROOS-kee)

Russian Orthodox
правослáвный (pruh-vah-
SLAHV-ny)

231

sad печа́льно (pee-CHAHL'-nuh)

safe безопа́сно (beez-ah-PAHS-nuh)

   (for valuables) сейф (m.) (syehf)

   safekeeping хране́ние (n.) (khrah-NYEH-nyeh)

salesman продаве́ц (m.) (pruh-dah-VYEHTS)

saleswoman продавщи́ца (f.) (pruh-dahv-SHEE-tsuh)

salt соль (f.) (sawl')

sandwich бутербро́д (m.) (boo-teer-BRAWT)

Saturday суббо́та (f.) (soo-BAW-tuh)

saucer таре́лка (f.) (tah-RYEHL-kuh)

say говори́ть (imp.) (guh-vah-REET')

screwdriver отвёртка (f.) (aht-VYAWRT-kuh)

sea мо́ре (n.) (MAWR-yeh)

season (time of year) вре́мя го́да (n.) (VRYEH-myuh GAW-duh)

second второ́й/втора́я/второ́е (ftah-ROY/ftah-RAH-yuh/ftah-RAW-yeh)

separate отде́льный (ahd-DYEHL'-ny)

September сентя́брь (m.) (seen-TYAH-buhr')

service облу́живание (n.) (ahb-SLOOZH-y-vuhn-ee-yuh)

services услу́ги (oo-SLOOG-ee)

set (hair) укла́дка (f.) (oo-KLAHT-kuh)

seven семь (syehm')

seventeen семна́дцать (seem-NAHT-seet')

seventy се́мьдесят (SYEHM-dee-seet)

seventh седьмо́й/седьма́я/седьмо́е (seed'-MOY/seed'-MAH-yuh/seed'-MAW-yeh)

several не́сколько (NYEH-skuhl'-kuh)

shade (in the) в тени́ (f.) (ftee-NEE)

   (color) отте́нок (m.) (ah-TYEHN-uhk)

shampoo шампу́нь (m.) (shahm-POON')

shave бри́ться/побри́ться (v.) (BREET-suh/pah-BREET-suh)

she она́ (ah-NAH)

shirt руба́шка (f.) (roo-BAHSH-kuh)

shoes о́бувь (f.) (AW-boof); ту́фли (pl.) (TOOF-lee)

shop магази́н (m.) (muh-gah-ZEEN)

shopping, go ходи́ть за поку́пками (kha-DEET' zah pah-KOOP-kuh-mee)

short коро́ткий (kah-RAWT-kee)

shoulder плечо́ (n.) (plee-CHAW)

show (art) вы́ставка (f.) (VY-stuhf-kuh)

   (movie) сеа́нс (m.) (see-AHNS)

   (performance) выступле́ние (n.) (vy-stoo-PLYEH-nyeh)

to show пока́зывать/
показа́ть *(puh-KAH-zy-vuht'
/puh-kah-ZAHT')*

shower душ (m.) *(doosh)*

sick, be боле́ть *(bah-LYEHYT')*

side сторона́ (f.) *(stuh-rah-NAH)*

  on the side (position)
сбо́ку *(ZBAW-koo)*

sideburns бакенба́рды
(pl.) *(buh-keen-BAHR-dy)*

sidewalk тротуа́р (m.) *(truh-too-AHR)*

sign подпи́сываться/
подписа́ться *(puht-PEES-y-vuht-suh/puht-pee-SAHT-suh)*

silk шёлк (m.) *(shawlk)*

silly глу́по *(GLOO-puh)*

silver серебро́ (n.) *(see-ree-BRAW)*

silverware прибо́ры
(pl.) *(pree-BAW-ry)*

sing петь/попе́ть *(pyehyt'/pah-PYEHYT')*

single room одноме́стный
но́мер (m.) *(ahd-nah-MYEHS-ny NAW-meer)*

sister сестра́ (f.) *(see-STRAH)*

sit сиде́ть *(see-DYEHT')*

  sit down сади́ться/
сесть *(sah-DEET-suh/SYAYST')*

six шесть *(shehst')*

sixteen шестна́дцать *(shys-NAHT-suht)*

sixth шесто́й *(shys-TOY)*

sixty шесмьдеся́т *(shys-dee-SYAHT)*

size разме́р (m.) *(rahz-MYEHR)*

skin ко́жа (f.) *(KAW-zhuh)*

skirt ю́бка (f.) *(YOOP-kuh)*

sleep спать (imp.) *(spaht')*

  sleeping car спа́льный
ваго́н (m.) *(SPAHL'ny vah-GAWN)*

slippers та́почки (pl.) *(TAH-pouhch-kee)*

slow ме́дленный
(adj.) *(MYEH-dlee-ny)*

slowly ме́дленно *(MYEH-dlee-nuh)*

small ма́ленький *(MAH-leen'-kee)*

smoke кури́ть/
закури́ть *(koo-REET'/zah-koo-REET')*

  smoking куря́щий
(adj.) *(koo-RYAH-shee)*

  smoked meat
копчёное мя́со (n.) *(kahp-CHAW-nuh-yuh)*

soap мы́ло (n.) *(MY-law)*

soccer футбо́л (m.) *(food-BAWL)*

socks носки́ (pl.) *(nahs-KEE)*

someone кто́-то *(KTAW-tuh)*

something что́-то *(SHTAW-tuh)*

somewhere где́-то *(GDYEH-tuh)*

son сын (m.) *(syn)*

soon ско́ро *(SKAW-ruh)*

  as soon as possible как
мо́жно скоре́е *(kahk MAWZH-nuh skah-RYAY-yuh)*

sorry, I am прости́те *(prah-STEE-tyeh)*

soup суп (m.) *(soop)*

south юг (m.) *(yook)*

souvenir сувени́р (n.) *(soo-veen-EER)*

Soviet сове́тский (sah-VYEHT-skee)

Soviet Union Сове́тский Сою́з (m.) (sah-VYEHT-skee sah-YOOS)

spark plugs запа́льные све́чи (pl.) (zah-PAHL'ny-yuh SVYEH-chee)

speak говори́ть/ сказа́ть (guh-vah-REET'/skah-ZAHT')

special осо́бый (ah-SAW-by)

spend (money) тра́тить/ потра́тить (TRAH-teet'/pah-TRAH-teet')

(time) проводи́ть/ провести́ вре́мя (pruh-vah-DEET'/pruh-vees-TEE VRYEH-myuh)

spicy о́строе (AW-struh-yuh)

spoon ло́жка (f.) (LAWSH-kuh)

Spring весна́ (f.) (vees-NAH)

square пло́щадь (f.) (PLAW-shut')

stamp (postage) ма́рка (f.) (MAHR-kuh)

stand (taxi) стоя́нка (f.) (stah-YAHN-kuh)

to stand стоя́ть/ постоя́ть (stah-YAHT'/puh-stah-YAHT')

start начина́ть/нача́ть (nuh-chee-NAHT'/nah-CHANT')

(automobile) заводи́ться /завести́сь (zuh-vah-DEE-tsuh/zuh-vees-TEES')

station (gasoline) бензоколо́нка (f.) (been-zuh-kah-LAWN-kuh)

(railroad) вокза́л (m.) (vahg-ZAHL)

(subway) ста́нция метро́ (f.) (STAHN-tsy-yuh mee-TRAW)

stay; stop остана́вливаться /останови́ться (ah-stah-NAH-vlee-vaht-suh/ah-stah-nah-VEET-suh)

steak бифште́кс (m.) (beef-SHTYEHKS)

stomach желу́док (m.) (zhy-LOO-duhk)

stomachache несваре́ние желу́дка (n.) (nee-svah-RYEH-nyuh zhy-LOOT-kuh)

stop (bus) остано́вка (f.) (ah-STAH-nawf-kuh)

store магази́н (m.) (muh-gah-ZEEN)

strange стра́нно (STRAH-nuh)

street у́лица (f.) (OO-lee-tsuh)

string верёвка (f.) (vee-RYAWF-kuh)

strong си́льный (SEEL'-ny)

subway метро́ (n.) (mee-TRAW)

sugar са́хар (m.) (SAH-khur)

suit костю́м (m.) (kahs-TYOOM)

suitcase чемода́н (m.) (chee-mah-DAHN)

summer ле́то (n.) (LYEH-tuh)

sun со́лнце (n.) (SAWN-tsuh)

Sunday воскресе́нье (n.) (vuhs-kree-SYEH-nyeh)

sunglasses со́лнечные очки́ (pl.) (SAWL-neech-ny-yeh ahch-KEE)

234

sunny со́лнечно (*SAWL-neech-nuh*)

sweater сви́тер (m.) (*SVEE-teer*)

swell пу́хнуть/ опу́хнуть (*POO-khnoot'/ah-POOKH-noot*)

swim купа́ться (imp.) (*koo-PAHT-suh*)

(swimming pool) бассе́йн (m.) (*bah-SYEHYN*)

swollen опу́хло (*ah-POOKH-luh*)

synagogue синаго́га (f.) (*see-nah-GAW-guh*)

T

table стол (m.) (*stawl*)

tablespoon столо́вая ло́жка (f.) (*stah-LAW-vuh-yuh LAWSH-kuh*)

to take (accept) бра́ть/ взя́ть (*braht'/vzyaht'*)

(by conveyance) отвози́ть/отвезти́ (*aht-vah-ZEET'/aht-vees-TEE*)

(by hand) относи́ть/ отнести́ (*aht-nah-SEET'/aht-nees-TEE*)

tax нало́г (m.) (*nah-LAWK*)

taxi такси́ (n.) (*tohk-SEE*)

tea чай (m.) (*chahy*)

teacher преподава́тель (-ница) (*pree-puh-dah-VAH-teel', -nee-tsuh*)

teaspoon ча́йная ло́жка (f.) (*CHAY-nuh-yuh LAWSH-kuh*)

telegram телегра́мма (f.) (*tee-lee-GRAHM-uh*)

telegraph посыла́ть/ посла́ть (v.) телегра́мму (*puh-sy-LAHT'/pah-SLAHT' tee-lee-GRAHM-oo*)

telephone телефо́н (m.) (*tee-lee-FAWN*)

telephone number но́мер телефо́на (*NAW-meer tee-lee-FAWN-uh*)

to telephone звони́ть/ позвони́ть (*zvah-NEET'/puh-zvah-NEET'*)

television телеви́зор (m.) (*tee-lee-VEEZ-uhr*)

tell сказа́ть (pf.) (*skah-ZAHT'*)

temperature температу́ра (f.) (*teem-pee-rah-TOO-ruh*)

temporarily вре́менно (*VRYEH-meen-nuh*)

ten де́сять (*DYEH-seet'*)

tenth деся́тый/деся́тая/ деся́тое (*dee-SYAH-ty/dee-SYAH-tuh-yuh/dee-SYAH-tuh-yeh*)

thank you спаси́бо (*spah-SEE-buh*)

theater теа́тр (m.) (*tee-AH-tuhr*)

theirs их (*eekh*)

then тогда́ (*tahg-DAH*)

there (location) там (*tahm*)

(direction, movement) туда́ (adv.) (*too-DAH*)

thermometer термо́метр (m.) (*teer-MAW-meet-uhr*)

they они́ (*ah-NEE*)

think ду́мать/ поду́мать (*DOO-muht'/pah-DOO-muht'*)

235

third тре́тий/тре́тья/
тре́тье *(TRYEH-tee/TRYEH-t'yuh /TRYEH-t'yeh)*

thirteen трина́дцать *(tree-NAHT-suht')*

thirty три́дцать *(TREET-suht')*

thousand ты́сяча *(TY-seech-uh)*

three три *(tree)*

throat го́рло (n.) *(GAWR-luh)*

thumb большо́й па́лец (m.) *(bahl'-SHOY PAH-leets)*

Thursday четве́рг (m.) *(cheet-VYEHRK)*

ticket биле́т (m.) *(bee-LYEHT)*
  ticket window ка́сса (f.) *(KAH-suh)*

tie (neck-) га́лстук (m.) *(GAHL-stook)*

time вре́мя (n.) *(VRYEH-myuh)*
  on time во́время *(VAW-vree-myuh)*

tip чаевы́е (pl.) *(chee-yee-VY-yeh)*

tire (automobile) ши́на (f.) *(SHY-nuh)*

tobacco таба́к (m.) *(tah-BAHK)*

today сего́дня *(see-VAW-dnyuh)*

toilet туале́т (m.) *(too-ah-LYEHT)*
  toilet paper туале́тная бума́га (f.) *(too-ah-LYEHT-nuh-yuh boo-MAH-guh)*

tomato помидо́р (m.) *(puh-mee-DAWR)*

tomorrow за́втра *(ZAHF-truh)*

tongue язы́к (m.) *(yee-ZYK)*

too (also) то́же *(TAW-zhuh)*

(much) сли́шком *(SLEESH-kuhm)*

tooth зуб (m.) *(zoop)*

toothbrush зубна́я щётка (f.) *(zoob-NAH-yuh SHAWT-kuh)*

toothpaste зубна́я па́ста (f.) *(zoob-NAH-yuh PAH-stuh)*

toothpick зубочи́стка (f.) *(zoo-bah-CHEEST-kuh)*

tourist тури́ст (m.)/ тури́стка (f.) *(too-REEST/too-REEST-kuh)*

tow отбукси́ровать *(ahd-book-SEER-uh-vuht')*

towel полоте́нце (n.) *(puh-lah-TYEHN-tsuh)*

train по́езд (m.) *(PAW-yeest)*

transfer де́лать/сде́лать переса́дку *(DYEH-luht'/ ZDYEH-luht' pee-ree-SAHT-koo)*

travel путеше́ствовать *(poo-tee-SHEHST-vuh-vuht')*

true пра́вда *(PRAHV-duh)*

Tuesday вто́рник (m.) *(FTAWR-neek)*

turn поворо́т (m.) *(puh-vah-RAWT)*
  to turn повора́чивать/ поверну́ть *(puh-vah-RAHCH-ee-vuht'/puh-veer-NOOT')*

twelve двена́дцать *(dvee-NAHT-suht')*

twenty два́дцать *(DVAH-tsuht')*

twice два ра́за *(dvah RAH-zuh)*

two два *(dvah)*

typical типи́чный *(tee-PEECH-ny)*

U

umbrella зонт (m.) *(zawnt)*

uncle дядя (m.) *(DYAH-dyuh)*

underpants трусы (pl.) *(troo-SY)*

understand понимать/ понять *(puh-nee-MAHT'/pah-NYAHT')*

United States of America Соединённые Штаты Америки *(sah-yee-dee-NYAW-ny-yeh SHTAH-ty ah-MYEH-ree-kee)*

university университет (m.) *(oo-nee-veer-see-TYEHT)*

up вверх *(vyehrkh)*

upstairs наверху (adv.) *(nuh-veer-KHOO)*

V

vacation отпуск (m.) *(AWT-poosk)*

veal телятина (f.) *(tee-LYAH-tee-nuh)*

vegetables овощи (pl.) *(AW-vuh-shee)*
   (greens) зелень (f.) *(ZYEH-leen')*

velvet бархат (m.) *(BAHR-khuht)*

very очень *(AW-cheen')*

veterinarian ветеринар (m.) *(vee-tee-ree-NAHR)*

view вид (m.) *(veet)*

village деревня (f.) *(dee-RYEHV-nyuh)*

vinegar уксус (m.) *(OOK-soos)*

visa виза (f.) *(VEE-zuh)*

visit посещать/посетить (v.) *(puh-see-SHAHT'/puh-see-TEET')*

visitor посетитель (m.) *(puh-see-TEE-teel')*

W

wait (for) подождать *(puh-dah-ZHDAHT')*

waiter официант (m.) *(ah-fee-tsy-AHNT)*

waitress официантка (f.) *(ah-fee-tsy-AHNT-kuh)*

want хотеть (imp.) *(kha-TYEHYT')*

warm тёплый (adj.) *(TYAWP-ly)*; тепло (adv.) *(tee-PLAW)*

wash стирать/ постирать *(stee-RAHT'/puh-stee-RAHT')*

water вода (f.) *(vah-DAH)*

watermelon арбуз (m.) *(ahr-BOOS)*

watch (timepiece) часы (pl.) *(chee-SY)*
   to watch смотреть/ посмотреть *(smah-TREHYT'/puh-smah-TREHYT')*

we мы *(my)*

weak слабый *(SLAH-by)*

weather погода (f.) *(pah-GAW-duh)*

Wednesday среда (f.) *(sree-DAH)*

week неделя (f.) *(nee-DYEH-luh)*

welcome, you're не за что *(NYEH-zuh-shtuh)*

west запад (m.) *(ZAH-puht)*

what что *(shtaw)*

237

when когда́ (kahg-DAH)
where где (gdyeh)
  where, from отку́да (aht-KOO-duh)
  where, to куда́ (koo-DAH)
which кото́рый (kah-TAWR-y)
while пока́ (pah-KAH)
white бе́лый (BYEH-ly)
who кто (ktaw)
why почему́ (puh-chee-MOO)
wide широ́кий (shy-RAW-kee)
wife жена́ (f.) (zhy-NAH)
wind ве́тер (m.) (VYEH-tuhr)
  windy ве́трено (VYEH-tree-nuh)
window окно́ (n.) (ahk-NAW)
wine вино́ (n.) (vee-NAW)
winter зима́ (f.) (zee-MAH)
wish жела́ть/пожела́ть (v.) (zhy-LAHT'/puh-zhy-LAHT')
woman же́нщина (f.) (ZHEHN-shee-nuh)
wonderful прекра́сно (pree-KRAHS-nuh)
wool шерсть (f.) (shehrst')
work рабо́тать (v.) (rah-BAW-tuht')
would бы (by)
wrap завёртывать/заверну́ть (v.) (zah-VYAWR-ty-vuht'/zuh-veer-NOOT')
wrapping paper обёрточная бума́га (f.) (ah-BYAWR-tuhch-nuh-yuh boo-MAH-guh)

wrist запя́стье (n.) (zah-PYAHS-tyuh)
write писа́ть/написа́ть (pee-SAHT'/nuh-pee-SAHT')
writing paper почто́вая/пи́счая бума́га (f.) (pahch-TAW-vuh-yuh/PEES-chuh-yuh boo-MAH-guh)

X

X ray рентге́н (m.) (reen-GYEHN)

Y

year год (m.) (gawt)
yellow жёлтый (ZHAWL-ty)
yes да (dah)
you ты/тебя́/тобо́й (sing.) (ty/tee-BYAH/tah-BOY)
  you вы/вас/вам/ва́ми (pl. or polite form) (vy, vahs, vahm, VAH-mee)
young молодо́й (muh-lah-DOY)
yours твой (sing.) (tvoy); ваш (pl.) (vahsh)

Z

zero ноль (m.) (nawl')
zoo зоопа́рк (m.) (zuh-ah-PAHRK)

RUSSIAN-ENGLISH DICTIONARY

А

абрико́с (m.) *(ah-bree-KAWS)*
apricot

ава́рия (f.) *(ah-VAH-ree-yuh)*
accident

а́вгуст (m.) *(AHV-goost)*
August

австри́ец (m.)/**австри́йка** (f.)
(ahf-STREE-yehts/ahf-STREE-kuh)
Austrian

авто́бус (m.) *(ahf-TAW-boos)*
bus

автовокза́л (m.) *(ahf-tuh-vahg-ZAHL)* bus station

автомагистра́ль (f.) *(ahf-tuh-muh-gee-STRAHL')* highway

администра́тор (m.) *(ahd-mee-nee-STRAH-tuhr)* administrator, manager

а́дрес (m.) *(AH-drees)* address

аккумуля́тор (m.) *(ah-koo-moo-LYAH-tuhr)* automobile battery

алкого́ль (m.) *(ahl-kah-GAWL')* alcohol

алло́ *(ah-LAW)* hello (telephone)

америка́нец (m.)/
америка́нка (f.) *(ah-mee-ree-KAH-nyehts/ah-mee-ree-KAHN-kuh)* American

америка́нский (adj.) *(ah-mee-ree-KAHN-skee)* American

анана́с (m.) *(ah-nah-NAHS)* pineapple

англи́йский *(ahn-GLEE-skee)* English

англича́нин (m.)/
англича́нка (f.) *(ahn-glee-CHAHN-een/Ahn-glee-CHAHN-kuh)* English

Англия (f.) *(AHN-glee-yuh)* England

анке́та (f.) *(ahn-KYEH-tuh)* form

апельси́н (m.) *(ah-peel'-SEEN)* orange

апре́ль (m.) *(ah-PRYEHL')* April

апте́ка (f.) *(ahp-TYEH-kuh)* pharmacy

арбу́з (m.) *(ahr-BOOS)* watermelon

аргенти́нец (m.)/
аргенти́нка (f.) *(ahr-geen-TEEN-eets/ahr-geen-TEEN-kuh)* Argentinian

аспири́н (m.) *(ahs-pee-REEN)* aspirin

Б

ба́бушка (f.) *(BAH-boosh-kuh)* grandmother

бага́ж (m.) *(bah-GAHSH)* baggage

бакенба́рды (pl.) *(bah-keen-BAHR-dy)* sideburns

бале́т (m.) *(bah-LYEHT)* ballet

балко́н (m.) *(bahl-KAWN)* balcony

бана́н (m.) *(bah-NAHN)* banana

ба́нк (m.) *(bahnk)* bank

ба́нк обме́на валю́ты *(bahnk ahb-MYEH-nuh vah-LYOO-ty)* exchange office

ба́р (m.) *(bahr)* bar

бара́нина (f.) *(bah-RAH-nee-nuh)* lamb

ба́рхат (m.) *(BAHR-khuht)* velvet

бассе́йн (m.) *(bah-SYEHY-uhn)* pool

бедро́ (n.) *(bee-DRAW)* hip

бе́з *(byeehs)* less, without

белоку́рый *(byeh-lah-KOO-ry)* blond

бельги́ец (m.)/**бельги́йка** (f.) (noun) *(beel'-GEE-yehts/beel'-GEE-kuh)* Belgian

бе́лый *(BYEH-ly)* white

бензи́н (m.) *(been-ZEEN)* gasoline

бензозапра́вочная ста́нция (f.) *(been-zuh-zah-PRAH-vuhch-nuh-yuh STAHN-tsee-yuh)* gas station

беспла́тно *(bees-PLAHT-nuh)* free of charge

беспо́шлиннный *(bees-PAWSH-ly-ny)* duty-free

библиоте́ка (f.) *(bee-blee-ah-TYEH-kuh)* library

бизнесме́н (m.) *(beez-nees-MYEHN)* businessman

биле́т (m.) *(bee-LYEHT)* ticket

би́рка (f.) *(BEER-kuh)* luggage tag

бифште́кс (m.) *(beef-SHTEHKS)* steak

ближа́йший *(blee-ZHAHY-shee)* nearest

бли́зкий *(BLEES-kee)* close

бли́зко *(BLEES-kuh)* near

блу́зка (f.) *(BLOOS-kuh)* blouse

блю́до (n.) *(BLYOO-duh)* dish (food)

боле́знь (f.) *(bah-LYEHZN')* illness

боле́ть (imp.)/**заболе́ть** (perf.) *(bah-LYEHT'/zah-bah-LYEHT')* to be ill, to hurt

больни́ца (f.) *(bahl'-NEE-tsuh)* hospital

бо́льно *(BAWL'nuh)* hurt

больно́й *(bahl'-NOY)* sick

большо́й *(bahl'-SHOY)* big

борода́ (f.) *(buh-rah-DAH)* beard

брази́лец (m.)/**бразилья́нка** (f.) (noun) *(brah-ZEEL-eets/brah-zeel-YAHN-kuh)* Brazilian

брасле́т (m.) *(brah-SLYEHT)* bracelet

бра́т (m.) *(braht)* brother

бра́ть (imp.)/**взя́ть** (perf.) *(braht'/vzyaht')* to take

бра́ть (imp.)/**взя́ть** (perf.) **напрока́т** *(braht'/vzyaht' nah prah-KAHT)* to rent

бри́тва (f.) *(BREET-vuh)* razor

бри́ть (imp.)/**побри́ть** (perf.) *(breet'/pah-BREET')* to shave

бро́вь (f.) *(brawf')* eyebrow

бро́шка (f.) *(BRAW-shkuh)* brooch

брю́ки (pl.) *(BRYOO-kee)* pants

букси́ровать (imp.)/**отбукси́ровать** (perf.) *(book-SEE-ruh-vuht'/ahd-book-SEE-ruh-vuht')* to tow

бу́лочка (f.) *(BOO-luhch-kuh)* roll (bread)

бума́га (f.) *(boo-MAH-guh)* paper

бутерброд (m.) *(boo-teer-BRAWT)* sandwich

бутылка (f.) *(boo-TYL-kuh)* bottle

бы *(by)* would

быть (imp.)/ **пробыть** (perf.) *(byt'/prah-BYT')* to be

В

в *(v)* to, in

вагон (m.) *(vah-GAWN)* railroad car

вагон-ресторан (m.) *(vah-GAWN ree-stah-RAHN)* dining car

валюта (f.) *(vah-LYOO-tuh)* currency

ванная (f.) *(VAH-nuh-yuh)* bathroom

варёное *(vah-RYAW-nuh-yuh)* boiled

варенье (n.) *(vah-RYEH-nyuh)* preserves

варьете (n.) *(vah-r'ee-TEH)* show

вата (f.) *(VAH-tuh)* cotton

вверх *(vyehrkh)* up

великий *(vee-LEE-kee)* very big, great

вентилятор (m.) *(veen-tee-LYAH-tuhr)* fan

верёвка (f.) *(vee-RYAWF-kuh)* string

верный *(VYEHR-ny)* true

верхний *(VYEHRKH-nee)* top

весна (f.) *(vees-NAH)* spring

вестибюль (m.) *(vee-stee-BYOOL')* lobby

ветрено *(VYEH-tree-nuh)* windy

ветчина (f.) *(vee-chee-NAH)* ham

вечер (m.) *(VYEH-cheer)* evening

вечером *(VYEH-chee-ruhm)* in the evening

вешалка (f.) *(VYEH-shuhl-kuh)* hanger

вещь (f.) *(vyehsh')* thing

взрослый *(VZRAW-sly)* adult

вид (m.) *(veet)* view

видаться (imp.)/ **повидаться** (perf.) *(vee-DAHT'-suh/pah-vee-DAHT'-suh)* to see, to meet

видеть (imp.)/**увидеть** (perf.) *(VEE-deet'/oo-VEE-deet')* to see

виза (f.) *(VEE-zuh)* visa

визитная карточка (f.) *(vee-ZEET-nuh-yuh KAHR-tuhch-kuh)* business card, hotel pass

вилка (f.) *(VEEL-kuh)* fork

вино (n.) *(vee-NAW)* wine

виноград (m.) *(vee-nah-GRAHT)* grapes

виски (n.) *(VEE-skee)* whiskey

вишня (f.) *(VEESH-nyuh)* cherries

включать (imp.)/**включить** (perf.) *(fklyoo-CHAHT'/fklyoo-CHEET')* to include

вниз *(vnees)* down

внутри *(vnoo-TREE)* indoors

вовремя *(VAW-vree-myuh)* on time

вода (f.) *(vah-DAH)* water

водитель (m.) *(vah-DEE-teel')* driver

водительские права (pl.) *(vah-DEE-teel'-skee-yeh prah-VAH)* driver's license

241

води́ть маши́ну (vah-DEET' mah-SHY-hny) to drive a car

заводи́ться (imp.)/ **завесми́сь** (perf.) (ah-DEET'-suh/zah-vees-TEES') to start up

во́дка (f.) (VAWT-kuh) vodka

водопрово́дчик (m.) (vah-duh-prah-VAWT-cheek) plumber

возвраща́ть (imp.)/ **возврати́ть** (perf.) (vahz-vrah-SHAHT'/vahz-vrah-TEET') to return

вокза́л (m.) (vahg-ZHAL) train station

во́лосы (pl.) (VAW-luh-sy) hair

во́р (m.) (vawr) thief

восемна́дцать (vuh-seem-NAHT-seet) eighteen

во́семь (VAW-seem') eight

во́семьдесят (VAW-seem'-dee-seet) eighty

воскресе́нье (n.) (vahs-kree-SYEH-nyeh) Sunday

восто́к (m.) (vah-STAWK) east

восьмо́й (vahs'-MOY) eighth

во́т (vawt) here

впереди́ (fpee-ree-DEE) in front

вра́ч (m.) (vrahch) doctor

вреди́ть (imp.)/**повреди́ть** (perf.) (vree-DEET'/puh-vree-DEET') to injure

вре́мя (n.) (VRYEH-myuh) time

встре́тить (imp.)/**встреча́ть** (perf.) (FSTRYEH-teet'/fstree-CHAHT') to meet

всё (fsyaw) everything

встава́ть (imp.)/ **вста́ть** (perf.) (fstah-VAHT'/fstaht') to get up

встре́ча (f.) (FSTRYEH-chuh) meeting

вто́рник (m.) (FTAWR-neek) Tuesday

второ́й (ftah-ROY) second

вхо́д (m.) (fkhawt) entrance

входи́ть (imp.)/**войти́** (perf.) (fkhah-DEET'/vah-ee-TEE) to enter

вчера́ (fchee-RAH) yesterday

вы (vy) you (formal, pl.)

выводи́ть (imp.)/**вы́вести** (perf.) (vy-vah-DEET'/VY-vees-tee) to remove

вызыва́ть (imp.)/**вы́звать** (perf.) (vy-zy-VAHT'/VY-zvuht') to call for

вы́леты (pl.) (VY-lee-ty) depatures

выпада́ть (imp.)/**вы́пасть** (perf.) (vy-pah-DAHT'/VY-puhst') to fall out

выпи́сывать (imp.)/**вы́писать** (perf.) (vy-PEE-sy-vuht'/VY-pee-suht') to write out

высо́кий (adj.) (vy-SAW-kee) high

выу́чивать (imp.)/**вы́учить** (perf.) (vy-OO-chee-vuht'/VY-oo-cheet') to learn

вы́ход (m.) (VY-khuht) exit

выходи́ть (imp.)/**вы́йти** (perf.) (vy-khah-DEET'/VY-ee-tee) to go out

Г

газе́та (f.) (gah-ZYEH-tuh) newspaper

га́лстук (m.) (GAHL-stook) necktie

гара́ж (m.) (gah-RAHSH) garage

where **где** (gdyeh) where
гид (m.) (geet) guide
гладить (imp.)/**погладить** (perf.) (GLAH-deet'/pah-GLAH-deet') to iron
глаз (m.) (glahs) eye
глупо (GLOO-puh) silly, stupid
говорить (imp.)/**сказать** (perf.) (guh-vah-REET'/skah-ZAHT') to speak
говядина (f.) (gah-VYAH-dee-nuh) beef
год (m.) (gawt) year
голландец (m.)/**голландка** (f.) (gah-LAHN-deets/gah-LAHNT-kuh) Dutch
голова (f.) (guh-lah-VAH) head
головная боль (f.) (guh-lahv-NAH-yuh bawl') headache
головокружение (n.) (guh-luh-vuh-kroo-ZHEH-nyeh) dizzyness
голубой (gah-loo-BOY) light blue
гора (f.) (gah-RAH) mountain
горло (n.) (GAWR-luh) throat
горничная (f.) (GAWR-neesh-nuh-yuh) maid
город (m.) (GAW-ruht) city
горошек (m.) (gah-RAW-shuhk) pea
горячий (gah-RYAH-chee) hot
гостиная (f.) (gah-STEE-nuh-yuh) living room
гостиница (f.) (gah-STEE-nee-tsuh) hotel
гостеприимство (n.) (guh-stee-pree-EEM-stvuh) hospitality
гость (m.) (gawst') guest

готовить (imp.)/**приготовить** (perf.) (gah-TAW-veet'/pree-gah-TAW-veet') to prepare
готовый (gah-TAW-vy) ready
граница (f.) (grah-NEE-tsuh) border
грек (m.)/**гречанка** (f.) (gryehk/gree-CHAHN-kuh) Greek
гриб (m.) (greep) mushroom
громкий (GRAWM-kee) loud
грудь (f.) (groot') chest, breast
грузовик (m.) (groo-zah-VEEK) truck
груша (f.) (GROO-shuh) pear
губа (f.) (goo-BAH) lip
гусь (m.) (goos') goose

Д

да (dah) yes
давать (imp.)/**дать** (perf.) (dah-VAHT'/daht') to give
давно (dah-VNAW) long ago, a long time
далеко (dah-lee-KAW) far
датчанин (m.)/**датчанка** (f.) (dah-CHAHN-een/dah-CHAHN-kuh) Danish
дача (f.) (DAH-chuh) country house
два (dvah) two
двадцать (DVAHT-seet') twenty
двенадцать (dvee-NAHT-seet') twelve
двигать (imp.)/**двинуть** (perf.) (DVEE-guht'/DVEE-noot') to move

243

дворе́ц (m.) *(dvah-RYEHTS)* palace

двухспа́льная крова́ть (f.) *(dvookh-SPAHL'-nuh-yuh krah-VAHT')* double bed

двухме́стный но́мер (m.) *(dvookh-MYEHS-ny NAW-meer)* double room

де́вушка (f.) *(DYEH-voosh-kuh)* young woman

девяно́сто *(dee-vee-NAW-stuh)* ninety

девятна́дцать *(dee-veet-NAHT-seet')* nineteen

девя́тый *(dee-VYAH-ty)* ninth

де́вять *(DYEH-veet')* nine

де́душка (m.) *(DYEH-doosh-kuh)* grandfather

дека́брь (m.) *(dee-KAH-buhr')* December

деклара́ция (f.) *(dee-klah-RAH-tsee-yuh)* declaration

де́лать (imp.)/**сде́лать** (perf.) *(DYEH-luht'/ZDYEH-luht')* to do

де́ло (n.) *(DYEH-luh)* business

день (m.) *(dyehn')* day

де́ньги (pl.) *(DYEHN'-gee)* money

дере́вня (f.) *(dee-RYEHV-nyuh)* countryside

держи́тесь пра́вой стороны́ *(deer-ZHEE-tyehs' PRAH-vuhy stah-rah-NY)* keep right

десе́рт (m.) *(dee-SYEHRT)* dessert

деся́тый *(dee-SYAH-ty)* tenth

де́сять *(DYEH-seet')* ten

до *(dah)* until, up to

де́ти (pl.) *(DYEH-tee)* children

дёшево *(DYAW-shuh-vuh)* cheap

дешёвый *(dee-SHYAW-vy)* inexpensive

джем (m.) *(dzhyehm)* jam

дива́н (m.) *(dee-VAHN)* couch

дли́нный *(DLEE-ny)* long

для *(dlyah)* for

днём *(dnyawm)* in the afternoon

до *(daw)* before

до свида́ния *(duh svee-DAH-nee-yuh)* goodbye

добира́ться (imp.)/**добра́ться** (perf.) *(dah-bee-RAHT'-suh/dah-BRAHT'-suh)* to reach, to get to

добро́ (n.) *(dah-BRAW)* good

до́брый (adj.) *(DAW-bry)* good, nice

доводи́ть (imp.)/**довести́** (perf.) *(dah-vah-DEET'/dah-vees-TEE)* to take, to drive

довози́ть (imp.)/**довезти́** (perf.) *(dah-vah-ZEET'/dah-vees-TEE)* to take to

доезжа́ть (imp.)/**дое́хать** (perf.) *(dah-yee-ZHAHT'/dah-YEH-khuht')* to reach, to arrive

дождь (m.) *(dawsht')* rain

до́лго *(DAWL-guh)* a long while

до́лжен *(DAWL-zhyn)* should, owe

до́ллар (m.) *(DAW-luhr)* dollar

дом (m.) *(dawm)* house, home

домкра́т (m.) *(dahm-KRAHT)* jack

доро́га (f.) *(dah-RAW-guh)* road

дорого́й *(dah-rah-GOY)* expensive

доро́жные че́ки *(dah-RAWZH-ny-yeh CHYEH-kee)* traveler's checks

доста́точно (adv.) *(dah-STAH-tuhch-nuh)* enough

до́чь (f.) *(dawch')* daughter

драгоце́нности (pl.) *(drah-gah-TSEH-nuh-stee)* jewelry

дру́г (m.) *(droog)* friend

друго́й *(droo-GOY)* different

дру́жба (f.) *(DROOZH-buh)* friendship

ду́мать (imp.)/**поду́мать** (perf.) *(DOO-muht'/pah-DOO-muht')* to think

духи́ (pl.) *(doo-KHEE)* perfume

ду́ш (m.) *(doosh)* shower

ды́ня (f.) *(DY-nyuh)* melon

деодора́нт (m.) *(dee-uh-dah-RAHNT)* deodorant

дю́жина (f.) *(DYOO-zhy-nuh)* dozen

дя́дя (m.) *(DYAH-dyuh)* uncle

Е

его́ *(yee-VAW)* him, his

еда́ (f.) *(yee-DAH)* food

её *(yee-YAW)* her, hers

е́здить (imp.)/**сьезбимь** (perf.) *(YEHZ-deet')* to drive

е́сли *(YEH-slee)* if

е́сть *(yehst')* is, are

е́сть *(yehst')* to eat

е́хать (imp.)/**пое́хать** (perf.) *(YEH-khuht'/pah-YEH-khuht')* to ride

ещё *(ee-SHAW)* still, again, another

Ж

жа́ловаться (imp.)/**пожа́ловаться** (perf.) *(ZHAH-luh-vuht'-suh/pah-ZHAH-luh-vuht'-suh)* to complain

жа́ль *(zhahl')* too bad

жа́р (m.) *(zhahr)* fever

жа́реный *(ZHAH-ree-ny)* fried

жда́ть (imp.)/**подожда́ть** (perf.) *(zhdaht'/puh-dahzh-DAHT')* to wait

жва́чка (f.) *(zhy-VAHCH-kuh)* chewing gum

жела́ть (imp.)/**пожела́ть** (perf.) *(zhy-LAHT'/puh-zhy-LAHT')* to wish, to want

желе́зная доро́га (f.) *(zhy-LYEHZ-nuh-yuh dah-RAW-guh)* railroad

жёлтый *(ZHAWL-ty)* yellow

желу́док (m.) *(zhy-LOO-duhk)* stomach

жена́ (f.) *(zhy-NAH)* wife

жена́т *(zhy-NAHT)* married

жечь (imp.)/**поджечь** (perf.) *(zhaych/pahd-ZHAYCH)* to burn

жи́р (m.) *(zhyr)* fat

жи́ть *(zheet')* to live

журна́л (m.) *(zhoor-NAHL)* magazine

З

за́ *(zah)* to

заблужда́ться (imp.)/**заблуди́ться** (perf.) *(zah-bloozh-DAHT'-suh/zah-bloo-DEET'-suh)* to get lost

245

забыва́ть (imp.)/**забы́ть** (perf.) *(zah-by-VAHT'/zah-BYT')* to forget

заво́д (m.) *(zah-VAWT)* factory

за́втра *(ZAHF-truh)* tomorrow

за́втрак (m.) *(ZAHF-truhk)* breakfast

задава́ть (imp.)/**зада́ть** (perf.) *(zah-dah-VAHT'/zah-DAHT')* to give

задава́ть (imp.)/**зада́ть** (perf.) **вопро́с** *(zah-dah-VAHT'/zah-DAHT' vah-PRAWS)* to ask a question

зажига́ние (n.) *(zuh-zhee-GAH-nee-yeh)* ignition

зака́з (m.) *(zah-KAHS)* reservation

зака́зывать (imp.)/**заказа́ть** (perf.) *(zah-KAH-zy-vuht'/zah-kah-ZAHT')* to order, to reserve

зака́нчивать (imp.)/**зако́нчить** (perf.) *(zuh-KAHN-chee-vuht'/zah-KAWN-cheet')* to finish

закрыва́ть (imp.)/**закры́ть** (perf.) *(zah-kry-VAHT'/zah-KRYT')* to close

закры́то *(zah-KRY-tuh)* closed

заменя́ть (imp.)/**замени́ть** (perf.) *(zuh-mee-NYAHT'/zah-mee-NEET')* to replace

замо́к (m.) *(zah-MAWK)* lock

за́мок (m.) *(ZAH-muhk)* castle

за́мужем *(ZAH-moozh-uhm)* married

за́нято *(ZAHN-yuh-tuh)* occupied

за́пад (m.) *(ZAH-puht)* west

запа́льные све́чи (pl.) *(zah-PAHL'-ny-yeh SVYEH-chee)* spark plugs

запасно́й *(zah-pahs-NOY)* spare

запека́ть (imp.)/**запе́чь** (perf.) *(zuh-pee-KAHT'/zah-PYEHCH')* to bake

запечёное *(zu-pee-CHYAW-nuh-yuh)* baked

запломби́ровать *(zuh-plahm-BEER-uh-vuht')* to fill a tooth

заполня́ть (imp.)/**запо́лнить** (perf.) *(zuh-pahl-NYAHT'/zah-PAWL-neet')* to fill

запрещённый *(zah-pree-SHYAW-ny)* forbidden

запча́сть (f.) *(zahp-CHAHST')* (automobile) part

запя́стье (n.) *(zah-PYAHST'-yuh)* wrist

зва́ть (imp.)/**позва́ть** (perf.) *(zvaht'/pah-ZVAHT')* to call

звони́ть (imp.)/**позвони́ть** (perf.) *(zvah-NEET'/puh-zvah-NEET')* to call, to ring

зда́ние (n.) *(ZDAH-nyeh)* building

зде́сь *(zdyehs')* here

здоро́вье (n.) *(zdah-RAWV'-yeh)* health

здра́вствуйте *(ZDRAH-stvoo-ee-tyeh)* hello (formal)

зелёный *(zee-LYAW-ny)* green

зе́ркало (n.) *(ZYEHR-kuh-luh)* mirror

зима́ (f.) *(zee-MAH)* winter

знако́миться (imp.)/**познако́миться** (perf.) *(znah-KAW-meet'-suh/puh-znah-KAW-meet'-suh)* to become acquainted

знако́мство (n.) *(znah-KAWM-stvuh)* acquaintance

знать *(znaht')* to know

зо́лото (n.) *(ZAW-luh-tuh)* gold

зонт (m.) *(zawnt)* umbrella

зоопа́рк (m.) *(zuh-ah-PAHRK)* zoo

зуб (m.) *(zoop)* tooth

зубна́я па́ста (f.) *(zoob-NAH-yuh PAH-stuh)* toothpaste

зубна́я щётка (f.) *(zoob-NAH-yuh SHAWT-kuh)* toothbrush

зубно́й врач (m.) *(zoob-NOY vrahch)* dentist

И

игра́ть (imp.)/**поигра́ть** (perf.) *(ee-GRAHT'/pah-ee-GRAHT')* to play

иде́я (f.) *(ee-DYEH-yuh)* idea

идти́ (imp.)/**пойти́** (perf.) *(ee-TEE/pah-ee-TEE)* to go (on foot)

из *(ees)* from

извеще́ние (n.) *(eez-vee-SHEHN-yuh)* voucher

извиня́ть (imp.)/**извини́ть** (perf.) *(ee-zvee-NEET'/ee-zvee-NYAHT')* to excuse

измеря́ть (imp.)/**изме́рить** (perf.) *(eez-mee-RYAHT'/eez-MYEH-reet')* to measure

израильтя́нин (m.)/**израильтя́нка** (f.) *(eez-ruh-eel'-TYAH-neen/eez-ruh-eel'-TYAHN-kuh)* Israeli

ико́на (f.) *(ee-KAW-nuh)* icon

икра́ (f.) *(ee-KRAH)* caviar

ирла́ндец (m.)/**ирла́ндка** (f.) *(eer-LAHND-eets/eer-LAHNT-kuh)* Irish

инди́ец (m.)/**индиа́нка** (f.) *(een-DEE-yehts/een-dee-AHN-kuh)* Indian

иностра́нный *(ee-nah-STRAH-ny)* foreign

интере́сно *(een-tee-RYEHS-nuh)* interesting

интересова́ться (imp.)/**заинтересова́ться** (perf.) *(een-tee-ree-sah-VAHT'-suh/zah-een-tee-ree-sah-VAHT'-suh)* to be interested

иска́ть *(ee-SKAHT')* to look for

иску́сство (n.) *(ees-KOOST-vuh)* art

испа́нец (m.)/**испа́нка** (f.) *(ee-SPAH-neets/ee-SPAHN-kuh)* Spanish

испо́рчен *(ees-PAWR-chuhn)* spoiled, ruined

италья́нец (m.)/**италья́нка** (f.) *(ee-tahl'-YAHN-eets/ee-tahl'-YAHN-kuh)* Italian

ию́ль (m.) *(ee-YOOL')* July

ию́нь (m.) *(ee-YOON')* June

Й

йод (m.) *(yawt)* iodine

К

к *(k)* to

кабине́т (m.) *(kuh-bee-NYEHT)* office

каза́ться (imp.)/**показа́ться** (perf.) *(kah-ZAHT'-suh/puh-kah-ZAHT'-suh)* to seem

как *(kahk)* how

како́й *(kah-KOY)* which

ка́мера (f.) *(KAH-mee-ruh)* chamber

ка́мера хране́ния (f.) *(KAH-mee-ruh khrah-NYEH-nee-yuh)* baggage lockers

Кана́да (f.) *(kah-NAH-duh)* Canada

кана́дец (m.)/**кана́дка** (f.) *(kah-NAH-deets/kah-NAHD-kuh)* Canadian

капу́ста (f.) *(kah-POO-stuh)* cabbage

каранда́ш (m.) *(kah-rahn-DAHSH)* pencil

карбюра́тор (m.) *(kahr-byoo-RAH-tuhr)* carburetor

кори́чневый *(kah-REECH-nee-vy)* brown

карма́н (m.) *(kahr-MAHN)* pocket

ка́рта (f.) *(KAHR-tuh)* map

карти́на (f.) *(kahr-TEE-nuh)* painting

карто́фель (m.) *(kahr-TAW-feel')* potatoes

ка́сса (f.) *(KAH-suh)* ticket office, cashier

католи́ческий *(kuh-tah-LEE-chees-kee)* Catholic

кафе́ (n.) *(kah-FEH)* cafe

ка́ша (f.) *(KAH-shuh)* cereal

ка́шель (m.) *(KAHSH-eel')* cough

ка́шлять (imp.)/**пока́шлять** (perf.) *(KAHSH-lyuht'/pah-KAHSH-lyuht')* to cough

кашта́н (m.) *(kahsh-TAHN)* chestnut

кварта́л (m.) *(kvahr-TAHL)* block

кварти́ра (f.) *(kvahr-TEE-ruh)* apartment

квита́нция (f.) *(kvee-TAHN-tsee-yuh)* receipt

киломе́тр (m.) *(kee-lah-MYEH-tuhr)* kilometer

килогра́мм (m.) *(kee-lah-GRAHM)* kilogram

кино́ (n.) *(kee-NAW)* movies

кио́ск (m.) *(kee-AWSK)* newsstand

кита́ец (m.)/**китая́нка** (f.) *(kee-TAH-eets/kee-tah-YAHN-kuh)* Chinese

класс (m.) *(klahs)* class

клие́нт(-ка) *(klee-YEHNT,-kuh)* client

клуб (m.) *(kloop)* club

клубни́ка (f.) *(kloob-NEE-kuh)* strawberry

ключ (m.) *(klyooch)* key

кни́га (f.) *(KNEE-guh)* book

ковёр (m.) *(kah-VYAWR)* rug

когда́ *(kahg-DAH)* when

ко́жа (f.) *(KAW-zhuh)* skin

коктейль (m.) *(kahk-TEHYL')* cocktail

колбаса́ (f.) *(kuhl-bah-SAH)* sausage

коле́но (n.) *(kah-LYEH-nuh)* knee

колле́га (m. and f.) *(kah-LYEHG-uh)* colleague

кольцо́ (n.) *(kahl'-TSAW)* ring

командиро́вка (f.) *(kuh-muhn-dee-RAWF-kuh)* business trip

коме́дия (f.) *(kah-MYEH-dee-yuh)* comedy

ко́мната (f.) *(KAWM-nuh-tuh)* room

конве́рт (m.) *(kahn-VYEHRT)* envelope

кондиционе́р (m.) *(kahn-dee-tsyah-NYEHR)* air conditioner

коне́ц (m.) *(kah-NYEHTS)* end

коне́чно *(kah-NYEHSH-nuh)* of course

ко́нсульство (n.) *(KAWN-sool-stvuh)* consulate

конто́ра (f.) *(kahn-TAWR-uh)* office

конфе́ты (pl.) *(kahn-FYEH-ty)* candy

конце́рт (m.) *(kahn-TSEHRT)* concert

конча́ть (imp.)/ко́нчить (perf.) *(kahn-CHAT'/KAWN-cheet')* to finish, to end

корзи́на (f.) *(kahr-ZEE-nuh)* basket

коро́ткий *(kah-RAWT-kee)* short

костю́м (m.) *(kah-STYOOM)* suit

ко́сть (f.) *(kawst')* bone

кото́рый *(kah-TAW-ry)* which

ко́фе (n.) *(KAW-fee)* coffee

краси́во *(krah-SEE-vuh)* prettily

краси́вый *(krah-SEE-vy)* beautiful

кра́сить (imp)/покра́сить (perf.) *(KRAH-seet'/pah-KRAH-seet')* to dye

кра́сный *(KRAH-sny)* red

кра́сть (imp.)/укра́сть (perf.) *(krahst'/oo-KRAHST')* to steal

креве́тки (pl.) *(kree-VYEHT-kee)* shrimp

креди́тная ка́рточка (f.) *(kree-DEET-nuh-yuh KAHR-tuhch-kuh)* credit card

кре́м (m.) *(kryehm)* lotion

кре́сло (n.) *(KRYEH-sluh)* armchair

крова́ть (f.) *(krah-VAHT')* bed

кро́вь (f.) *(krawf')* blood

кро́лик (m.) *(KRAW-leek)* rabbit

кру́жево (n.) *(KROO-zhy-vuh)* lace

кто́ *(ktaw)* who

куда́ *(koo-DAH)* where to

кукуру́за (f.) *(koo-koo-ROO-zuh)* corn

купа́льник (m.) *(koo-PAHL'-neek)* bathing suit

купа́ться (imp.)/искупа́ться (perf.) *(koo-PAHT'-suh/pis-koo-PAHT'-suh)* to swim, to bathe

кури́ть (imp.)/закури́ть (perf.) *(koo-REET'/zah-koo-REET')* to smoke

ку́рица (f.) *(KOO-ree-tsuh)* chicken

куса́ть (imp.)/укуси́ть (perf.) *(koo-SAHT'/oo-koo-SEET')* to bite

ку́хня (f.) *(KOOKH-nyuh)* kitchen, cooking

Л

ла́дно *(LAH-dnuh)* okay

ла́к (m.) *(lahk)* lacquerware

ла́мпочка (f.) *(LAHM-puhch-kuh)* light bulb

ле́вый *(LYEH-vy)* left

лёгкие (pl.) *(LYAWKH-kee-yeh)* lungs

лёгкий *(LYOKH-kee)* light

лёд (m.) *(lyawt)* ice

лека́рство (n.) *(lee-KAHRST-vuh)* medicine

лён (m.) *(LYAWN)* linen

ле́нта (f.) *(LYEHN-tuh)* ribbon

ле́то (n.) *(LYEH-tuh)* summer

ликёр (m.) *(lee-KYAWR)* liqueur

лимо́н (m.) *(lee-MAWN)* lemon

ли́ния (f.) *(LEE-nee-yuh)* line

литр (m.) *(LEE-tuhr)* liter

лифт (m.) *(leeft)* elevator

лицо́ (n.) *(lee-TSAW)* face

лоб (m.) *(lawp)* forehead

ло́дка (f.) *(LAWT-kuh)* boat

ложи́ться (imp.)/лечь (perf.) *(lah-ZHYT'-suh/lyehch')* to lie down

ло́жка (f.) *(LAWSH-kuh)* spoon

лома́ть (imp.)/слома́ть (perf.) *(lah-MAHT'/slah-MAHT')* to break

лук (m.) *(look)* onion

лу́чше *(LOO-cheh)* better

люби́мый *(lyoo-BEE-my)* favorite

лю́ди (pl.) *(LYOO-dee)* people

M

магази́н (m.) *(muh-gah-ZEEN)* store

май (m.) *(mahy)* May

ма́ленький *(MAH-leen'-kee)* small

ма́ло *(MAH-luh)* few, little

маникю́р (m.) *(mah-nee-KYOOR)* manicure

ма́рка (f.) *(MAHR-kuh)* stamp

ма́рля (f.) *(MAHR-lyuh)* gauze

март (m.) *(mahrt)* March

маршру́т (m.) *(mahr-SHROOT)* itinerary

ма́ска для лица́ (f.) *(MAH-skuh dlyah lee-TSAH)* facial

масли́на (f.) *(mah-SLEE-nuh)* olive

ма́сло (n.) *(MAH-sluh)* butter, oil

матч (m.) *(mahch)* game, match

мать (f.) *(maht')* mother

маши́на (f.) *(mah-SHY-nuh)* car

медици́нский *(mee-dee-TSYN-skee)* medical

ме́дленнее *(MYEH-dlee-nyeh-yeh)* slower

ме́дленно *(MYEH-dlee-nuh)* slowly

ме́дленный *(MYEH-dlee-ny)* slow

медсестра́ (f.) *(meet-see-STRAH)* nurse

ме́жду *(MYEHZH-doo)* between

междугоро́дный *(meezh-doo-gah-RAWD-ny)* between cities

междунаро́дный *(meezh-doo-nah-RAWD-ny)* international

мексика́нец (m.)/мексика́нка (f.) *(meek-see-KAH-neets/meek-see-KAHN-kuh)* Mexican

ме́лочь (f.) *(MYEH-luhch')* coins, change

меню́ (n.) *(mee-NYOO)* menu

меня́ть (imp.)/поменя́ть (perf.)/разменя́ть (perf.) *(mee-NYAHT'/puh-mee-NYAHT'/ruhz-mee-NYAHT')* to change, to exchange

ме́рить (imp.)/**поме́рить** (perf.) *(MYEH-reet'/pah-MYEH-reet')* to measure, to try on

ме́сто (n.) *(MYEH-stuh)* place, seat

ме́сяц (m.) *(MYEH-seets)* month

метро́ (n.) *(mee-TRAW)* subway

меша́ть (imp.)/**помеша́ть** (perf.) *(mee-SHAHT/pah-mee-SHAHT')* to bother, to mix

мили́ция (f.) *(mee-LEE-tsee-yuh)* police, militia

миллио́н (m.) *(mee-LYAWN)* one million

ми́лый *(MEE-ly)* nice

минда́ль (m.) *(meen-DAHL')* almond

минера́льный *(mee-nee-RAHL'-ny)* mineral

мину́та (f.) *(mee-NOOT-uh)* minute

мно́го *(MNAW-guh)* a lot, many

мо́жно *(MAWZH-nuh)* one may

мой *(moy)* my

молодо́й *(muh-lah-DOY)* young

молоко́ (n.) *(mah-lah-KAW)* milk

моло́чный *(mah-LAWCH-ny)* dairy

монасты́рь (f.) *(muh-nah-STYR')* convent, monastery

мо́ре (n.) *(MAWR-yeh)* sea

морко́вь (f.) *(mahr-KAWF')* carrots

моро́женое (n.) *(mah-RAW-zhy-nuh-yuh)* ice cream

мост (m.) *(mawst)* bridge

мочь (imp.)/**смочь** (perf.) *(mawch'/smawch')* to be able

муж (m.) *(moozh)* husband

музе́й (m.) *(moo-ZYEHY)* museum

му́зыка (f.) *(MOO-zy-kuh)* music

мука́ (f.) *(moo-KAH)* flour

мы́ло (n.) *(MY-luh)* soap

мыть (imp.)/**вы́мыть** (perf.) *(myt'/VY-myt')* to wash

мя́гкий *(MYAKH-kee)* soft

мя́со (n.) *(MYAH-suh)* meat

Н

на *(nah)* on, for

На по́мощь! *(nah PAW-muhsh'!)* Help!

на́до *(NAH-duh)* one must

нажима́ть (imp.)/**нажа́ть** (perf.) *(nuh-zhy-MAHT/nah-ZHAHT')* to press

наза́д (adv.) *(nah-ZAHT)* back, backwards, ago

назнача́ть (imp.)/**назна́чить** (perf.) **вре́мя** *(nah-znah-CHAHT'/nah-ZNAH-cheet' VRYEH-myuh)* to make an appointment

называ́ться (imp.)/**назва́ться** (perf.) *(nah-zy-VAHT'-suh/nah-ZVAHT'-suh)* to be called

наконе́ц *(nah-kah-NYEHTS)* finally

нало́г (m.) *(nah-LAWK)* tax

напи́ток (m.) *(nah-PEE-tuhk)* drink, beverage

настоя́щий *(nah-stah-YAH-shee)* real

251

находи́ться (imp.) *(nah-KHAW-deet'-suh/nah-ee-TEES')* to find oneself, to be located

национа́льность (f.) *(nuh-tsyah-NAHL'-nuhst')* nationality; ethnic origin

национа́льный *(nah-tsyah-NAHL'-ny)* national

нача́ло (n.) *(nah-CHAH-luh)* beginning

начина́ть (imp.)/**нача́ть** (perf.) *(nuh-chee-NAHT'/nah-CHAHT')* to begin

наш *(nahsh)* our

не *(nee)* not

недалеко́ *(nee-duh-lee-KAW)* near

неде́ля (f.) *(nee-DYEHL-yuh)* week

недо́лго *(nee-DAWL-guh)* a short while

нельзя́ *(neel'-ZYAH)* it is impossible, it is not allowed

не́мец (m.)/**не́мка** (f.) *(NYEH-meets/NYEHM-kuh)* German

неме́цкий (adj.) *(nee-MYEHTS-kee)* German

немно́жко *(nee-MNAWSH-kuh)* a little

непра́вда *(nee-PRAHV-duh)* false

не́сколько *(NYEH-skuhl'-kuh)* a few

нести́ (imp.)/**снести́** (perf.) *(nee-STEE/snee-STEE)* to carry

нет *(nyeht)* no

ни́жний *(NEEZH-nee)* bottom

ничего́ *(nee-chee-VAW)* nothing

но *(naw)* but

но́вости (pl.) *(NAW-vuhs-tee)* news

Но́вый го́д (m.) *(NAW-vy gawt)* New Year

нога́ (f.) *(nah-GAH)* leg, foot

но́готь (m.) *(NAW-guht')* nail

нож (m.) *(nawsh)* knife

ноль (m.) *(nawl')* zero

но́мер (m.) *(NAW-meer)* number, hotel room

норве́жец (m.)/**норве́жка** (f.) (noun) *(nahr-VYEH-zheets/nahr-VYEHZH-kuh)* Norwegian

нос (m.) *(naws)* nose

носи́льщик (m.) *(nah-SEEL'-sheek)* porter

носо́к (m.) *(nah-SAWK)* sock

ночь (f.) *(nawch')* night

ноя́брь (m.) *(nah-YAH-buhr')* November

нра́виться (imp.)/**понра́виться** (perf.) *(NRAH-veet-suh/pahn-RAH-veet-suh)* to like

ну́жно (adv.) *(NOOZH-nuh)* needed, necessary

О

обе́д (m.) *(ah-BYEHT)* lunch

обёрточная бума́га (f.) *(ah-BYAWR-tuhch-nuh-yuh boo-MAH-guh)* wrapping paper

обжа́реное *(ahb-ZHAHR-ee-nuh-yuh)* broiled

обжига́ться (imp.)/**обже́чься** (perf.) *(ahb-zhy-GAHT-suh/ahb-ZHYEHCH-suh)* to be burned

о́блако (n.) *(AW-bluh-kuh)* cloud

обме́н (m.) *(ahb-MYEHN)* exchange

обме́нивать (imp.)/**обме́нять** (perf.) *(ahb-MYEH-nee-vuht'/ ahb-meen-YAHT')* to exchange

обожа́ть (imp.) *(ah-bah-ZHAHT')* to adore

обра́тно *(ah-BRAHT-nuh)* back

обслу́живание (n.) *(ahp-SLOO-zhy-vuhn-yuh)* service

о́бщий *(AWP-shee)* general

объе́зд (m.) *(ahb-YEHST)* detour

о́вощи (pl.) *(AW-vuh-shee)* vegetables

ограниче́ние ско́рости (n.) *(ah-gruh-nee-CHYEH-nee-yeh SKAW-ruhst-ee)* speed limit

огуре́ц (m.) *(ah-goo-RYEHTS)* cucumber

одева́ться (imp.)/**оде́ться** (perf.) *(ah-dee-VAHT-suh/ah-DYEHT-suh)* to get dressed

оде́жда (f.) *(ah-DYEHZH-duh)* clothes

одея́ло (n.) *(ah-dee-YAH-luh)* blanket

оди́н *(ah-DEEN)* one

оди́ннадцать *(ah-DEEN-uht-seet')* eleven

одноме́стный *(ahd-nah-MYEHS-ny)* single

односторо́ннее движе́ние (n.) *(ah-dnuh-stah-RAWN-nyeyeh dvee-ZHYEH-nee-yeh)* one-way traffic

ожере́лье (n.) *(ah-zhe-RYEHL'-yee)* necklace

ожо́г (m.) *(ah-ZHAWK)* burn

озно́б (m.) *(ah-ZNAWP)* chill

океа́н (m.) *(ah-kee-AHN)* ocean

окно́ (n.) *(ah-KNAW)* window

о́коло *(AW-kuh-luh)* near, next to

октя́брь (m.) *(ahk-TYAH-buhr')* October

он (m.) *(awn)* he, it

она́ (f.) *(ah-NAH)* she, it

опа́сно *(ah-PAHS-nuh)* dangerous

о́пера (f.) *(AW-pee-ruh)* opera

опера́тор (m.) *(ah-pee-RAH-tuhr)* operator

о́птик (m.) *(AWP-teek)* optometrist

о́пухоль (f.) *(AW-poo-khuhl')* swelling

ора́нжевый *(ah-RAHN-zhy-vy)* orange

орке́стр (m.) *(ahr-KYEH-stuhr)* orchestra

о́сень (f.) *(AW-seen')* autumn

осетри́на (f.) *(ah-see-TREE-nuh)* sturgeon

остава́ться (imp.)/**оста́ться** (perf.) *(ah-stah-VAHT'-suh/ah-STAHT'-suh)* to remain

оставля́ть (imp.)/**оста́вить** (perf.) *(ah-stah-VLYAHT'/ah-STAH-veet')* to leave

остана́вливаться (imp.)/**останови́ться** (perf.) *(ah-stah-NAH-vlee-vuht-suh/ah-stuh-nah-VEET-suh)* to stop, to stay

остано́вка (f.) *(ah-stah-NAWF-kuh)* (bus) stop

осторо́жно (adv.) *(ah-stah-RAWZH-nuh)* careful

осторо́жный *(ah-stah-RAWZH-ny)* careful

о́стрый *(AW-stry)* spicy, sharp

253

остыва́ть (imp.)/осты́ть (perf.) (ah-sty-VAHT'/ah-STYT') to get cold

от (aht) from

отвёртка (f.) (aht-VYAWRT-kuh) screwdriver

отводи́ть (imp.)/отвести́ (perf.) (aht-vah-DEET'/aht-vees-TEE) to take, to bring

отде́льный (ahd-DYEHL'-ny) separate

оте́ц (m.) (ah-TYEHTS) father

открыва́ть (imp.)/откры́ть (perf.) (aht-kry-VAHT'/aht-KRYT') to open

откры́тка (f.) (aht-KRYT-kuh) postcard

откры́то (aht-KRY-tuh) open

отку́да (aht-KOO-duh) where from

отли́чный (aht-LEECH-ny) excellent

относи́ть (imp.)/отнести́ (perf.) (aht-nah-SEET'/aht-nee-STEE) to carry away

отопле́ние (n.) (ah-tah-PLYEH-nyeh) heat

отправля́ть (imp.)/отпра́вить (perf.) (aht-prah-VLYAHT'/aht-PRAH-veet') to send

о́тпуск (m.) (AWT-poosk) vacation

отсю́да (aht-SYOO-duh) from here

отходи́ть (imp.)/отойти́ (perf.) (aht-khah-DEET'/aht-uh-ee-TEE) to leave, to move away from

официа́нт (m.) (ah-fee-TSYAHNT) waiter

о́чень (AW-cheen') very

очки́ (pl.) (ahch-KEE) glasses

ошиба́ться (imp.)/ошиби́ться (perf.) (ah-shee-BAHT'-suh/ah-shee-BEET'-suh) to make a mistake

оши́бка (f.) (ah-SHEEP-kuh) mistake

П

па́дать (imp.)/упа́сть (perf.) (PAH-duht'/oo-PAHST') to fall

па́лец (m.) (PAH-leets) finger

пальто́ (n.) (pahl'-TAW) coat

па́мятник (m.) (PAH-meet-neek) monument

па́ра (f.) (PAH-ruh) pair

парикма́хер (m.) (pah-reek-MAH-kheer) barber

парикма́херская (f.) (pah-reek-MAH-kheer-skuh-yuh) barber shop, beauty parlor

паркова́ть (imp.)/запаркова́ть (perf.) (pahr-kah-VAHT'/zuh-puhr-kah-VAHT') to park

па́смурно (PAH-smoor-nuh) cloudy

па́спорт (m.) (PAHS-puhrt) passport

па́стор (m.) (PAH-stuhr) minister

Па́сха (f.) (PAHS-khuh) Easter

пе́нсия (f.) (PYEHN-see-yuh) pension

пе́пельница (f.) (PYEH-peel'-nee-tsuh) ashtray

пе́рвая по́мощь (f.) (PYEHR-vuh-yuh PAW-muhsh') first aid

пе́рвые блю́да (pl.) *(PYEHR-vy-yeh BLYOO-duh)* soups, first courses

пе́рвый *(PYEHR-vy)* first

переводи́ть (imp.)/**перевести́** (perf.) *(pee-ree-vah-DEET'/pee-ree-vees-TEE)* to translate

перево́дчик (m.) *(pee-ree-VAWT-cheek)* translator

перегрева́ться (imp.)/**перегре́ться** (perf.) *(pee-ree-gree-VAHT-suh/pee-ree-GRYEHT-suh)* to overheat

переда́ча (f.) *(pee-ree-DAH-chuh)* program

переезжа́ть (imp.)/**перее́хать** (perf.) *(pee-ree-yee-ZHAHT'/pee-ree-YEH-khuht)* to move

переключе́ние (n.) *(pee-ree-klyoo-CHEH-nee-yeh)* gears

перело́м (m.) *(pee-ree-LAWM)* break, fracture

переса́дка (f.) *(pee-ree-SAHT-kuh)* transfer

пе́рец (m.) *(PYEH-reets)* pepper

пермане́нт (m.) *(peer-mah-NYEHNT)* permanent wave

перро́н (m.) *(pee-RAWN)* platform

пе́рсик (m.) *(PYEHR-seek)* peach

пе́ть *(pyeht')* to sing

печа́льно *(pee-CHAHL'-nuh)* sadly

печёнка (f.) *(pee-CHAWN-kuh)* liver (dish)

пе́чень (f.) *(PYEH-cheen')* liver

пешехо́д (m.) *(pee-shee-KHAWT)* pedestrian

пешко́м *(peesh-KAWM)* on foot

пи́во (n.) *(PEE-vuh)* beer

пиро́г (m.) *(pee-RAWK)* pastry

писа́ть (imp.)/**написа́ть** (perf.) *(pee-SAHT'/nuh-pee-SAHT')* to write, to draw

письмо́ (n.) *(pees'-MAW)* letter

пита́ние (n.) *(pee-TAH-nee-yeh)* nourishment

пи́ть *(peet')* to drink

пи́ща (f.) *(PEE-shuh)* food

пласти́нка (f.) *(plah-STEEN-kuh)* record

плати́ть (imp.)/**заплати́ть** (perf.) *(plah-TEET'/zuh-plah-TEET')* to pay

плато́к (m.) *(plah-TAWK)* handkerchief

пла́тье (n.) *(PLAHT'-yee)* dress

плёнка (f.) *(PLYAWN-kuh)* roll of film

плечо́ (n.) *(plee-CHAW)* shoulder

пло́мба (f.) *(PLAWM-buh)* filling

пломби́ровать (imp.)/**запломби́ровать** (perf.) *(plahm-BEER-uh-vuht'/zuh-plahm-BEER-uh-vuht')* to fill

плоскогу́бцы (pl.) *(pluh-skah-GOOP-tsy)* pliers

плохо́й *(plah-KHOY)* bad

пло́хо *(PLAW-khuh)* badly

пло́щадь (f.) *(PLAW-shuht')* square

пля́ж (m.) *(plyahsh)* beach

побере́жье (n.) *(pah-bee-RYEHZH'-yeh)* coast

поворо́т (m.) *(puh-vah-RAWT)* turn

255

повторя́ть (imp.)/повтори́ть (perf.) *(puhf-tah-RYAHT'/puhf-tah-REET')* to repeat

повя́зка (f.) *(pah-VYAHZ-kuh)* bandage

пого́да (f.) *(pah-GAW-duh)* weather

пода́рок (m.) *(pah-DAHR-uhk)* gift

подпи́сывать (imp.)/подписа́ть (perf.) *(puht-PEE-sy-vuht/paht-pee-SAHT')* to sign

подру́га (f.) *(pah-DROO-guh)* friend (female)

по-друго́му *(pah-droo-GAW-moo)* differently, different

подстри́чься (imp.)/подстри́чься (perf.) *(paht-stree-GAHT'-suh/paht-STREECH'-suh)* to get a haircut

поду́шка (f.) *(pah-DOOSH-kuh)* pillow

подходи́ть (imp.)/подойти́ (perf.) *(puht-khah-DEET'/puh-duh-ee-TEE')* to suit

подъезжа́ть (imp.)/подъе́хать (perf.) *(pahd-yee-ZHAHT'/pahd-YEH-khuht')* to approach

по́езд (m.) *(PAW-eest)* train

пое́здка (f.) *(pah-YEHST-kuh)* a trip

пожа́луйста *(pah-ZHAHL-stuh)* please

пожа́р (m.) *(pah-ZHAHR)* fire

по́здно *(PAWZ-nuh)* late

по́зже *(PAW-zheh)* later

пока́зывать (imp.)/показа́ть (perf.) *(pah-KAH-zy-vuht'/puh-kah-ZAHT')* to show

покупа́ть (imp.)/купи́ть (perf.) *(puh-koo-PAHT'/koo-PEET')* to buy

пол (m.) *(pawl)* floor

по́лдень (m.) *(PAWL-deen')* noon

по́лночь (f.) *(PAWL-nuhch')* midnight

по́лный *(PAWL-ny)* full

полови́на (f.) *(pah-lah-VEE-nuh)* half

полоте́нце (n.) *(puh-luh-TYEHN-tsuh)* towel

получа́ть (imp.)/получи́ть (perf.) *(puh-loo-CHAHT'/pah-loo-CHEET')* to receive

помидо́р (m.) *(pah-mee-DAWR)* tomato

помога́ть (imp.)/помо́чь (perf.) *(pah-mah-GAHT'/pah-MAWCH')* to help

понеде́льник (m.) *(pah-nee-DYEHL'-neek)* Monday

понима́ть (imp.)/поня́ть (perf.) *(pah-nee-MAHT'/pah-NYAHT')* to understand

попада́ть (imp.)/попа́сть (perf.) *(puh-pah-DAHT'/pah-PAHST')* to find oneself in, to wind up

попо́зже *(pah-PAW-zheh)* later

пора́ *(pah-RAH)* time

поре́зать (perf.) *(pah-RYEH-zuht')* to cut

порт (m.) *(pawrt)* port

португа́лец (m.)/португа́лка (f.) *(puhr-too-GAHL-eets/puhr-too-GAHL-kuh)* Portuguese

по́рция (f.) *(PAWR-tsee-yuh)* portion

поря́док (m.) *(pah-RYAH-duhk)* order

поса́дка (f.) *(pah-SAHT-kuh)* stopover

посеща́ть (imp.)/посети́ть (perf.) *(pah-see-SHAHT'/pah-see-TEET')* to visit

по́сле *(PAW-slee)* after

после́дний *(pah-SLYEHD-nee)* last

посо́льство (n.) *(pah-SAWL'-stvuh)* embassy

посте́ль (f.) *(pah-STYEHL')* bed

посыла́ть (imp.)/посла́ть (perf.) *(puh-sy-LAHT'/puh-SLAHT')* to send

посы́лка (f.) *(pah-SYL-kuh)* package

потоло́к (m.) *(pah-tah-LAWK)* ceiling

пото́м *(pah-TAWM)* then, next

почему́ *(puh-chee-MOO)* why

по́чта (f.) *(PAWCH-tuh)* mail, post office

почти́ *(pahch-TEE)* almost

почто́вый я́щик (m.) *(pahch-TAW-vy YAH-shyk)* mailbox

по́шлина (f.) *(PAWSH-lee-nuh)* duty

по́яс (m.) *(PAW-yuhs)* waist; belt

правосла́вный *(pruh-vah-SLAHV-ny)* Russian Orthodox

пра́вый *(PRAH-vy)* right

пра́здник (m.) *(PRAHZ-neek)* holiday

пра́чечная (f.) *(PRAH-cheech-nuh-yuh)* laundry

предлага́ть (imp.)/предложи́ть (perf.) *(preed-lah-GAHT'/preed-lah-ZHEET')* to offer, to suggest

предпочита́ть (imp.)/предпоче́сть (perf.) *(preet-puh-chee-TAHT'/preet-pah-CHYEHST')* to prefer

представи́тель (m.) *(preet-stah-VEE-teel')* representative

представля́ть (imp.)/предста́вить (perf.) *(preet-stahv-LYAHT'/preet-STAH-veet')* to present, to introduce, to imagine

прекра́сно *(pree-KRAHS-nuh)* perfect, excellent

преподава́тель (m.) *(pree-puh-dah-VAH-teel')* teacher

приве́т *(pree-VYEHT)* hello (informal)

приводи́ть (imp.)/привести́ (perf.) *(pree-vah-DEET'/pree-vees-TEE)* to bring (on foot)

привози́ть (imp.)/привезти́ (perf.) *(pree-vah-ZEET'/pree-vees-TEE)* to bring (by vehicle)

приглаша́ть (imp.)/пригласи́ть (perf.) *(pree-glah-SHAHT'/pree-glah-SEET')* to invite

приёмная (f.) *(pree-YAWM-nuh-yuh)* reception

прилёты (pl.) *(pree-LYAW-ty)* arrivals

принима́ть (imp.)/приня́ть (perf.) *(pree-nee-MAHT'/pree-NYAHT')* to accept, to take приноси́ть (imp.)/ принести́ (perf.) *(pree-nah-SEET'/pree-nees-TEE)* to bring

приходи́ть (imp.)/прийти́ (perf.) *(pree-khah-DEET'/pree-TEE)* to arrive

приходи́ться (imp.)/ прийти́сь (perf.) *(pree-KHAW-deet-suh/pree-TEES')* to have to

прия́тель (m.) *(pree-YAH-teel')* friend

прия́тный *(pree-YAHT-ny)* pleasant, nice

пробле́ма (f.) *(prah-BLYEH-muh)* problem

про́бовать (imp.)/ попро́бовать (perf.) *(PRAW-buh-vuht'/pah-PRAW-buh-vuht')* to try

пробы́ть *(prah-BYT')* to stay

проводи́ть (imp.)/провести́ (perf.) *(prah-vah-DEET'/prah-vees-TEE)* to conduct, to spend

програ́мма (f.) *(prah-GRAH-muh)* program

продолжа́ть (imp.)/ продо́лжить (perf.) *(pruh-dahl-ZHAHT'/prah-DAWL-zheet')* to continue

прое́зд (m.) *(prah-YEHST)* passage

проездна́я пла́та (f.) *(pruh-yeezd-NAH-yuh PLAH-tuh)* fare

прожива́ть *(puh-zhy-VAHT')* to live

проспе́кт (m.) *(prah-SPYEHKT)* avenue

просту́да (f.) *(prah-STOO-duh)* a cold

проте́з (m.) *(prah-TYEHS)* denture

протеста́нтский *(pruh-tees-TAHNT-skee)* Protestant

профе́ссия (f.) *(prah-FYEH-see-yuh)* profession

прохо́д (m.) *(prah-KHAWT)* aisle

проходи́ть (imp.)/пройти́ (perf.) *(pruh-khah-DEET'/pruh-ee-TEE)* to go

проце́нт (m.) *(prah-TSEHNT)* percent

проща́ть (imp.)/прости́ть (perf.) *(prah-SHAHT'/prah-STEET')* to forgive

пря́мо *(PRYAH-muh)* directly

прямо́й *(pree-MOY)* direct, straight

пря́ность (f.) *(PRYAH-nuhst')* condiment

пти́ца (f.) *(PTEE-tsuh)* bird, fowl

пу́говица (f.) *(POO-guh-veet-suh)* button

пу́динг (m.) *(POO-deenk)* pudding

путеше́ствовать *(poo-tee-SHEHST-vuh-vuht')* to travel

пу́ть (m.) *(poot')* way, path

пятна́дцать *(peet-NAHT-seet')* fifteen

пя́тница (f.) *(PYAHT-nee-tsuh)* Friday

пятно́ (n.) *(peet-NAW)* spot

пя́тый *(PYAH-ty)* fifth

пять *(pyaht')* five

пятьдеся́т *(pee-dee-SYAHT)* fifty

пьéса (f.) *(P'YEH-suh)* play

Р

рабóтать *(rah-BAW-tuht')* to work

раввин (m.) *(rah-VEEN)* rabbi

радиáтор (m.) *(rah-dee-AH-tuhr)* automobile radiator

рáдио (n.) *(RAH-dee-uh)* radio

рáз *(rahs)* time, occasion, one

раздевáться (imp.)/ **раздéться** (perf.) *(rahz-dee-VAHT-suh/rahz-DYEHT-suh)* to undress

размéнивать (imp.)/ **разменя́ть** (perf.) *(rahz-MYEH-nee-vuht'/rahz-mee-NYAHT')* to change

размéр (m.) *(rahz-MYEHR)* size

разрешáть (imp.)/**разрешить** (perf.) *(rahz-ree-SHAHT'/rahz-ree-SHEET')* to allow

райóн (m.) *(rah-YAWN)* area

рáнний (adj.) *(RAH-nee)* early

рáно (adv.) *(RAH-nuh)* early

рáньше *(RAHN'-sheh)* earlier

рассчитывать (imp.)/ **рассчитáть** (perf.) *(rahs-SHEE-ty-vuht'/rahs-shee-TAHT')* to calculate

растяжéние (n.) *(rahs-tee-ZHYEH-nyeh)* sprain

расчёска (f.) *(rahs-SHYAWS-kuh)* comb

ребёнок (m.) *(ree-BYAW-nuhk)* child

ребрó (n.) *(ree-BRAW)* rib

регистрáция (f.) *(ree-gee-STRAH-tsee-yuh)* registration

редиска (f.) *(ree-DEES-kuh)* radish

рейс (m.) *(ryehys)* flight

рекá (f.) *(ree-KAH)* river

рекомендовáть (imp.)/ **порекомендовáть** (perf.) *(ree-kuh-meen-dah-VAHT'/pah-ree-kuh-meen-dah-VAHT')* to recommend

ремéнь (m.) *(ree-MYEHN')* belt

рентгéн (m.) *(reent-GYEHN)* X ray

ресница (f.) *(rees-NEE-tsuh)* eyelash

ресторáн (m.) *(ree-stah-RAHN)* restaurant

рецéпт (m.) *(ree-TSEHPT)* prescription

рис (m.) *(rees)* rice

родиться *(rah-DEET'-suh)* to be born

Рождествó (n.) *(rahzh-deest-VAW)* Christmas

розéтка (f.) *(rah-ZYEHT-kuh)* outlet

рóзыск (m.) *(RAWZ-ysk)* search

рóм (m.) *(rawm)* rum

ромáн (m.) *(rah-MAHN)* novel

рóт (m.) *(rawt)* mouth

рубáшка (f.) *(roo-BAHSH-kuh)* shirt

рýбль (m.) *(ROO-buhl')* ruble

рукá (f.) *(roo-KAH)* arm, hand

рýсский *(ROO-skee)* Russian

рýчка (f.) *(ROOCH-kuh)* pen

ручнáя клáдь (f.) *(rooch-NAH-yuh klaht')* carry-on luggage

рыба (f.) *(RY-buh)* fish

рынок (m.) *(RY-nuhk)* market

259

c (s) with, from

са́д (m.) *(saht)* garden

сади́ться (imp.)/**се́сть** (perf.) *(sah-DEET'-suh/syehst')* to sit

сала́т (m.) *(sah-LAHT)* salad

салфе́тка (f.) *(sahl-FYEHT-kuh)* napkin

са́мый *(SAH-my)* most

сапо́г (m.) *(sah-PAWK)* boot

сарди́на (f.) *(sahr-DEE-nuh)* sardine

са́хар (m.) *(SAH-khuhr)* sugar

сбо́ку *(ZBAW-koo)* on the side

свёкла (f.) *(SVYAW-kluh)* beets

све́т (m.) *(svyeht)* light

светофо́р (m.) *(svee-tah-FAWR)* traffic light

све́тлый (adj.) *(SVYEHT-ly)* light

сви́тер (m.) *(SVEE-teer)* sweater

свини́на (f.) *(svee-NEE-nuh)* pork

свобо́дно *(svah-BAWD-nuh)* free

свой *(svoy)* his, hers, one's own

свяще́нник (m.) *(svee-SHYEH-neek)* priest

сдава́ть (imp.)/**сда́ть** (perf.) *(zdah-VAHT'/zdaht')* to hand over

сда́ча (f.) *(ZDAH-chuh)* change

се́вер (m.) *(SYEH-veer)* north

сего́дня *(see-VAWD-nyuh)* today

седьмо́й *(seed'-MOY)* seventh

сейча́с *(see-CHAHS)* now

селёдка (f.) *(see-LYAWT-kuh)* herring

семна́дцать *(seem-NAHT-seet')* seventeen

се́мь *(syehm')* seven

се́мьдесят *(SYEHM'-dee-seet)* seventy

семья́ (f.) *(seem'-YAH)* family

сентя́брь (m.) *(seen-TYAH-buhr')* September

се́рдце (n.) *(SYEHR-tseh)* heart

середи́на (f.) *(see-ree-DEE-nuh)* middle

серебро́ (n.) *(see-ree-BRAW)* silver

се́рьги (pl.) *(SYEHR'-gee)* earrings

серьёзный *(seer'-YAWZ-ny)* serious

се́рый *(SYEH-ry)* gray

сестра́ (f.) *(see-STRAH)* sister

сза́ди *(ZAH-dee)* in back

сигаре́та (f.) *(see-gah-RYEHT-uh)* cigarette

синаго́га (f.) *(see-nah-GAW-guh)* synagogue

си́ний *(SEE-nee)* dark blue

синя́к (m.) *(see-NYAHK)* bruise

ско́лько *(SKAWL'-kuh)* how much

ско́рая по́мощь (f.) *(SKAW-ruh-yuh PAW-mush')* ambulance

ско́ро *(SKAW-ruh)* soon

скуча́ть *(skoo-CHAHT')* to miss, to be bored

слаби́тельное (n.) *(slah-BEE-teel'-nuh-yuh)* laxative

сла́бый *(SLAH-by)* weak

сла́дкий *(SLAHT-kee)* sweet

сле́ва *(SLYEH-vuh)* on the left

сле́дующий (SLYEH-doo-yoo-shee) next

сли́ва (f.) (SLEE-vuh) plum

сли́вки (pl.) (SLEEF-kee) cream

сли́шком (SLEESH-kuhm) too

слова́рь (m.) (slah-VAHR') dictionary

сло́во (n.) (SLAW-vuh) word

слу́жба (f.) (SLOOZH-buh) service

слу́шать (imp.)/послу́шать (perf.) (SLOO-shuht'/pah-SLOO-shuht') to listen

слы́шать (imp.)/услы́шать (perf.) (SLY-shuht'/oo-SLY-shuht') to hear

смотре́ть (imp.)/посмотре́ть (perf.) (smah-TRYEHT'/pah-smah-TRYEHT') to look at

снару́жи (snah-ROO-zhee) outdoors

снег (m.) (snyehk) snow

собира́ть (imp.)/собра́ть (perf.) (sah-bee-RAHT'/sah-BRAHT') to gather, to make ready

собо́р (m.) (sah-BAWR) cathedral

Сове́тский Сою́з (sah-VYEHT-skee sah-YOOS) Soviet Union

Соединённые Шта́ты Аме́рики (sah-yee-dee-NYAW-ny-yeh SHTAH-ty ah-MYEH-ree-kee) United States of America

соединя́ть (imp.)/соедини́ть (perf.) (sah-yee-dee-NYAHT'/sah-yee-dee-NEET') to connect

сок (m.) (sawk) juice

солёные огурцы́ (pl.) (sah-LYAW-ny-yeh ah-goor-TSY) pickles

со́лнце (n.) (SAWN-tsuh) sun

соль (f.) (sawl') salt

со́рок (SAW-ruhk) forty

со́ус (m.) (SAW-oos) sauce

спа́льня (f.) (SPAHL'-nyuh) bedroom

спа́льный (adj.) (SPAHL'-ny) sleeping

спаса́тель (m.) (spah-SAH-teel') lifeguard

спаси́бо (spah-SEE-buh) thank you

спать (spaht') to sleep

специа́льный (spee-TSYAHL'-ny) special

спе́ция (f.) (SPYEH-tsee-yuh) spice

спеши́ть (imp.)/поспеши́ть (perf.) (spee-SHYT'/puh-spee-SHEET') to hurry

спина́ (f.) (spee-NAH) back

спи́чки (pl.) (SPEECH-kee) matches

споко́йный (spah-KOY-ny) calm, peaceful

спра́вки (pl.) (SPRAHF-kee) information booth

спу́щенная ши́на (f.) (SPOO-shee-nuh-yuh SHY-nuh) flat tire

сра́зу (SRAH-zoo) immediately

среда́ (m.) (sree-DAH) Wednesday

сре́дний (SRYEHD-nee) medium, average

сро́чный (SRAWCH-ny) urgent

261

ста́вить (imp.)/**поста́вить** (perf.) *(STAH-veet'/pah-STAH-veet')* to put

стака́н (m.) *(stah-KAHN)* a glass

сталь (f.) *(stahl)* steel

ста́нция (f.) *(STAHN-tsee-yuh)* station

ста́рый *(STAH-ry)* old

стекло́ (n.) *(stee-KLAW)* glass

стира́ть (imp.)/**постира́ть** (perf.) *(stee-RAHT'/puh-stee-RAHT')* to wash, to do laundry

сто *(staw)* one hundred

сто́ить *(STAW-eet')* to cost

стол (m.) *(stawl)* table, desk

сто́лик (m.) *(STAWL-eek)* table

столо́вая (f.) *(stah-LAW-vuh-yuh)* dining room, cafeteria

сторона́ (f.) *(stah-rah-NAH)* side, direction

стоя́нка (f.) *(stah-YAHN-kuh)* stop, parking

стра́нно *(STRAH-nuh)* strange

страхо́вка (f.) *(strah-KHAWF-kuh)* insurance

стри́жка (f.) *(STREESH-kuh)* haircut, hairdo

студе́нт (m.) *(stoo-DYEHNT)* student

суббо́та (f.) *(soo-BAW-tuh)* Saturday

сувени́р (m.) *(soo-vee-NEER)* souvenir

су́мка (f.) *(SOOM-kuh)* bag

суп (m.) *(soop)* soup

сухари́ (pl.) *(soo-khah-REE)* melba toast

сухо́й *(soo-KHOY)* dry

счёт (m.) *(shawt)* bill

счётчик (m.) *(SHAWT-cheek)* meter

счита́ть (imp.)/**сосчита́ть** (perf.) *(shee-TAHT'/suh-shee-TAHT')* to count

США *(sshAH)* U.S.A.

сын (m.) *(syn)* son

сыр (m.) *(syr)* cheese

Т

таба́к (m.) *(tah-BAHK)* tobacco

табле́тка (f.) *(tah-BLYEHT-kuh)* pill

тако́й *(tah-KOY)* such

такси́ (n.) *(tahk-SEE)* taxi

тамо́жня (f.) *(tah-MAWZH-nyuh)* customs

танцева́ть (imp.)/**потанцева́ть** (perf.) *(tahn-tsah-VAHT'/pah-tuhn-tsah-VAHT')* to dance

та́почки (pl.) *(TAH-puhch-kee)* slippers

таре́лка (f.) *(tah-RYEHL-kuh)* plate

твёрдый *(TVYAWR-dy)* hard

теа́тр (m.) *(tee-AH-tuhr)* theater

телеви́зор (m.) *(tee-lee-VEE-zuhr)* television set

телегра́мма (f.) *(tee-lee-GRAH-muh)* telegram

теле́жка (f.) *(tee-LYEHSH-kuh)* baggage cart

телефо́н (m.) *(tee-lee-FAWN)* telephone

телефони́стка (f.) *(tee-lee-fah-NEEST-kuh)* operator

теля́тина (f.) *(tee-LYAH-tee-nuh)* veal

тёмный *(TYAWM-ny)* dark

температу́ра (f.) *(teem-pee-rah-TOO-ruh)* temperature

тёплый *(TYAW-ply)* warm

термо́метр (m.) *(teer-MAW-mee-tuhr)* thermometer

теря́ть (imp.)/потеря́ть (perf.) *(teer-YAHT'/pah-teer-YAHT')* to lose

тётя (f.) *(TYAW-tyuh)* aunt

типи́чный *(tee-PEECH-ny)* typical

това́р (m.) *(tah-VAHR)* goods

тогда́ *(tahg-DAH)* then

то́же *(TAW-zhuh)* also

то́лько *(TAWL'-kuh)* only

то́рмоз (m.) *(TAWR-muhs)* automobile brakes

то́рт (m.) *(TAWRT)* cake

тошни́ть *(tahsh-NEET')* to be nauseous

тротуа́р (m.) *(trah-too-AHR)* sidewalk

тре́тий *(TRYEH-tee)* third

тре́ть (f.) *(tryeht')* a third

три *(tree)* three

три́дцать *(TREET-seet)* thirty

трина́дцать *(tree-NAHT-seet')* thirteen

тру́дно *(TROOD-nuh)* difficult

трусы́ (pl.) *(troo-SY)* underpants

туале́т (m.) *(too-ah-LYEHT)* toilet

туале́тная бума́га (f.) *(too-ah-LYEHT-nuh-yuh boo-MAH-guh)* toilet paper

туда́ *(too-DAH)* there

тума́н (m.) *(too-MAHN)* fog

тури́ст(-ка) *(too-REEST,-kuh)* tourist

ту́рок (m.)/турча́нка (f.) *(TOOR-uhk/toor-CHAHN-kuh)* Turk

ту́т *(toot)* here

ту́фли (pl.) *(TOO-fly)* shoes

тушёное *(too-SHAW-nuh-yuh)* braised

ты́сяча (f.) *(TY-seech-uh)* one thousand

У

у *(oo)* belonging to, at

убира́ть (imp.)/убра́ть (perf.) *(oo-bee-RAHT'/oo-BRAHT')* to clean

убо́рщица (f.) *(oo-BAWR-shee-tsuh)* maid

удаля́ть (imp.)/удали́ть (perf.) *(oo-dah-LYAHT'/oo-dah-LEET')* to extract

удово́льствие (n.) *(oo-dah-VAWL'-stvee-yuh)* satisfaction, pleasure

уезжа́ть (imp.)/уе́хать (perf.) *(oo-ee-ZHAHT'/oo-YEH-khuht')* to leave

у́зкий *(OOS-kee)* narrow

указа́ть (imp.)/ука́зывать (perf.) *(oo-kah-ZAHT'/oo-KAH-zy-vuht')* to show

укла́дка (f.) *(oo-KLAHT-kuh)* set (hair)

уко́л (m.) *(oo-KAWL)* injection

уку́с (m.) *(oo-KOOS)* bite

у́лица (f.) *(OO-lee-tsuh)* street

улы́бка (f.) *(oo-LYP-kuh)* smile

универма́г (m.) *(oo-nee-veer-MAHK)* department store

универса́м (m.) *(oo-nee-veer-SAHM)* supermarket

263

университе́т (m.) *(oo-nee-veer-see-TYEHT)* university

употребля́ть (imp.)/ **употреби́ть** (perf.) *(oo-puh-tree-BLYAHT'/oo-puh-tree-BEET')* to use

услу́га (f.) *(oo-SLOO-guh)* service

усы́ (pl.) *(oo-SY)* mustache

у́тка (f.) *(OOT-kuh)* duck

у́тро (n.) *(OO-truh)* morning

утю́г (m.) *(oo-TYOOK)* iron

у́хо (n.) *(OO-khuh)* ear

уходи́ть (imp.)/**уйти́** (perf.) *(oo-khah-DEET'/oo-ee-TEE)* to leave (on foot)

Ф

фа́ра (f.) *(FAH-ruh)* headlight

февра́ль (m.) *(fee-VRAHL')* February

фильм (m.) *(feel'm)* movie

финн (m.)/**фи́нка** (f.) *(feen/FEEN-kuh)* Finnish

фиоле́товый *(fee-ah-LYEHT-uh-vy)* purple

фона́рь (m.) *(fah-NAHR')* flashlight

фонта́н (m.) *(fahn-TAHN)* fountain

фотографи́ровать (imp.)/ **сфотографи́ровать** (perf.) *(fuh-tuh-grah-FEER-uh-vuht'/sfuh-tuh-grah-FEER-uh-vuht')* to photograph

францу́з (m.)/ **францу́женка** (f.) *(frahn-TSOOS/frahn-TSOO-zheen-kuh)* French

францу́зский (adj.) *(fran-TSOOS-kee)* French

фру́кты (pl.) *(FROOK-ty)* fruit

футбо́л (m.) *(food-BAWL)* soccer

Х

хала́т (m.) *(khah-LAHT)* robe

хвата́ть (imp.)/**хвати́ть** (perf.) *(khvah-TAHT'/khvah-TEET')* to suffice

химчи́стка (f.) *(kheem-CHEEST-kuh)* dry cleaner

хлеб (m.) *(khlyehp)* bread

хло́пок (m.) *(KHLAW-puhk)* cotton

холо́дный *(khah-LAW-dny)* cold

хоро́ший *(khah-RAW-shee)* good

хорошо́ *(khah-rah-SHAW)* good, fine

хоте́ть (imp.)/**захоте́ть** (perf.) *(khah-TYEHT'/zah-khah-TYEHT')* to want

храни́ть *(khrah-NEET')* to store

худе́ть (imp.)/**похуде́ть** (perf.) *(khoo-DYEHT'/puh-khoo-DYEHT')* to lose weight

худо́жник (m.) *(khoo-DAWZH-neek)* artist

Ц

цвет (m.) *(tsvyeht)* color

цвето́к (m.) *(tsvee-TAWK)* flower

цена́ (f.) *(tsy-NAH)* price

центр (m.) *(TSEHN-tuhr)* center

цепо́чка (f.) *(tsee-PAWCH-kuh)* chain

це́рковь (f.) *(TSEHR-kuhf)*
church

Ч

чаевы́е (pl.) *(chee-yee-VY-yeh)*
tip

ча́й (m.) *(chahy)* tea

ча́с (m.) *(chahs)* hour

часы́ (pl.) *(chee-SY)* watch,
clock

ча́шка (f.) *(CHAHSH-kuh)* cup

чек (m.) *(chehk)* check

челове́к (m.) *(chee-lah-VYEHK)*
person

че́люсть (f.) *(CHEH-lyoost')*
jaw

чемода́н (m.) *(chee-mah-DAHN)*
suitcase

че́рез *(CHEH-rees)* across,
over

чёрный *(CHYAWR-ny)* black

чесно́к (m.) *(chees-NAWK)*
garlic

четве́рг (m.) *(cheet-VYEHRK)*
Thursday

че́тверть (f.) *(CHEHT-veert')*
one fourth; a quarter

четвёртый *(cheet-VYAWR-ty)*
fourth

четы́ре *(chee-TY-ree)* four

четы́рнадцать *(chee-TYR-nuht-seet')* fourteen

чини́ть (imp.)/**почини́ть**
(perf.) *(chee-NEET'/puh-chee-NEET')* to fix

чи́стить (imp.)/**почи́стить**
(perf.) *(CHEE-steet'/pah-CHEE-steet')* to clean, to dry-clean

что *(shtaw)* what, that

что́бы *(SHTAW-by)* in order to

что́-нибудь *(SHTAW-nee-boot')*
anything

чу́вствовать *(CHOOST-vuh-vuht')* to feel

Ш

ша́ль (f.) *(shahl')* shawl

шампа́нское (n.) *(shahm-PAHN-skuh-yuh)* champagne

шампу́нь (m.) *(shahm-POON')*
shampoo

ша́пка (f.) *(SHAHP-kuh)* hat

швед (m.)/**шве́дка** (f.)
(shvyeht/SHVYEHT-kuh) Swede

швейца́рец (m.)/**швейца́рка**
(f.) *(shvay-TSAHR-eets/shvay-TSAHR-kuh)* Swiss

ше́я (f.) *(SHEH-yuh)* neck

шёлк (m.) *(shawlk)* silk

ше́рсть (f.) *(shehrst')* wool

шестна́дцать *(shyst-NAHT-seet')* sixteen

шесто́й *(shys-TOY)* sixth

шесть *(shehst')* six

шестьдеся́т *(shyst'-dee-SYAHT)*
sixty

ши́на (f.) *(SHEE-nuh)*
automobile tire

широ́кий *(shee-RAW-kee)*
wide

шить (imp.)/**приши́ть** (perf.)
(shyt'/pree-SHYT') to sew

шокола́д (m.) *(shuh-kah-LAHT)*
chocolate

шоссе́ (n.) *(shah-SEH)*
highway

шофёр (m.) *(shah-FYAWR)*
driver

265

штопать (imp.)/**заштопать**
(perf.) (SHTAW-puht'/zah-
SHTAW-puht) to mend
шумный (SHOOM-ny) noisy

Щ
щётка (f.) (SHYAWT-kuh)
brush
щиколотка (f.) (SHEE-kuh-luht-
kuh) ankle

Э
экскурсия (f.) (eek-SKOOR-see-
yuh) excursion
электричество (n.) (ee-leek-
TREE-cheest-vuh) electricity
эти (EH-tee) these
это (EH-tuh) this
этот (EH-tuht) this

Ю
юбка (f.) (YOOP-kuh) skirt
юг (m.) (yook) south
юрист (m.) (yoo-REEST) lawyer

Я
я (yah) I
яблоко (n.) (YAH-bluh-kuh)
apple
язык (m.) (yee-ZYK) tongue,
language
яйцо (n.) (yee-TSAW) egg
январь (m.) (yeen-VAHR')
January
янтарь (m.) (yeen-TAHR')
amber
японец (m.)/**японка** (f.) (yee-
PAW-neets/yee-PAWN-kuh)
Japanese

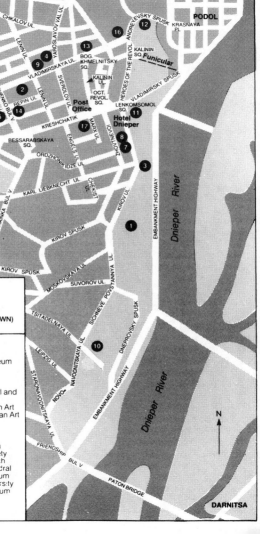

KIEV

(NOT ALL STREETS SHOWN)

Points of Interest

1 Askold's Grave
2 Central Lenin Museum
3 Former Marinsky Palace
4 Golden Gate
5 Museum of Oriental and Western Art
6 Museum of Russian Art
7 Museum of Ukrainian Art
8 October Palace of Culture
9 Opera
10 Pecherskaya Lavra
11 Philharmonic Society
12 St Andrew's Church
13 St Sophia's Cathedral
14 Shevchenko Museum
15 Shevchenko University
16 State History Museum
17 Tchaikovsky Conservatory

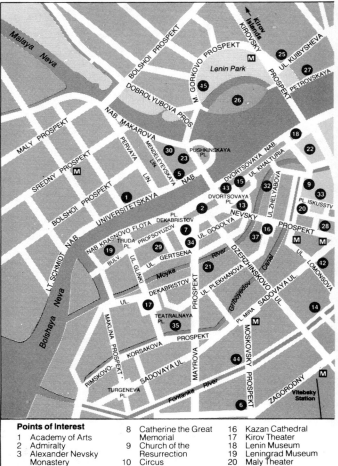

Points of Interest

1. Academy of Arts
2. Admiralty
3. Alexander Nevsky Monastery
4. Anchikov Palace
5. Anthropology and Zoology Museums
6. Arch of Triumph
7. Bronze Horseman
8. Catherine the Great Memorial
9. Church of the Resurrection
10. Circus
11. Cruiser Aurora
12. Engineers' Castle
13. General Staff
14. Gorky Theater
15. Hermitage Museum
16. Kazan Cathedral
17. Kirov Theater
18. Lenin Museum
19. Leningrad Museum
20. Maly Theater
21. Marinsky Palace
22. Marsovo Pole
23. Naval Museum
24. October Concert Hall

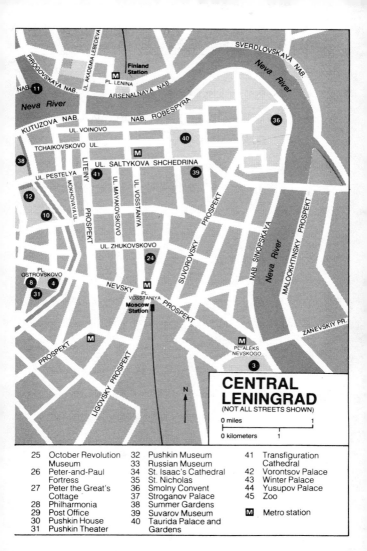

CENTRAL LENINGRAD
(NOT ALL STREETS SHOWN)

0 miles 1
0 kilometers 1

N

25 October Revolution Museum	32 Pushkin Museum	41 Transfiguration Cathedral
26 Peter-and-Paul Fortress	33 Russian Museum	42 Vorontsov Palace
27 Peter the Great's Cottage	34 St. Isaac's Cathedral	43 Winter Palace
28 Philharmonia	35 St. Nicholas	44 Yusupov Palace
29 Post Office	36 Smolny Convent	45 Zoo
30 Pushkin House	37 Stroganov Palace	
31 Pushkin Theater	38 Summer Gardens	Ⓜ Metro station
	39 Suvarov Museum	
	40 Taurida Palace and Gardens	

Map labels:
SVERDLOVSKAYA NAB.
Neva River
PIROGOVSKAYA NAB.
UL. AKADEMIA LEBEDEVA
Finland Station
PL. LENINA
ARSENALNAYA NAB.
NAB. ROBESPYRA
KUTUZOVA NAB.
UL. VOINOVO
TCHAIKOVSKOVO UL.
UL. SALTYKOVA SHCHEDRINA
LITEINY
MOKHOVAYA UL.
UL. PESTELYA
UL. MAYAKOVSKOVO
UL. VOSSTANIYA
SUVOROVSKY PROSPEKT
NAB. SINOPSKAYA
Neva River
MALOOKHTINSKY PROSPEKT
UL. ZHUKOVSKOVO
PL. OSTROVSKOVO
NEVSKY
PL. VOSSTANIYA
Moscow Station
PROSPEKT
ZANEVSKIY PR.
PL. ALEKS NEVSKOGO
LIGOVSKY PROSPEKT

EMERGENCY NUMBERS

Slova — Finds a job where
the ~~Lord~~ will use him.

NAMES AND ADDRESSES